Conversations with
Billy Collins

Literary Conversations Series
Monika Gehlawat
General Editor

Conversations with Billy Collins

Edited by John Cusatis

University Press of Mississippi / Jackson

The University Press of Mississippi is the scholarly publishing agency of the Mississippi Institutions of Higher Learning: Alcorn State University, Delta State University, Jackson State University, Mississippi State University, Mississippi University for Women, Mississippi Valley State University, University of Mississippi, and University of Southern Mississippi.

www.upress.state.ms.us
The University Press of Mississippi is a member of the Association of University Presses.

Several poems appear in the text.
Taylor, Henry. "Paradelle: Nocturne de la Ville," from *The Paradelle: An Anthology*. Copyright © 2005 by Theresa M. Welford. Reprinted with the permission of Red Hen Press and Theresa M. Welford.

Billy Collins, "Etymology" from *The Apple That Astonished Paris*. Copyright © 1988, 1996 by Billy Collins. Reprinted with the permission of The Permissions Company, LLC on behalf of the University of Arkansas Press, uapress.com

Billy Collins, "Candle Hat" from *Questions about Angels*. Copyright © 1991 by Billy Collins. Reprinted with the permission of University of Pittsburgh Press.

Billy Collins, "The Start," "Nurse," and "Comparisons." © Billy Collins. Printed by permission.

First printing 2022
∞

Library of Congress Cataloging-in-Publication Data

Names: Cusatis, John, editor.
Title: Conversations with Billy Collins / John Cusatis.
Other titles: Literary conversations series.
Description: Jackson : University Press of Mississippi, 2022. |
    Series: Literary conversations series | Includes index.
Identifiers: LCCN 2021062380 (print) | LCCN 2021062381 (ebook) |
    ISBN 9781496840660 (hardback) | ISBN 9781496840677 (trade paperback) |
    ISBN 9781496840691 (epub) | ISBN 9781496840684 (epub) |
    ISBN 9781496840714 (pdf) | ISBN 9781496840707 (pdf)
Subjects: LCSH: Collins, Billy—Interviews. | Poets, American—20th century—
    Interviews. | Poets, American—21st century—Interviews.
Classification: LCC PS3553.O47478 Z46 2022 (print) |
    LCC PS3553.O47478 (ebook) | DDC 811/.54 [B]—dc23/eng/20220128
LC record available at https://lccn.loc.gov/2021062380
LC ebook record available at https://lccn.loc.gov/2021062381

British Library Cataloging-in-Publication Data available

Books by Billy Collins

Poetry

Pokerface. Pasadena, California: Kenmore Press, 1977.

Video Poems. Long Beach, California: Applezaba Press, 1980.

The Apple That Astonished Paris. Fayetteville: University of Arkansas
  Press, 1988.

Questions about Angels. New York: Quill / William Morrow, 1991; University
  of Pittsburgh Press, 1991.

The Art of Drowning. Pittsburgh: University of Pittsburgh Press, 1995.

Picnic, Lightning. Pittsburgh: University of Pittsburgh Press, 1998; London:
  Eurospan, 2003.

Taking off Emily Dickinson's Clothes: Selected Poems. London: Picador, 2000.

Sailing Alone around the Room: New and Selected Poems. New York:
  Random House, 2001.

Nine Horses. New York: Random House, 2002; London: Picador, 2003.

The Trouble with Poetry and Other Poems. New York: Random House, 2005;
  London: Picador, 2006.

She Was Just Seventeen. Lincoln, Illinois: Modern Haiku Press, 2006.

Ballistics. New York: Random House, 2008. London: Picador, 2009.

Horoscopes for the Dead. New York: Random House 2011. London:
  Picador, 2011.

Aimless Love. New York: Random House 2013. London: Picador, 2013.

The Rain in Portugal. New York: Random House, 2016; London:
  Picador, 2017.

Whale Day. New York: Random House, 2020; London, Picador, 2020.

Edited Anthologies

Poetry 180: A Turning Back to Poetry. New York: Random House, 2003.

180 More: Extraordinary Poems for Every Day. New York: Random House, 2005.

The Best American Poetry 2006, New York: Scribner Poetry, 2006.

Bright Wings: An Illustrated Anthology of Poems about Birds. New York: Columbia University Press, 2009.

Children's Books

Voyage. Piermont, New Hampshire: Bunker Hill Publishing, 2014.

Contents

Introduction

In his 2016 interview with Billy Collins, Princeton Theological Seminary president Craig Barnes begins, "We live in a day that values science and technology and big data. Why do we need poetry?" Collins responds, "Well, because of those things," to which the audience reacts with resounding applause. "Poetry is little data, or a datum," he continues; "it asks us to tap the brakes, slow down," to look at the world "one datum at a time"—like we did as children. And as Collins's literary heroes, the English Romantics, did. "Wordsworth said, 'The child is father of the man,'" Collins told a group of AP English students in 2019, "It's important to keep your child alive inside of you."

"Artists—poets, musicians, dancers, whatever—are people who have not let the child inside wither away," Collins explained to the students. "All children are basically artists in a very unconscious and unselfconscious way." Adolescence, he says, ushers in self-consciousness and inhibits the spontaneity, candor, and attentiveness to the world one associates with children. Another culprit, his work implies, is formal education. In one of the earliest of his ninety-two poems that have appeared in *Poetry*, "First Reader," he celebrates the initial joy of learning to read, discovering "the infinite, clicking, / permutations of the alphabet's small and capital letters." He recalls his early Dick and Jane reader: "It was always Saturday and he and she / were always pointing at something and shouting, "Look!" But he concludes by lamenting the effect of the rigid, authoritarian atmosphere of the classroom: "Alphabetical ourselves in the rows of classroom desks, / we were forgetting how to look, learning how to read."

In a much earlier poem, "Instructions to the Artist," published in *The Paris Review* in the fall of 1977 and only slightly reworked for inclusion in Collins's second major book, *Questions about Angels*, where "First Reader" also appeared, he applauds childhood's creative impulse: "Never be ashamed of kindergarten / It is the alphabet's only temple." But somewhere in a child's education, Collins suggests, this temple is desecrated, and language, along with its most consecrated form of expression, poetry, loses its allure. He explains to Margaret Renkl in 2010, "Children are delighted and astounded to discover at some point in their life that the thing that they use to eat their cereal with sounds almost exactly like that big white thing in the sky at night—moon-spoon. It feels good on their lips and it connects these two wildly different things, and that's one of the very primal pleasures of poetry." Unfortunately, he explains to Renkl, "boys and girls often have the natural pleasures of poetry beaten out of them by the time they get out of high school. Two reasons why: forceful emphasis on interpretation and using poems that are very dated—poems that were written a hundred years ago." If it hadn't been for his discovery of the Beat poets during his Catholic school education, Collins stated in our 2016 interview, he too might have been denied the primal pleasure poetry affords readers. Poets such as Allen Ginsberg, Gregory Corso, and Lawrence Ferlinghetti, he said, "formed a revolutionary disruption of the manners of the traditional poetry we were being taught (by priests and brothers, I might add)."

Throughout the twenty-one interviews collected within these pages, Collins speaks candidly and colorfully about his aim to create poetry that does not neglect what Wordsworth considered one of the central aims of poetry: pleasure. In his essay "Poetry, Pleasure and the Hedonist Reader," Collins points out that Wordsworth uses the word *pleasure* nearly fifty times in his own poetic manifesto, "Preface to *The Lyrical Ballads.*" A poem's meaning, Collins feels, is over-emphasized in the classroom, at the expense of the other sources of pleasure, such as sound, metaphoric language, and what he often refers to as "imaginative travel." He writes in his early poem "Introduction to Poetry" that students have been conditioned to "tie the poem to a chair with rope / and torture a confession out of it." The emphasis on teaching meaning, he has suggested, made difficulty a central criterion for good poetry, which inevitably turned students away from it. He tells Terry Gross in his first of four interviews on *Fresh Air*, "I don't think readers enjoy being led down a flight of stairs into an unlit basement, and that's the feeling I get from reading quite a few contemporary poems."

Collins aimed to remedy this problem during his two terms as United States Poet Laureate by beginning a program called Poetry 180, which started as a website and led to two print anthologies. In his introduction to *Poetry 180: A Turning Back to Poetry*, he recalls a student at a high school he visited describing her experience with contemporary poetry. "When I read a modern poem," she explained, "it's like my brother has his foot on the back of my neck in the swimming pool." Collins hoped that a collection of "poems whose injection of pleasure is immediate" would not instill a feeling of helplessness but rather cause students to make a 180 degree turn back to poetry. He also offered 180 contemporary poems, one for each day of the school year, and not intended to be taught or analyzed. He told Grace Cavalieri in 2001, "My sense is, if a student hears a poem every day, there's probably one poem out there, at least one, for every student. All it takes is one poem to get you hooked."

For Collins, the poems that most easily get readers "hooked" are the ones that speak directly to them. "What I look for in the first few lines is whether someone is talking to me or just doing a word painting or throwing out some complicated imagery that I am not willing to stop and examine," he told students in 2019. "The conversational style is certainly the most basic way to get the reader on board and make the reader feel included." The reader for Collins is half of the poetic equation; without him or her, the poem is incomplete. He told George Plimpton in 2001, "I want the reader to be in the sidecar, ready. Then off we go." He and his reader begin in "a hospitable place," he explained, but soon journey to a location that is "disorienting." He explained to students in a 2010 interview, "Archibald MacLeish said, 'a poem should not mean but be.' In other words, let's not analyze; let's just let it be. But the way I look at poetry is that a poem should not *mean* but *move*. I'm interested in the poem being a little bit of imaginative travel that moves from the simple to the complex." If the poem *begins* complex, Collins has said, and the reader is disoriented at the start, he will most likely abandon the journey. "I like to say the poem begins in Kansas and goes to Oz," he tells Craig Barnes. "What's wrong with a lot of poems . . . is that they start in Oz. They start in an already bizarre landscape, and you feel like you have to play catch up, but you don't really want to."

One of Collins's signature poetic attributes is the affable voice of his persona, who welcomes and orients the reader at the outset, a persona, he claims, who has his roots in English Romantic poetry. He explained to Andy Kuhn in 2014, "My persona is really a modernized version of that character drawn primarily from Wordsworth and Coleridge. He is by nature a day dreamer whose favorite toys are his thoughts. Not content to leave the natural world alone, he uses its scenes as launching pads for imaginative flights." Collins links his success as a poet to the development of this persona, whose voice, he claims, grew out of his extensive reading. He remarked to high school students in 2010, "Your voice in poetry has an external source, and the source of the voice is basically the poetry books in the library. You form a voice through reading, and through borrowing tonal effects or stylistic mannerisms from other poets."

Yet another of Collins's distinct traits was not assimilated from reading the Romantics, but according to him, inherited from his father and granted license from contemporary poets such as Philip Larkin, Kenneth Koch, and Ron Koertge: *humor*. Wordsworth and Coleridge, he jokes in his interview with Barnes, "got rid of humor and sex and substituted landscape." Yet, Collins uses humor to treat serious subjects, a topic he discusses with Terry Gross in regard to one of his most popular poems, "Forgetfulness," which gains its levity through the yoking of a grave topic and a colloquial style: "Long ago you kissed the names of the nine Muses good bye / And watched the quadratic equation pack its bag." Collins explains, "I think it has a kind of instant appeal because it's about something that's both humorous—we make fun of forgetfulness, absent-minded professors and people walking around with their glasses on their head looking for them—but at the same time the loss of memory is frightening. I try to handle both aspects." He comments further on this balance of gravity and levity to Grace Cavalieri: "I think that's an aim for me: to express the beauty, the sadness, and the sheer ridiculousness of life at the same time."

Even death is treated flippantly in Collins's poetry. He recognizes in "Life Expectancy," from his latest volume, *Whale Day*, that he can no longer assume that he "would be around longer / than the squirrel dashing up a tree / or the nightly raccoons in the garbage." In "Helium," from his 2016 book, *The Rain in Portugal*, he is appalled that the local businesses he passes in an Ohio town, such as Balloon Designs by Pauline, may outlive him. A preoccupation with death, he explains to Diane Rehm in 2020, is fundamental to poetry: "I think it's probably the oldest theme in poetry, going back to Roman poetry and the theme of *carpe diem*, that we must seize the day because we don't have all the diems in the world. An awareness of mortality tends to intensify life." In "The Garland," from *Whale Day*, he imagines his dead self, laughing joyously in the face of death.

And while Collins considers poetry a way of expressing one's reverence for the mystery of existence, his *ir*reverence does not exclude his deceased poetic heroes. The child is alive inside him as he mischievously mocks the formality and often the pretentiousness of his poetic predecessors and contemporaries. "I like turning back on my influences and liberating myself from them," he explains to English students in 2019. "I have written a poem called 'Taking Off Emily Dickinson's Clothes.' I wrote a poem mocking 'The Love Song of J. Alfred Prufrock.'" He's also written a parody called "Sonnet," one of his many metapoems, self-consciously creating itself as it unravels, that celebrates the form while mocking it. And most famously, in 1997, he published "Paradelle for Susan" in the *American Scholar*, alerting readers in a fictitious footnote that "the paradelle is one of the more demanding French forms" and illustrating the challenging restrictions laid down by its eleventh-century creators with such lines as the final one: "Darken the mountain, time and find was my into it was with to to." He kept the joke going before exposing the ruse in his 2001 interview with the *Paris Review*. "I knew the editor, Joseph Epstein, had a sense of literary humor. They published the poem and that, I assumed, was that, until Epstein wrote to tell me about the mail they were getting," he explained to George Plimpton. "Subscribers were sending angry letters questioning the magazine's judgment for having published such a slovenly poem. How could the journal of the Phi Beta Kappa Society endorse such literary incompetence? One person said it was the worst paradelle he'd ever read. No kidding." When asked to respond to the angry outpouring of letters, Collins did not back down. "The paradelle is an extremely difficult form, my defense ran," he says. "I did the best that I could." The form, whose name suggests "parody of a villanelle" caught on, resulting in an anthology of paradelles being published by major poets, including Pulitzer Prize winner Henry Taylor, whose 2001 interview with Collins includes a reading of his paradelle. *The Paradelle: An Anthology*, published by Red Hen Press in 2006 included an introduction by Collins.

The childlike alacrity with which Collins responds to language, learning, and life in general has been central to his globe-spanning popularity. The poetry itself is ultimately responsible for the prestige he enjoys as a contemporary poet whose work continues to appear in periodicals such as the *New Yorker*, *The Atlantic*, and the *Paris Review*, while occupying several pages in the canon-affirming *Norton Anthology of American Literature*. Yet he attributes his being catapulted to international fame in the late 1990s largely to public radio. Margaret Renkl commented in 2010, "Even before you were appointed poet laureate, the *New York Times* called you "the most popular poet in America," to which Collins responds, "I don't know why I became popular. To tell you the truth, it's basically NPR." His 1998 interview on *Fresh Air*, and frequent subsequent appearances on shows such as *Talk of the Nation*, allowed him to read to three million people, he says "instead of twenty-five."

Contrary to his modest estimate of attendees at his readings, Collins's appearances for the past two decades have been delivered to packed auditoriums, with enthusiastic applause following each of his poems, rather than the polite hush poets tend to receive. His rigorous reading tour was paused, naturally, in the spring of 2020 due to the onset of the coronavirus pandemic. "I'm taking this seriously," he wrote in an email to me on April 4, 2020, "because at my age with tarnished lungs, the corona would take me out of the picture, and as you know, I like the picture a lot." In conjunction with his seventy-ninth birthday, however, Collins conducted a short reading live on Facebook. He quickly reunited with his quarantined audience and continued the readings for thirty minutes each weeknight until his eightieth birthday, with roughly three hundred loyal viewers and thousands more tuning in to the recorded reading. He explained to Diane Rehm in November 2020, "I said right in the beginning, on the very first broadcast, 'I'm not going to read poems to comfort you or make you feel better about yourself. I'm just going to read good poems.'"

Collins continued delivering the readings for two nights a week in the spring of 2021, reading good poems from others and from his own work, which, as the broadcast proved, are above all, life-affirming, even when they are pointing out the "sheer ridiculousness of life." "For some people, it takes a catastrophe or a brush with death to stimulate a kind of existential awareness," he stated in our 2021 interview. "Suddenly, they feel the need to carpe their diems. But poetry by example shows that all it takes is stillness and quiet focus." Just as Dick and Jane in his first reading primer did, Collins's poems, though a little more tacitly, shout, "Look!" After all, he asks in his 2016 poem "Greece," "Is not poetry a megaphone held up / to the whispering lips of death?"

John Cusatis

Chronology

1941　William James Collins is born on March 22, 1941, in New York City, the only child of William S. Collins, an electrician turned insurance broker, and Katherine Collins, who grew up on a farm in Ontario, Canada. Collins's mother quits her job as a nurse to raise the couples' only child, reciting poems to him and engendering a love for reading.

1946　Billy Collins enters public kindergarten and subsequently completes his primary education in Catholic elementary school, serving as an altar boy and a member of the Boy Scouts of America. Collins develops an abiding affinity for Warner Brothers cartoons, while devouring the *Lassie* and *Hardy Boys* series.

1955　Enrolls in Archbishop Stepinac High School in White Plains, New York, publishing his first poems in his school literary magazine, *The Phoenix*. His father brings home copies of *Poetry* magazine from his Wall Street office, and the teenager discovers contemporary poets whose work is a welcome alternative to the "school poetry" he had been introduced to by his teachers. He later discovers the Beats—Kerouac, Ginsberg, Ferlinghetti, and Corso—whom he imitates in his early attempts at writing poetry.

1957　A junior in high school, Collins submits poems to *Poetry* magazine, which are rejected; however, the sixteen-year-old poet receives an encouraging note from editor Henry Rago.

1959　Graduates from Archbishop Stepinac and enrolls at Holy Cross, a Jesuit college in Worcester, Massachusetts; begins writing for the school's literary journal while finding a new poetic model, Wallace Stevens, and takes an interest in writers such as Samuel Beckett, Jean Genet, and Albert Camus.

1963　Graduates from Holy Cross with a BA in English. Enrolls at University of California Riverside. One of his teachers is the poet Robert Peters, who gives him a copy of Gaston Bachelard's *The*

	Poetics of Space, which has a lingering impact. He also befriends the California poet Jack Spicer.
1965	Graduates from UC Riverside with an MA in English and begins graduate studies there. Reads Richard Brautigan's *Trout Fishing in America* in manuscript, initiating an affection for the work of the offbeat counterculture novelist and poet.
1968	Begins teaching at Lehman College of the City University of New York.
1971	Completes his doctoral dissertation, "The World's Ear: The Romantic Search for an Audience," focusing on the British Romantic poets, and earns a PhD in English from UC Riverside. He has short poems, in the style of Brautigan, published in *Rolling Stone*, and others begin appearing in small press magazines.
1975	Cofounds *Mid-Atlantic Review* with Walter Blanco and Stephen Bailey, which features the work of such poets as Robert Peters, Charles Bukowski, and Ron Koertge.
1977	"Instructions to the Artist," which appears in a modified form in *Questions about Angels*, is published in the fall issue of *The Paris Review*. Kenmore Press publishes Collins's first chapbook, *Pokerface*, in 200 hand-stitched copies.
1979	Marries Diane Olbright, an architect, on January 21, and the couple settle in Westchester County, New York. They divorce in 2013.
1980	Long Beach, California, publisher Applezaba Press releases Collins's second chapbook, *Video Poems*.
1985	At the suggestion of his friend and fellow poet Ron Koertge, Collins sends poems to the poet Miller Williams, director of University of Arkansas Press, who returns them—placing the strongest ones in a paper clip—offers encouraging advice, and invites him to resubmit.
1987	"Brooklyn Museum of Art" appears in the May 18, 1987, issue of the *New Yorker*, where Collins becomes a contributor for more than three decades.
1988	University of Arkansas Press publishes Collins's first full-length collection, *The Apple That Astonished Paris*. *Poetry* magazine features three poems, "Winter Syntax," "Books," and "A History of Weather," in its April issue, beginning an enduring and prolific publication history with the magazine. Collins receives a fellowship from the National Endowment for the Arts.
1991	University of Pittsburgh Press publishes *Questions about Angels*,

which Edward Hirsch selects as winner of the National Poetry Series.

1992   Named a Literary Lion by the New York Public Library. "Nostalgia" is chosen by guest editor Charles Simic to be included in *The Best American Poetry 1992*, the first of sixteen times Collins's poems appear in this annual anthology.

1993   Awarded a Guggenheim Fellowship.

1994   *Poetry* magazine names Collins "Poet of the Year."

1995   University of Pittsburgh Press publishes *The Art of Drowning*.

1997   Begins lengthy tenure as Visiting Writer at Sarah Lawrence College in New York City. The mock formal poem "Paradelle for Susan" appears in the *American Scholar*, resulting in a deluge of letters to the publisher from disconcerted readers. Collins releases *The Best Cigarette*, an audio recording of thirty-three of his poems.

1998   University of Pittsburgh Press publishes *Picnic, Lightning*. Collins appears for the first time on Garrison Keillor's *Prairie Home Companion*, reading selections from his new book, an appearance that substantially augments his popularity.

1999   In a December 19 profile in the *New York Times*, Bruce Weber labels Collins "the most popular poet in America." Collins's book sales continue to soar, and his frequent international poetry readings attract unprecedented numbers.

2001   Appointed Poet Laureate of the United States, serving two terms. As laureate, Collins establishes the "Poetry 180" website in an effort to engage high school students with poetry and helps support the Poetry Society of America's "Poetry in Motion," which places poems on public buses and subways. A June 22 appearance on NPR's *Fresh Air* further enhances his visibility and popularity. Following a lengthy permissions battle with University of Pittsburgh Press, Random House publishes *Sailing Alone around the Room: New and Selected Poems*, offering Collins a six-figure contract, secured by his agent Chris Calhoun, for his next three books. Lehman College names Collins Distinguished Professor of English.

2002   Random House publishes *Nine Horses*. Collins reads "The Names," honoring the victims and survivors of the 9/11 bombings, before a joint session of Congress on the first anniversary of the terrorist attacks.

2003   Random House publishes the anthology *Poetry 180*. Named Poet Laureate of New York, serving two terms.

2004   The Poetry Foundation names Collins the recipient of the Mark Twain Award for humor.

2005   Random House publishes *The Trouble with Poetry* and the anthology *180 More* and releases *Billy Collins Live*, a cd of a New York performance that includes an introduction by comedian and actor Bill Murray.

2006   Serves as guest editor of *The Best American Poetry*. Modern Haiku Press publishes a limited fine letter press edition of Collins's haikus, *She Was Just Seventeen*. Inspired by his *American Scholar* submission, Red Hen Press publishes *The Paradelle*, an anthology for which Collins provides "A Brief Introduction."

2008   Random House publishes *Ballistics*. Collins is named Senior Distinguished Fellow at Rollins Winter Park Institute. Discusses poetry and lyric writing with Paul Simon at the 92nd St. Y in New York City. The two pick up the discussion on three future occasions at Chautauqua Institute, Emory University, and Rollins College.

2009   Columbia University Press publishes *Bright Wings: An Illustrated Anthology of Poems about Birds*, edited by Collins and illustrated by David Sibley.

2010   Contributes the introduction to a new edition of Richard Brautigan's *Trout Fishing in America* released by Mariner Books.

2011   Random House publishes *Horoscopes for the Dead*. At the request of President and Mrs. Obama, Collins joins poet Rita Dove and others for "An Evening of Poetry at the White House" on May 11.

2012   Random House publishes *Aimless Love: New and Selected Poems*, which is a *New York Times* Best Seller. Appears in his first of two TEDTalks for NPR's Ted Radio Hour, discussing and presenting five animated adaptations of his poems, which were produced for the Sundance Channel.

2013   Reads his work in the Blue Room of the White House on October 23 at the request of First Lady Michelle Obama and Dr. Jill Biden, wife of Vice-President Joe Biden, during a visit from Kulsoom Nawaz, wife of Pakistan prime minister Nawaz Sharif.

2014   Receives the Norman Mailer Prize for "Distinguished Poetry." Publishes *Voyage*, a children's book illustrated by Karen Romagna. Paul McCartney joins Collins at Rollins College in October to discuss literature, songwriting, and his music career.

2015   Begins national tour with singer-songwriter Aimee Mann, whom he met when both were invited to the White House in 2011.

2016   Elected to the Academy of American Arts and Letters. Receives the Peggy V. Helmerich Distinguished Author Award from the Tulsa Library Trust for his "major contribution to the field of literature and letters." Collins retires from Lehman College after nearly five decades. Random House publishes his eleventh major collection, *The Rain in Portugal*, a *New York Times* Best Seller. The book features "Speed Walking on August 31, 2013," a tribute to Nobel Laureate Seamus Heaney, which appeared in the program for the late Irish poet's memorial service in 2013.

2019   Marries Suzannah Gilman, an attorney and writer, on July 21 in Southampton, New York.

2020   In March, during the early days of the Covid-19 pandemic in America, Collins begins a live thirty-minute daily poetry reading and discussion called *The Poetry Broadcast* on Facebook, which sustains a large, loyal global audience. In September, Random House publishes his twelfth major collection, *Whale Day*, selections of which appeared in the *New Yorker*, *The Atlantic*, and the *Paris Review* in the months preceding publication.

2021   Celebrates his eightieth birthday and the one-year anniversary of *The Poetry Broadcast* in March.

**Conversations with
Billy Collins**

Describing Ordinary Feelings

Terry Gross / 1998

This is the first of four interviews Terry Gross conducted with Billy Collins on her NPR show, *Fresh Air*. The interview aired on April 7, 1998 and was instrumental in introducing Collins's work to an expansive audience of American readers. Reprinted with the permission of WHYY, Inc. *Fresh Air* with Terry Gross is produced by WHYY in Philadelphia and distributed by NPR.

Terry Gross: This is *Fresh Air*. I'm Terry Gross. Our director, Roberta Shorrock, recently brought me a poem by Billy Collins about memory, or more precisely, about losing your memory, "Forgetfulness." I thought it perfectly described the frustrations of not being able to recall a book, or a name, or part of your life. Billy Collins has plenty of poems that perfectly describe ordinary feelings. As part of our celebration of National Poetry Month, we invited him to read a few and talk about his work. Billy Collins has won several poetry awards. He has been published in the 1992, '93, and '97 editions of the anthology *Best American Poetry*. He is a professor of English at City University of New York. His latest collection of poems is called *Picnic, Lightning*. Well, Billy, I want you to read your poem "Forgetfulness." I think you've described this as your "Over the Rainbow" poem. Is this like your greatest hit?

Billy Collins: It is my one hit. I feel embarrassed about reading it so many times, but then again, The Coasters never stopped singing "Charlie Brown." They never got tired of that. I think it has a kind of instant appeal because it's about something that's both humorous—we make fun of forgetfulness, absent-minded professors and people walking around with their glasses on their head looking for them—but at the same time the loss of memory is frightening. I try to handle both aspects.

Gross: Would you read it for us?

Collins: Sure. [Reads "Forgetfulness"]

Gross: Oh, this is the story of my life. [Laughs] I really like this poem.

Collins: [Laughs] Anyone over ten can relate to that.

Gross: That's right. I think it is probably particularly frightening to feel like you're losing your memory when you're a writer because so much of your material comes from your life, which you've lived and are beginning to forget.

Collins: Indeed. It starts with forgetting books. John Updike said that he was about halfway through Melville's novel *Redburn*, I think it was, before he realized that he'd read it before. And he came to that realization because he found his own notations in the margin. So, losing the library that you have spent so many years collecting in your mind can be a startling loss.

Gross: Now, the poem about forgetfulness that you just read us, do you know it by heart?

Collins: I do know that one by heart, yes. [Laughs]

Gross: [Laughs] That's good. How did you get to memorize it? Is it just from having read it a lot?

Collins: I think it's just from having read it a lot. Now that poetry has dropped end rhyme, at least, and regular meter, it's much more difficult to memorize. But one thing that helps you memorize a poem is the rhythmic quality of it. If it has a certain sure-footed rhythm, it's much easier to get it into your head. I think that's the case with that poem.

Gross: Well, it's spring, and a lot of people are starting to plan vacations. It is vacation planning time if you're lucky enough to have the time and money to afford to go on a vacation. You have a great poem about having to stay home, not being able to go on that vacation. [Laughs] The poem is called "Consolation." Will you tell us the story behind the poem before you read it to us?

Collins: Sure. I had planned to go to Europe with my wife one summer, but because of circumstances beyond our control, we had to scrub those plans, and we stayed home for the summer. I was trying to convince myself in this poem of the merits of just hanging around the house and not going anywhere. The poem is an unconvincing consolation. But, nonetheless, I'll read the poem. [Reads "Consolation"]

Gross: One of the things I really like about your poetry is, well, how plainspoken it is, in a way. It's about very ordinary experience, and it uses an ideal version of ordinary language.

Collins: I think poetic language is, in fact, *that*. It's language that is tidied. It's language that is steamed clean or purified, language that comes under principles of organization and even neatness that are missing in conversation, and even in well-written prose, perhaps.

Gross: Did your poems always stick to ordinary life and always have the directness that they have? Or did you ever write in other styles?

Collins: No, I wrote in *awful* styles when I started. Mostly slavishly imitative styles.

Gross: Of whom?

Collins: William Carlos Williams, Wallace Stevens, Ferlinghetti, producing really awful versions, almost unintentional parodies of these people, and it was really before I found my voice. That expression is one I am not happy with. It sounds like your voice has slipped behind the sofa cushions. Eventually, I started to write poems that I felt only *I* could've written. I think that's the point you either get to or you don't in writing poems. I felt that I had released a lot of myself into the poems, and they did become, as you said, more relaxed. They start out using a very conversational tone. I think it's a sign of my overall interest in attracting and keeping readers. My poems have different subjects, but I think the ultimate subject of all these poems is the engagement that takes place between the poem and the reader.

Gross: Well, I know exactly what you mean, and there are a lot of poems where I'll really love the beginning, and then I just totally get lost deeper in, and the imagery becomes so obscure. I might like the way the language sounds, but I have no idea sometimes what the poet is communicating.

Collins: Yes, I think there are several reasons for obscurity in poetry, and one of them is to hide the banality of what's really being said. I'm not greatly concerned with the large social issue of what the audience is for American poetry, but I'm very deeply concerned about the audience for *my* poetry. I try to address that concern in every poem I write, usually by starting out on some familiar note so that the poem at least *begins* with something we have in common. Or something that's impossible to question, like "I'm sitting here looking out the window at a bird." Then, I feel the poem can take the reader on a ride into less familiar territory, perhaps, to a place of surprise toward the end. But I really think that I'm supplying half of an engagement; the second half takes place in the reader's mind. A closed book of poems on a shelf is about as vital as a can of beans sitting in the darkness of a pantry.

Gross: I know what you mean, and I think as a reader, one of the things I gravitate toward in your poems is a sense of recognition, you know? Oh yeah, I know that feeling! I've had that feeling. I've experienced the forgetfulness that you're describing. I've experienced not being able to take that vacation. [Laughs]

Collins: I think the case might be that most of the poems that I'm writing, and the ones I've been reading of my own, are not so much memory driven, but they are more conceptually driven. Not by a big concept, but maybe just by a little notion. I tend not to write about my past in the autobiographical way of poems that include, as their nervous subject, the poet's family or his or her childhood. There seems to be today two kinds of poets: one has had a miserable childhood, and the other has had a happy childhood. The people with happy childhoods write about a variety of things, and the people with miserable childhoods just write about the misery of their childhood. Also, I don't want to presume that anyone is interested in my past. What the reader is interested in is a notion or subject that overlaps the reader's experience.

Gross: There's a poem I want you to read called "Osso Buco." This is really a poem about contentment. Is contentment a difficult thing to write about?

Collins: It is nearly impossible to write about contentment because serious poetry, at least since the Romantics, around beginning of the nineteenth century, takes sadness as a given. I think people are very suspicious of literary works that include or center on pleasure, happiness, contentment. But, of course, these things are part of our lives.

Gross: But the kind of contentment that this poem is describing, it isn't even like ecstasy or the big happiness. It's merely contentment.

Collins: It's a common kind of contentment induced by food, but the poem gets a little more complicated than that later on.

Gross: Why don't you read it for us?

Collins: I'd be glad to. [Reads "Osso Buco"]

Gross: How did you decide to write that poem?

Collins: I don't know where the poems are going. Most poets say that, but it does tend to be true. I wanted to write a poem in praise of the pleasure of eating this terrific meal. I didn't know where the poem would go. I think of poems as little journeys or rides, as kind of cheap forms of transportation. I like to end up in a very different place at the end of the poem from where we were at the beginning. Here, I start at the kitchen table, and I end up in the middle of the Earth. That's the kind of travel that interests me. It's like driving a car at night, where the headlights allow you to see far enough ahead to continue going, but you can't see any point beyond that.

Gross: You teach.

Collins: I do.

Gross: And you do a lot of poetry workshops. You actually have a poem that's very funny about trying to give constructive feedback to poets who are writing not very good poems. I'm going to ask you to read just a short excerpt of this poem, "Workshop."

Collins: Okay.

Gross: Can you start with the "Maybe it's just me" part?

Collins: Sure. I'm speaking here in the voice of someone in a workshop who is trying to analyze or understand a poem, which we gather is a poem that lies in the back of this one. And what we gather from the attempt is that it is resistant to understanding. [Reads from "Workshop"]

Gross: Is there a specific poem you're referring to in this?

Collins: No, just the terribly disorganized and seemingly nonsensical poem that's being discussed here at great length.

Gross: [Laughing] Right. When you're critiquing such a poem in one of your workshops, do you have nice ways or just direct ways of expressing what you think of the poem?

Collins: Well, I try to be as nice as possible, to a point. It's important to separate the writer from the poem. The workshop is the beginning of a poem's independence. As a rule, the poet is expected not to talk during the discussion. I think you try to establish the sovereignty of the poem, and once you do that, the comments that you offer are really comments about the poem, not the poet. So, nothing should be taken as a personal offense, even though people feel intimately connected to what they've written. The idea is to help the poem stand on its two feet and achieve some separation from the poet. In workshops, poems are moving away from their writers and into the world.

Gross: Do you find that you've had a lot of students who try much too hard to find that big metaphor to put into a poem?

Collins: Yes, the advice is always, "Save something for the next poem," [Laughter] if they try to jam life, consciousness, death, the vortex of loneliness, etc. into one poem. It's a common mistake to start too big, and a failure to look around one's self in the moment to see that poems really are strewn all around us, potentially, but what we need to do is be *attentive*. I think it's that kind of vigilance to daily life, to what lies around us, that can trigger poems rather than the big ideas that are best delivered from a cliff overlooking a raging sea.

Gross: You're very good in your poems at describing how effortless writing sometimes can be and how difficult it can be at other times. In a poem called "Tuesday, June 4, 1991" you write, "I feel like the secretary to the morning whose only / responsibility is to take down its bright, airy dictation / until it's time to go to lunch with the other girls, / all of us ordering the cottage cheese with half a pear." [Laughs] But then you have another poem about how hard it is to write, and I was trying to find that poem this morning, and I couldn't find it, so maybe you know the poem I'm talking about.

Collins: I'm not sure which poem. Sometimes the writing is easy and sometimes it's hard. There's kind of a downhill poem, the kind that does tend to write itself slightly. Then, there's a very uphill poem that requires a tremendous amount of sweat. It's very different for different poets. I think for some poets, it's ninety percent revision. I've compared it to what I consider the two styles of cooking. One style of cook cleans as he goes along, right? You kind of dice up a carrot and then you have to clean the cutting board. And the other type of cook makes a huge mess and cleans it up later. Some writers want to get it right the first time. They can't proceed with the next sentence until the first one is correct. And my style is more to make a mess, just to crash through and keep something of the spontaneity of the moment because the person who comes back to revise the poem is really a different person. It's like Heraclitus saying you can't stick your foot into the same stream twice. It's not even the same foot! The person who comes back the next morning or the next month to revise is a slightly different creature. And I'd rather not have the poem be a collaboration between these two competing sides of myself. I'd rather have the heart of it, at least the thrust of it, come out of one moment, one sitting, one mood . . . all at one time.

Gross: Now, most of your poems are not very autobiographical. They're about discrete moments in time, but they're not going over your childhood, the story of your life. How much of that is because of wanting to maintain a sense of privacy?

Collins: I think it's more trying to maintain a sense of audience, really. I know from experience that most people, for instance, are not interested in anyone's family but their own. Or if they are, it's in a much less intense way.

Gross: But wait, they're interested in reading about other people's families who are *like* their own?

Collins: Yes, I suppose so. I think you read to discover not the poet, but you read to discover yourself. I don't want the poem to get stuck in the past. The past is just a means to an end, which is the present. Many of my poems start in this discrete moment, a little haiku-like. Haiku is the great form that boxes in a tiny moment. And I like to have the poem begin with the occasion of its own present. I'm a little bored with poems that begin and stay in the past. I feel that fiction can do that better than poetry.

Gross: You're, I think, very aware of the different languages we have for different things. One of your poems, in part, is about the language of catalogs, particularly, fancy female lingerie catalogs. [Laughs] The poem I'm thinking of is called "Victoria's Secret," and maybe you could say a few words about writing the poem before you read us an excerpt from it.

Collins: Well, we're all familiar with this catalog. It comes to our house very frequently, a number of times a week it seems.

Gross: [Laughing] That's right.

Collins: It has lots of guises, manifestations, but it's basically the same catalog in different form, and I don't know why we get this catalog. [Laughter] My wife must've ordered something, like a belt or a pair of sunglasses at some point, but it's very distracting to have this with the mail almost every day. And again, as a way of dealing with it, I wrote this poem. And the poem tries to recapture the process of actually leafing through the magazine, and it also tries to include a lot of the amazing jargon that is in the copy next to the pictures. It's kind of a long poem because the catalog is so long, but maybe what I will do is read portions of it. [Reads from "Victoria's Secret"]

Gross: Billy, how did this really funny poem about the models in the Victoria's Secret catalog and the fancy-schmancy language describing the fancy-schmancy lingerie end up in sleep and dreams and this larger meditation on life?

Collins: I think it follows the pattern of a number of my poems that have tried to begin with something amusing, perhaps—although this goes on a bit in this poem—but finally the humor is an attempt to disarm the reader, to make the reader a little more susceptible to something that might be more serious and that might come toward the end of the poem. Humor in poetry is a touchy thing because it's considered to be opposed to seriousness. But I consider humor a kind of door into the serious. I think it's a way of gaining access to deeper themes.

Gross: A lot of your poems have to do with sleep and dreams. Several of them end there. They're just totally about that. And I'm wondering if sleep is often restful for you? [Laughs]

Collins: Or I'm just lazy is what you're implying. Well, Keats is the great poet of sleep and dreams and drowsiness, which can be a receptive state of mind. It might be that I just have too much time on my hands. Max Beerbohm once said that the hardest thing about being a poet was knowing what to do with the other twenty-three and a half hours of the day.

Gross: Right. How long are you really going to sit there and write?

Collins: That's right.

Gross: So do you take a lot of naps?

Collins: I do when I can, yes. [Laughter] And I think waking up from a nap or from sleep is a very good state in which to think about things to write about and even to begin writing. Before the language of the world has a chance to infiltrate your ears, before you hear the radio or someone else talking or read a newspaper. I think that's a good time to write because I think language can be fresher in those occasions when you're still connected to the unconscious.

Gross: You have a poem called "The Night House," which is in part about sleep and a difference between the waking mind and the unconscious mind, the sleeping mind.

Collins: Yes, another great time to write, of course, is in response to insomnia, and I suppose that poem is a meditation on insomnia, plus also the idea that strange things happen when we're asleep. You know how in those old cartoons, the teapot, the toaster, and all sorts of things in the kitchen come alive, but here the parts of ourselves go off in odd directions. Shall I read it?

Gross: Please.

Collins: [Reads "The Night House"]

Gross: That's a beautiful poem.

Collins: Thank you, Terry. [Laughs]

Gross: [Laughs] On those nights when you can't sleep, when you do have insomnia, do you panic about life in general?

Collins: Well, that nervousness, the anxiety, or the coffee that doesn't let you sleep is something that makes the pen jitter. This is the stuff that poets wag their tails over. It is a nervous response, a sign that there's some turbulence or some disturbance in your inner life. And for me, one of the functions, or one of the beauties, of poetry, is that it's something to *do* with your inner life; it's an activity. The writing and the construction of poems is an external activity that brings the inner life out of yourself and gives you a way to deal with it, maybe even create an understanding of it.

Gross: Another theme that you often write about is music. You obviously really love music: soul music, jazz, a lot of poems about jazz. You even have a poem about reading the saxophonist Art Pepper's autobiography and a wonderful poem about piano lessons. Would you talk a little bit about the interplay between music and poetry for you? I should preface this by saying that poetry about jazz is often a really frightening prospect because there are a lot of really bad jazz poems, in which the poet does a really lousy job of trying to use words to sound like a bebop solo.

Collins: Exactly. [Laughs]

Gross: It ends up just sounding like a failed hipster instead. I don't think that your poems try to approximate bop solos. I think they try to approximate your feelings about music.

Collins: That's very well put because I think there's a lot of really bad jazz poetry, and it's bad for the reasons that you say. What those poets are doing has been called the *imitative fallacy.* They're trying to make the poem come off as sounding like jazz. For me, if I write about jazz, it's simply as subject matter or part of the atmosphere of the moment. I have a poem about learning to play a difficult song on the piano. I have meditations on listening to music, on how a particular piece by Thelonious Monk seems to accompany the snow that's falling outside the window. I think the music puts one in a slightly meditative state, and there's a lot of different angles to jazz. And there's something in common I suppose because writing should at least give the illusion of having an improvisational spirit to it, that it doesn't seem completely planned out. It seems to be finding its way through itself the way an alto solo would.

Gross: I'd like you to end with a poem called "Nightclub." And perhaps you can introduce it for us before you read it.

Collins: Okay. This is a poem about jazz in some ways, but I literally started writing it when I was at the typewriter one day, and there was an album playing in the background. It was a famous album with Johnny Hartman and John Coltrane. It was playing in the other room, though, and all I could hear were words like "you're so beautiful, and I'm such a fool to be in love with you" and that kind of thing. I just wrote those words down and realized that there are so many songs that have that theme to them, and then the poem took off from there. [Reads "Nightclub"]

Gross: Billy Collins, I love your poems. I want to thank you so much for reading some of them for us. I wish we had time for some more.

Collins: The pleasure's been all mine, Terry.

Interview with Billy Collins

Alletha Saunders / 2001

This interview appeared in *Fugue, the literary digest of the University of Idaho,* No. 21 (Summer 2001): 64–71. It was conducted while Collins served as Distinguished Visiting Writer, a few months prior to his being named United States Poet Laureate. Reprinted by permission of *Fugue.*

Alletha Saunders: What was your first experience with poetry?

Billy Collins: Mother Goose, the mother of us all.

Saunders: What is it about poetry that draws or compels you to use it?

Collins: I don't "use" it. I write and read it. I write it because a) it is the highest game that can be played, and b) it offers the opportunity of the continuation of the human voice beyond the grave. I want to be a literary ghost.

Saunders: You call poetry the highest game that can be played. Can you explain what you meant by that and why it is so?

Collins: I should qualify that. What I meant was that poetry is the highest game that can be played with language. That might even serve as a quicky definition of poetry-the deployment of language at its highest level of playfulness. In poetry, language is put to its most extreme uses. The limits of its possibilities are tested. Poetry is the place where the language is most aware of itself, of the strange and fresh ways it is being used. In the dictionary, words stand in a line looking all logical and sure of their places and chaperoned by a definition. And in most prose, language does its job by pointing to things. "Cat" points to the cat. "Baseball" brings the baseball to mind. But in poetry, language is returned to its once magical state. The words are surprised to be there. Some seem relieved, others embarrassed. The poet has brought them out of the orphanage for a day at the beach.

Saunders: What do you see as the function of humor in poetry?

Collins: I would distinguish between poems that set out to be funny—this would include light verse—and poems that discover something humorous as they go along. I enjoy reading some of the first category, but I write in the second. For me humor is a way of seeing the world and a check against the overly serious poems I used to write and still hate to read. When I think of its effect on the reader—and this is only an afterthought—I would say humor is a disarming device, a way of seducing the reader and giving him or her a reason to continue reading. When we respond to humor, we may laugh, but in poetry we usually react silently; yet we can feel something opening inside, a receptivity begins. That reader is in a position to be led into the deeper corners of the poem where the laughter will be replaced by something else, which we may call "something else."

Saunders: What do you think the next new thing to come along in poetry will be or what would you like it to be?

Collins: The future holds no interest for me (he said flicking his ash on the carpet).

Saunders: Do you have particular writing habits that you think are good for beginning poets to cultivate?

Collins: First off, I should say that whenever I am asked to give advice about writing or to explain how I write, I feel like someone who has been asked to explain to a classroom of Martians how to kiss. It's something you discover on your own, and at some level, it's hard to do it wrong.

I have no work habits whatsoever. If I did, I would probably write less because I would resent having to stick to a schedule or be at my desk at a certain time.

"Whatever works" sounds like a bumper sticker, but that is what it comes down to. Catullus said, "Never a day without a line," which is good advice, though weeks have gone by without a line (or a peep) out of me. For me writing in the early morning is best, that is, before my head has been contaminated with the public language of the radio, the breakfast table, the unwanted email. But young poets tend to write at night. Dangerous. You are apt to think you are the only person on earth, the only light in the house. If I feel tempted to write at night, I just turn all the lights off. At night you can be more productive drinking with your friends or sleeping.

Saunders: In workshop settings, a common statement is "Perhaps this poem is really two poems?" Do you ever find this to be the case in early drafts of your own work?

Collins: No. Again, the part that may seem not to belong to the poem gets tossed out, not set aside to make another poem out of later. That is a kind of piece-work I would not be comfortable with. I don't want to picture myself at a desk looking through a pile of little scraps saying, "Oh here's a little thing I saved from that all night session from a couple of weeks ago." Start freshly. New day, blank yellow pad, sharpened #2 pencil. Off you go.

Saunders: Are there times when you find it accomplishes more to throw drafts away, why?

Collins: I throw drafts away all the time, and I wish more people did. If a poem has no flow as I am writing it, I will often pitch it and start again later. The poem should have a bolt of energy running through it (the Chinese call it chi) and if I cannot feel it, the draft is burned—crumpled into a ball and rolled on the carpet with the others. If you have a kitten, they love playing with rolled up balls of paper, and that may be all a failed draft is good for. Why make a reader unhappy when you can make a kitten happy? They tell you in workshops to save everything. You could use it later. Rubbish. Pitch it. If you use it later, it will seem attached to the poem by duct tape. If you burn the rice, you throw it out and start again. I would say throw the pot out too. What the hell. A great satisfaction lies in throwing things out. Ask any monk. Did you ever see a monk holding a garage sale?

Saunders: In the process of writing and revising your poetry, do you find the exploration of an idea sometimes more satisfying (intellectually, poetically, etc.) than the final product?

Collins: No. Although much of the fun is in getting there, getting there itself is crucial. If the poem cannot find a way to end itself, or if the poet cannot supply an ending, then the whole enterprise is thrown into question. To the reader, a poem may seem to be about love or separation or celebration or whatever. But to the poet who is in the process of writing the poem, the poem is about only one thing: its completion. The "inspiration" for starting a poem may remain a kind of mystery. The impetus shaken out of the sleeve. But what inspires the poet to continue to write beyond this initial impulse is a deeply rooted desire for completion. To make a thing that can stand on its own after you leave the room.

Saunders: How do you know when you are finished revising a poem?

Collins: I know I am finished revising a poem when I feel that instead of straightening its tie so that it will look a little better, I begin wondering whether it maybe shouldn't be wearing a suit at all, and that perhaps it should change its mind about going to the party. Maybe rent a video.

Saunders: How has your revision process changed with success?

Collins: Success has nothing to do with it, at least I would like to believe. I put less and less time into revision because I think that I am learning more and more how the poem should go on the first writing, how to steer the poem correctly so that revision never means overhauling the poem radically, rather making small adjustments. If something *that* crucial were wrong with the poem, I would just pitch it. Again, I am not a string saver. If a poem is aborted at some point, I throw it out and start again. Or throw it out and don't write for a week or two.

You never know what line may be your last. Of course, the distinction between "writing" and "revision" is false. When I am writing I am always revising. And when I revise, am I not writing? William Matthews put it best when he said that revision is not cleaning up after the party; it *is* the party.

Saunders: Do you have friends evaluate a poem before you submit it to a magazine?

Collins: Never. I still believe in the romantic conviction that poetry writing is a private and solitary activity. If I did ask my friends to evaluate it, I suspect I would not have any friends. I would be hurt by their suggestions; they would be irked by my panting. We would find new ways to avoid each other.

Saunders: Are there two or three books you would say are must haves for any aspiring poet?

Collins: I would recommend these to an aspiring whatever: Robert Burton, *An Anatomy of Melancholy*; Gaston Bachelard, *The Poetics of Space*; Fernando Pessoa, *Always Astonished*.

Saunders: You've said in this interview that you wanted "to be a literary ghost." Why?

Collins: Gee, I said that? Perhaps I meant that I saw poetry as a way of sustaining one's voice beyond the grave. If you manage to write a couple of poems that really last—I'm not saying I have achieved that—then they can never shut you up. You will still be talking after all the lights have been turned off and the chairs turned upside down on the tables. There you will be: a literary ghost, scaring the children with your poems.

Billy Collins, The Art of Poetry No. 83

George Plimpton / 2001

This interview appeared in the *Paris Review*, Issue 159, Fall 2001. It was conducted by the journal's first editor, George Plimpton, shortly after Collins was named United States Poet Laureate. Copyright © 2001 by the *Paris Review*, used by permission of The Wylie Agency LLC.

The big news, of course, is that Billy Collins has been appointed the new poet laureate by the Library of Congress, now the newest of a distinguished list that among others includes Robert Penn Warren, Joseph Brodsky, Robert Pinsky, and most recently, Stanley Kunitz.

Collins's credentials, despite starting a career as a poet at the late age of forty, are impressive indeed. His various wonderfully named collections of poetry include *Video Poems, Pokerface, Questions about Angels, The Art of Drowning, The Apple That Astonished Paris, Taking Off Emily Dickinson's Clothes,* and *Picnic, Lightning. Sailing Alone around the Room: New and Selected Poems* will be published this fall. His last three collections of poems have broken sales records for poetry. A well-known voice on National Public Radio, his public readings, perhaps better described as performances, are invariably put on before packed audiences.

His work is identified largely by its humor, which he speaks of as being "a door into the serious"—a comment echoed by John Updike's sentiment: "Billy Collins writes lovely poems . . . limpid, gently startling, more serious than they seem, they describe all the worlds that are and were and some others besides."

Collins lives in Somers, New York, a few miles from Katonah, which is about an hour's ride on the commuter train from Grand Central Station. The Katonah station is unique in that it is set in the middle of town, so that one steps out of the train just a yard or so from the main street and the arts and crafts shops that line the far side. Collins's home, a few miles away, is a renovated farmhouse that dates back to the 1860s. His wife, Diane, was away at work (she is an architect), but on hand was the family dog, Jeannine, a mixed-breed collie named after a song popularized by Cannonball Adderly. Collins often breaks away from work to play Adderly-mode jazz on a piano in the living room.

Jeannine made it clear she wanted to be taken outside for exercise—which entailed running down a steep slope of lawn to retrieve a frazzled-looking frisbee, so indented with teeth marks as to resemble (as Collins put it) "the end of a worried writer's pencil." Jeannine finally seemed wearied enough to allow Collins to invite his guest back in the house for the interview.

In manner, Billy Collins is very much like what one would expect from reading his poems—quick to add a touch of humor to whatever he has to say, however serious the topic, but leaving no doubt that he is a very dedicated practitioner of his art. He teaches at Lehman College of the City University of New York; one envies his students for their chance to study comparative literature from such a source. And yet there is nothing of the formal Ivory Tower mien about Collins: he is, for example, a passionate golfer, and what time he can take off from the lecture circuit (he is in considerable demand, giving over forty readings a year) and his teaching duties at Lehman, he spends touring the historic golf courses of the country with his golfing friend and literary agent, Chris Calhoun. Perhaps his informal side is best reflected by his given name: he was christened William after his father, thus Willy for a while, and then Billy, which he has kept as his nom de plume as much in reaction to the pretentiousness of those writers who use their initials, or one initial and a given name, as in W. James Collins, or whatever.

The interview took place in the small comfortable study of his home— shelves of books, a pair of paintings, one an abstract by Dan Christensen, the other a 1930s subway scene by George Tooker.

Billy Collins: I'd like to get something straightened out at the beginning: I write with a Uni-Ball Onyx Micropoint on nine-by-seven bound notebooks made by a Canadian company called Blueline. After I do a few drafts, I type up the poem on a Macintosh G3 and then send it out the door.

George Plimpton: Well, that's certainly the kind of information we're after, but can you tell us about the actual making of what you send out? Could you go through the genesis of a poem?

Collins: There's a lot of waiting around until something happens. Some poets like David Lehman and William Stafford set out on these very willful programs to write a poem a day. They're extending what Catullus said about "never a day without a line." But most poets don't write a poem a day. For me it's a very sporadic activity. Until recently, I thought "occasional poetry" meant that you wrote only occasionally. So there's a lot of waiting, and there's a kind of vigilance involved. I think what gets a poem going is an initiating line. Sometimes a first line will occur, and it goes nowhere; but other times—and this, I think, is a sense you develop—I can tell that the line wants to continue. If it does, I can feel a sense of momentum— the poem finds a reason for continuing. The first line is the DNA of the poem; the rest of the poem is constructed out of that first line. A lot of it has to do with tone because tone is the key signature for the poem. The basis of trust for a reader used to be meter and end-rhyme. Now it's tone that establishes the poet's authority. The first few lines keep giving birth to more and more lines. Like most poets, I don't know where I'm going. The pen is an instrument of discovery rather than just a recording implement. If you write a letter of resignation or something with an agenda, you're simply using a pen to record what you have thought out. In a poem, the pen is more like a flashlight, a Geiger counter, or one of those metal detectors that people walk around beaches with. You're trying to discover something that you don't know exists, maybe something of value.

Plimpton: What inspires that first line? Is it something you see? Is it a passing thought, a line of someone else's work?

Collins: There can be remote influences, but I think the line itself comes out of talking to yourself. It's a matter of paying attention to the detritus that floats through your head all the time—little phrases that through your own self-talking, your talk monitor, sometimes pop up. Also, I try to start the poem conversationally. Poems, for me, begin as a social engagement. I want to establish a kind of sociability or even hospitality at the beginning of a poem. The title and the first few lines are a kind of welcome mat where I am inviting the reader inside. What I do with the reader later can be more complicated, but the beginning of the poem is a seductive technique for me, a way of making a basic engagement. Then I hope the poem gets a little bit ahead of me and the reader.

Plimpton: What about revision?

Collins: I try to write very fast. I don't revise very much. I write the poem in one sitting. Just let it rip. It's usually over in twenty to forty minutes. I'll go back and tinker with a word or two, change a line for some metrical reason weeks later, but I try to get the whole thing just done. Most of these poems have a kind of rhetorical momentum. If the whole thing doesn't come out at once, it doesn't come out at all. I just pitch it.

Plimpton: You throw it out?

Collins: People say, Don't throw anything away. This is standard workshop advice: Always save everything. You could use it in another poem. I don't believe that. I say, get rid of it. Because if it got into a later poem it would be Scotch-taped on. It would not be part of the organic, you know, chi, the spine that the poem has, the way it all should be one continuous movement.

Plimpton: What was that word you used?

Collins: Chi. I think they use that in feng shui. It's the Chinese sense of energy that runs through things. Poems that lack that seem very mechanically put together, like a piece here and a part there. Because of the workshop and the MFA phenomenon there's much too much revision going on. Revision can grind a good impulse to dust. Of course, the distinction between revision and writing is kind of arbitrary because when I am writing I am obviously revising. And when I revise, I'm writing, aren't I? I love William Matthews's idea—he says that revision is not cleaning up after the party; revision *is* the party! That's the fun of it, making it right, getting the best words in the best order.

Plimpton: Could you tell us about growing up, your family?

Collins: Both of my parents were born in 1901 and both lived into their nineties, the two of them just about straddling the century. My father was from a large Irish family from Lowell, Massachusetts, a mill town, incidentally Kerouac's birthplace and the site of his first novel. I've never been to Lowell, but I was just invited by an editor of a magazine to go up there and write about my father and look at the Jack Kerouac place. I have a poem called "Lowell," which is about the coincidence of my father being born in the same town as Jack Kerouac. You couldn't find two more disparate characters. The end of the poem says something like, "He would have told Neal Cassady to let him out at the next light."

My mother was born on a farm in Canada. She was the one who taught me to read by reading to me. I have a feeling that was one of the most important experiences of my life. At some point I could read by myself, but I didn't want to be weaned away from that—I wanted to be read to. I have a secret theory that people who are addicted to reading are almost trying to recreate the joy, the comfortable joy of being read to as a child by a parent or a friendly uncle or an older sibling. Being read to as a child is one of the great experiences in life. Of course, I was always fascinated by the ability to read, and I'll make this confession: before I could read, I *pretended* I could. My parents would have company over at our house, and I would get out a volume of *Compton's Encyclopedia*, at the age of four or five, and sit there in an armchair and pretend to be reading—I would look very studious. I was the youngest phony in America. My parents would wink at their friends and, thinking that I had taken everybody in, I'd head off to bed.

Plimpton: What did your mother read to you?

Collins: *Black Beauty* and *The Yearling*, sentimental animal fiction. I was down giving a reading in Gainesville, Florida, last year, and I was taken out to the home of Marjorie Rawlings. It's kind of funky and frozen in time. Even her car is there. Once I had one of those bad measles where you have to stay in bed for a long time. They had to pull the shades down in those days. Well, you know the *Lassie* stories, Albert Payson Terhune's books—my father brought home the entire collection of seventeen collie novels, and I tore through them. They're all the same book. Then The Hardy Boys. Those were my earliest addictions to literature after *Mother Goose*. My mother also recited poetry. She had hundreds of lines of poetry in her head, mostly learned as a schoolgirl in Canada. She lived to be ninety-five, and up to her death she could rattle off stanza after stanza. I force all my students to memorize. Some take to it and others don't. I'll often say, "You need to memorize a minimum of fourteen lines," and they'll take a poem of seventeen lines and memorize fourteen lines and then stop. There are just three more lines, for God's sake, couldn't you just push a little bit! Other students will memorize thirty or forty lines with ease and pleasure. I feel, no matter what, they'll at least have a poem in their head. They can leave the class not remembering my name or anything I said during the year, but damnit they'll have fourteen lines of somebody.

Plimpton: When did you start writing?

Collins: I started writing very early. I have a memory of the first time I was inspired to write. I was in the back of my parents' car on the FDR Drive in New York City. I was about ten. I was in the backseat and I saw a sailboat on the East River. I remember asking my mother for a pencil or a pen, and I wrote something down. I don't know what I wrote down. But I do remember it was the first time I saw something and felt some kind of responsibility to record some reaction to it. It was my first act of literature! But my first real book wasn't published until I was in my forties. A late bloomer. I stayed kind of underground, never took a workshop, never associated much with other poets.

Plimpton: You published some poems in *Rolling Stone*.

Collins: I published a lot of poems in the back pages of *Rolling Stone*. Little four to six-line poems, tucked in among the record reviews. They were mostly kind of pothead poems. *Rolling Stone* is no literary magazine, but it had a huge readership, and they paid about thirty-five dollars a poem. This was back in the early seventies. I wrote very short poems in those days. I thought writing poetry was like blowing out birthday candles—you had to do it in one breath. It took me a while to figure out how to write a longer poem. I learned how to expand the poem outward. I think it was a matter of letting more of my life into the poems. I had been keeping myself at a distance, writing poems that were quite divorced from my real life. I don't know how or why exactly, but I got to the point where my life got into my poetry.

The magazine that really influenced me was *Poetry*. It used to come to my father's office on Wall Street. I'm not sure how it came there. No one in the office read it. The company chairman was a kind of philanthropist. Maybe one day he wrote a check and the magazine kept coming.

My father knew I was interested in poetry, and he brought this magazine home every month. That was the first time I heard contemporary voices in poetry. Until that point, in high school, I had only been exposed to "school poetry" like Longfellow and Whittier. Here in *Poetry* I heard these people *talking*. They sounded relaxed, and that connected me to the tone of modern poetry. At the age of eighteen I sent some poems to *Poetry*. I got a note back from Henry Rago encouraging me—not to send again, mind you, but to continue writing. I was so in the dark, I thought maybe everyone got a letter like this. Maybe they did. But the next time I sent anything to *Poetry* was almost twenty-five years later. In 1987 I sent poems to Joseph Parisi. He took some, and he's been taking poems ever since. I'd waited twenty-five years to strike again! Probably the editors of magazines would appreciate it if more of their young writers waited a respectful amount of time before they started resubmitting!

Plimpton: What were you doing during the twenty-five years?

Collins: I was still writing but writing badly under various influences. Actually, I don't think you can be really badly influenced by anyone, as long as it makes you write. Borges says, "I was a young man, so, of course, I had to disguise myself." I was disguising myself as Lawrence Ferlinghetti for a while, then for a long time as Wallace Stevens and Hart Crane. I went to graduate school, got a PhD, and began a career as a professor. The poet emerged gradually. I was under the mistaken modernist belief that there was an unbreakable connection between value and difficulty, so I wrote a lot of impenetrable poetry.

Plimpton: Was there a time when your true self suddenly emerged, an epiphany: I mustn't be a Stevens; I mustn't be a Ferlinghetti?

Collins: I think "finding your voice" is a false concept. It leads you to believe that it's out there somewhere, like it's behind the sofa cushions. I think your voice is always inside of you, and you find it by releasing things into your work that you have inside. I grew by allowing aspects of myself that I had previously excluded into the poetry. I think all poets—younger poets particularly—have a private sense of decorum, meaning they feel there are certain things they should write about and other things they shouldn't. I don't even think this is conscious in most cases, but like other young poets I would put on my poetry goggles when I wrote, and I would see only these so-called *poetic* things I should write about, and the rest of my life was very disconnected from that. There was, for instance, no humor. I thought poetry should be humorless. The Romantic poets drove sex and humor out of poetry. If you look before 1798 you find plenty of sex and humor. Just look at "The Rape of the Lock," or Chaucer, for that matter. They don't call Shakespeare's comedies *comedies* for nothing. But Wordsworth and Coleridge drove those two things out of poetry—humor was consigned to the subcategory of light verse. I don't know what happened to the sex. It's back now. Philip Larkin said it started in 1964.

There's still a sense of decorum dominant in American poetry. Philip Levine is famous for being the poet of the blue-collar worker. He's a fine poet, but his reputation really shows how few people write about work. Most poets are teachers now, attached to universities the way they used to attach themselves to cafés, but very few poets write about teaching. Something else that is excluded is wives and husbands. Particularly wives. Married poets don't write about their wives. It's like the *W* word.

Plimpton: Has teaching affected your work?

Collins: Many writers say the university life is in conflict with their own work, but for me it's really just the opposite. I've been teaching in the City University of New York system for about thirty years. I keep teaching *The Norton Anthology*, and many of my poems show an awareness of that. I have a poem called "Lines Composed over Three Thousand Miles from Tintern Abbey." I have a poem about splitting wood that begins with the word *frost*: "Frost covered this decades ago," referring to frost covering the ground. I figured you can't write a poem about splitting wood without using the word *frost*—then at least you've nodded to him. I have a poem called "Musée des Beaux Arts Revisited," a rewriting of the Auden poem. Also "Monday Morning," which is a rewriting of the first stanza of Stevens's "Sunday Morning." I make open allusions instead of veiled allusions, and teaching—taking that ride again and again on those poems—has kept them alive for me.

Plimpton: Did you have any early feedback?

Collins: Miller Williams, who was my first editor as well as the poet who read at Clinton's second inauguration, was a very influential person in my career. He was editor of the University of Arkansas Press and published my first real book, *The Apple That Astonished Paris*. The title comes from a comment by Cézanne, who said at one point, "With an apple I want to astonish Paris." I thought, What an amazing contrast between a little thing and a big thing, a natural thing and a man-made thing. Such strange braggadocio: "With an apple I want to astonish Paris!" I had gotten a manuscript together. A friend of mine suggested, "Send it down to Miller Williams." So I sent Miller Williams about forty-five poems. I got a quick response; he'd taken a paper clip and put it around seventeen of these poems. He said in the letter, "You have seventeen really good poems here, and the others don't live up to that standard. If you can write twenty-five or thirty more poems as good as those seventeen, I'll publish your book." I started in almost right away and went through a very productive period, basically just trying to please this guy Miller Williams whom I'd never met and did not meet until quite recently. It was instruction by paper clip. He didn't have to explain. As soon as I saw the seventeen poems, I knew what I had. I threw the other ones out.

Plimpton: You had that much faith in that paper clip?

Collins: That paper clip was worth an MFA. A year and a half or so later I sent him down the poems, and he said, "We've got a book here."

Plimpton: If you had to construct a poet out of whole cloth, so to speak, what attributes would you give him or her?

Collins: A Frankenstein monster! First, a sense of attentiveness. Then wanting to hang around the language. If you look a word up in the dictionary, and twenty minutes later you're still wandering around in the dictionary, you probably have the most basic equipment you need to be a poet. It's just liking the texture of language. I think there's another thing, a kind of attitude—an attitude of not ever getting used to being alive, of not ever taking your life for granted.

There's a very deep strain of existential gratitude that runs through a lot of poetry. It's certainly in haiku. Almost every haiku says the same thing: it's amazing to be alive here. There's a little haiku: "A cherry tree in blossom / In the distance / I hear a dog barking." Those two things have nothing to do with each other, except the fact that the poet was there to see and hear them. So the haiku is saying, "I was here. Kilroy was here." To appreciate the wonder of that, you have to imagine the absence of that, of not being there, of nonexistence, right? I consider poets to be a part of a larger group of people who don't have to survive major surgery or go through a windshield in order to feel grateful for being alive. It shouldn't require such traumatic experiences to feel grateful. So I think a love of language and a sense of gratitude would be two ingredients in the recipe for making a poet.

Plimpton: Anything else?

Collins: And laziness! Not being able to write more than half an hour a day. You know Max Beerbohm's line that the hardest thing about being a poet is knowing what to do with the other twenty-three and a half hours of the day.

Plimpton: Do you have any trouble with the other twenty-three and a half hours?

Collins: No, no, I have plenty to do. I mean, there's always the piano and walking the dog, and I'm very good at just playing with my own tail. While the novelist is banging on his typewriter, the poet is watching a fly in a windowpane.

Plimpton: You mentioned this ability to move from writing shorter poems to longer poems.

Collins: I learned how to do that by reading Coleridge's conversation poems, going back and reading his longer lyrics to figure out how he could get a second wind. My poems used to shut down very quickly. I would write a few lines, then the poem would close in on itself with some kind of witty remark and get offstage.

Plimpton: Have you ever considered writing a novel?

Collins: No. One of the differences between being a novelist and a poet is that the novelist kind of moves into your house. I mean, it takes three days or three weeks to read a novel. I think of the novelist as a houseguest. The poet is more someone who just appears. You know, a door opens, and there's the poet! He says something about life or death, closes the door and is gone. Who was that masked man? I like that kind of sudden appearance. Not overstaying your welcome, you might say.

Plimpton: Very rarely do you have poets who write novels.

Collins: Nicholas Christopher and Stephen Dobyns are contemporaries that come to mind. And Ronald Koertge. But success at both is rare. Look at Joyce. He completely redefined the novel, but his poems are useless. One exception is Nabokov's *Pale Fire*—an amazing poem with or without the notes. Writing poetry and writing fiction are as different as playing two very different musical instruments, like a clarinet and a piano. They're both producing music; they might both be playing in the key of E-flat, but the pianist might not have a clue what to do with a clarinet or a bassoon or a trombone. They're very different skills. I wouldn't know how to write a short story. I read fiction, I've taught fiction, but I can't write fiction. I was thinking the other day that in fiction, unless it's a nineteenth-century novel where you start with the person's birth and end with his death, there's always a sense that the character existed before you started reading about him. With a short story you jump into a person's life, and at the end of the story, the person's life (unless you've killed him off) will continue into an imaginary future dimension. But nothing precedes a poem but silence, and nothing follows a poem but silence. A poem is an interruption of silence, whereas prose is a continuation of noise. Plus, fiction is basically about other people, whereas poetry is about the poet. Two very different spheres of interest.

Plimpton: What do you tell the people in your writing classes? Is there sort of a principle that you start out with? What are your opening remarks to a classroom of would-be writers?

Collins: I don't know if I'd say this at the beginning, but the most difficult question you can put to people who want to write poetry is this: Ask yourself if what you are trying to say can be said in any other form—story, memoir, letter, phone call, e-mail, magazine article, novel. If the answer is yes, stop writing poetry. Put it in an e-mail, write a memoir, write a letter to your granny, use whatever form will accommodate what you're going to say. Stop writing poetry unless you're doing things that you can *only* do in poetry. And that means exercising your imaginative freedom because in a poem you have the greatest imaginative freedom possible in language. You have no allegiance to plot, consistency, plausibility, character development, chronology. You can fly. Clear the trees at the end of the runway, and off you go. So if you're not taking advantage of the giddy imaginative liberty that poetry offers, you should try a form that's a little more restrictive. Of course, if I say that in the first class, it's kind of deadening. Maybe it's better left for the last class.

Plimpton: Do you keep in touch with other poets, your contemporaries?
Collins: No, only the dead.

See, because my first real book wasn't published until I was in my forties, I wasn't really part of a poetry society. I didn't have friends who were poets. My friends were just my friends, names you would fail to recognize in an instant, as someone put it. I went to Holy Cross College, and Robert Frost came there once. Since I was on the literary magazine, we had dinner with him. Nobody said a word. Two Jesuits sat next to him and talked. We looked into our soup. We were afraid of making idiots out of ourselves.

For me poetry was always a solo act. A romantic idea maybe, but I thought that poetry was something you did in solitude, and the idea of sharing your work with anybody was completely antithetical to what I thought poetry was all about. So I was invisible until ten years ago. Well, I remember going to a little reception soon after *The Apple That Astonished Paris* came out—it had nothing to do with my book—and I ran into Henry Taylor, who has since become a good friend. In this crowded reception, he looked over to his wife who was on the other side of the room, pointed at me and yelled, Sarah! "*The Apple That Astonished Paris!*" It was the first time I had been referred to by the title of my book, and I felt I had been elevated to authorship at that very moment. I had always written with the expectation of having readers, and now that seemed to be coming true.

Plimpton: Who's the first reader? Do you read poems to your wife?

Collins: I hand them to her or just leave them out on the kitchen table. I don't read them out loud. I don't put her in a folding chair and get up there behind a lectern. She's a very sharp editor. She finds opportunities for clarification and can sense if the poem is going on too long. I don't show my poems to any other poets. I sometimes read a book of poems where the poet says, I want to thank the following eight poets who read this manuscript. That would seem to make it into a collaborative activity, like making a quilt.

Plimpton: How many do you produce in a month?

Collins: It varies. Maybe between three and zero.

Plimpton: Three would be a good month?

Collins: Three keepers. For most poets that would be a book every two years.

Plimpton: You've mentioned elsewhere that you don't see yourself as a writer of books of poems but a writer of poems.

Collins: Each poem is a single, separate act. Every poet has his or her obsessions, and after the fact, you can go back and see these connections between poems in a certain volume, but I never think of writing a book. When I have enough, I just rake them into a pile and see if they add up to a book. When I go to make a book, which isn't that often, I take all the poems and put them out on the floor in no particular order. Then I just walk around on top of them in my stocking feet. I take my time, and eventually this poem over here will want to be with this poem over there, and I'll take it, and I'll put them together. I don't know why. It's not because they're both about death or both about dogs, but that they just want to be with each other. It's almost like a party—people kind of get together in little circles. Eventually, three or four or five different piles will form. For the life of me, I wouldn't be able to label them and say these are the x poems or these are the y poems, but they seem to exhibit affinities that I am not really privy to. But no one reads a book of poems from beginning to end anyway. I mean, editors do and relatives maybe, but I never do. When I get a book of poems, I look for a fancy title or a short one. Most readers approach a book of poems like a flipbook, which for me underscores the notion that we turn to poetry because we're looking for something. It's really a matter of an author's vanity to spend a lot of time orchestrating a book, unless it's very thematic. When his *Collected Poems* was published, Auden just arranged them by date, showing his preference for the chronological over the thematic, and acknowledging the fact that books of poems are not really read from beginning to end.

Plimpton: When you look back at old poems in making these selections, do you see any similarities or find things in poems that you hadn't noticed before?

Collins: Only one thing: I have a lot of mice in my poems.

Plimpton: Mice?

Collins: That's the only revelation. There are mice all over the place. I think it wasn't until we bought a house and had our own mice that they started coming into the poems. But they're all over the place now.

Plimpton: Why do you think that is?

Collins: It's probably two sources. I think the mice come from cartoons, first of all. And it might be a literary love I learned from John Clare, the peasant poet who would walk around the countryside and look into birds' nests and count the eggs and notice the speckles on the eggs, always with a sensitivity to these little creatures rustling through the grass.

Plimpton: Do you have a concept of the reader?

Collins: She's this girl in high school who broke my heart, and I'm hoping that she'll read my poems one day and feel bad about what she did. No, the reader for me is someone who doesn't care about me or has no vested interest. I start the poem assuming that I have to engage his or her interest. There is no pre-existing reason for you to be interested in me and certainly not in my family, so there must be a lure at the beginning of a poem. I want the reader to be in the sidecar, ready. Then off we go. Then we can take a ride from what seemed to be a hospitable and friendly environment into an environment that's perhaps disorienting, manipulative, or a little off-balancing. I want to start in a very familiar place and end up in a strange place. The familiar place is often a comic place, and the strange place is indescribable except by reading the poem again. I love Patrick Kavanaugh's sense that tragedy is merely undeveloped comedy. I feel there's a time to be clear and a time to be mysterious in a poem. Poems that fail for me are often poems in which the poet is being mysterious about something that should be clear, or simplifying something that should be left mysterious. It's a matter of knowing what cards should be turned over and what cards should be kept face down. Poems that turn too many cards over don't respect the mysteriousness of life, and poems that turn over no cards are a game not really worth playing. My advice to poets is turn more cards over or don't turn so many cards over. I don't want to know about that. I don't want to see that card. If you've written a poem about your brother who is in the hospital undergoing surgery, well, tell us that. Why should that be a secret? Tell us the circumstances of the poem. But how you feel about this brother you've always felt competitive with, angry with, how you feel about him being close to death now—should remain mysterious. You can't do that justice in twenty lines.

Plimpton: I'm not sure I quite understood that.

Collins: Let me describe a typical scenario in a workshop where a poem gets passed around the table. Everyone has a copy of the poem; the poet reads it, and there's a polite silence. Then someone says, "Well, it's an interesting title." More silence. Someone says, "That ending's weird." Anyway, ten minutes later, we conclude that no one knows what's going on. No one has a clue, right? So you turn to the poet for help, and she says, "Well, I wrote this poem when my brother was in the hospital undergoing surgery." All of a sudden, the poem becomes seventy-three percent clearer. She kept that a secret. She wanted to make that mysterious. That shouldn't be a mystery! Call the poem "Poem Written in the Hours When My Brother Was Undergoing Surgery" and then tell us what's going on. How you feel about your brother can be couched in imagery, fraught with uncertainty. You must remain ambivalent about such matters.

It's like in shopping malls you have that arrow that says, "You are here." The beginning of the poem should at least give you that kind of informa-tion. The Romantic lyrics are so good about that because the poet always starts off by telling you where he is. You know, I'm sitting in my backyard in a lime-tree bower, or, I'm sitting up on a hill, or, I'm lying in a field, or, I'm three miles above Tintern Abbey. Location. The poem always starts with a geographical grounding wire, then moves off into areas of amazing spec-ulation and fanciful imaginative realms.

Plimpton: What about influences? You mentioned Crane and Ferlinghetti.

Collins: Danilo Kiš, the critic, says that asking about influences is treat-ing an author like a baby found in a basket outside a hospital and trying to fig-ure out who the parents are. A foundling!

There are nonpoetic influences, influences that shape your imagination. For me Warner Brothers cartoons were very influential in the way my mind works. I was a *Merrie Melodies* and *Looney Tunes* devotée through most of my childhood and adulthood. Another influence was learning the Latin responses of the mass as an altar boy. I can remember being out in Southampton at a modest house my parents rented in the summer. The altar boy test was in the fall. I would study the Latin responses every evening. Of course, I didn't know Latin. I was eleven or twelve years old, and I was no John Stuart Mill. Underneath the Latin in red would be the phonetic spellings, so I was just memorizing syllables. I'd memorize *Soo-shi-pee-ah-om-me-no-sa-cre-fi-chi-om*. I didn't know what I was saying! I was memorizing hundreds of syllables that brought me into the pure sound of the language, almost like nonsense, like jabberwocky, a delight in the *sound* of things. Another example of that is my interest in bridge columns. I don't play bridge. I have no idea how to play bridge, but I always read Alan Truscott's bridge column in the *Times*. I advise students to do the same unless, of course, they play bridge. You find language like, "South won with dummy's ace, cashed the club ace and ruffed a diamond." There's always drama to it: "Her thirteen imps failed by a trick." There's obviously lots at stake, but I have no idea what he's talking about. It's pure language. It's a jargon I'm exterior to, and I love reading it because I don't know what the context is, and I'm just enjoying the language and the drama, almost like when you hear two people arguing through a wall, and the wall is thick enough so you can't make out what they're saying, though you can follow the tone.

Plimpton: Presumably the cartoon background as an influence would have to do with humor?

Collins: Yes, a sense of animating the inanimate, a kind of speediness, an odd sense of possibility, an elastic world where things can change shape and you can pull a refrigerator out of your back pocket! Or get flattened by a steam roller and spring back into shape.

Plimpton: And there's no death, yes?

Collins: No death, no. There's just bouncing and shape-changing. It's odd, you know, for me to step outside of myself and talk about matters like influence. I'm reminded of a moment when Paul Desmond was being interviewed, which sums up a question from the outside and an answer from the inside. The interviewer said, "How do you account for all the melancholy in your playing, Mr. Desmond?" And he said, "Well, probably because I'm not playing any better."

Plimpton: That's a strange answer.

Collins: The answer meant you just try to do a good job. The artist is not thinking about life or death or sadness. He's trying to do a good job. He's not thinking theme or content. A poem I wrote was published in a college textbook. And after the poem there were these "study questions." I didn't have a clue! There's a huge gulf between doing and then being accountable for what you do. It's like going up to a guy who's trout fishing in a stream, wading out there and asking, "What do you think of the overfishing of the tuna? Any thoughts on the history of fish?"

Plimpton: Do you write occasional verse in the proper use of the word?

Collins: You could say every poem is an occasional poem because walking in the woods or cutting an apple is for me an occasion.

Plimpton: Is that when you spend your time talking aloud?

Collins: Well, I walk every morning for a couple of miles with the dog. That's as much for me as it is for her; it's head clearing. Wordsworth apparently composed while he was walking. The meter of the walk gave the poem its meter. For me it's more gazing around with an open mind or an empty head. What's important to me is having a time of the day when I'm in a receptive mode, when I'm ready for any incoming mail.

Plimpton: Is there ever a sense of urgency: My God, why haven't I . . . ?

Collins: Oh, sure. I mean, the ultimate urgency is that you think you're a goner; you think it's over. Coleridge's "Dejection: An Ode," for example, is about the wellsprings being depleted. It addresses the precariousness of writing, particularly of writing lyric poems. Writing the short poem might take a day, but then that's over, and you go back to zero with great regularity; whereas you can work on a novel for five years, and when you wake up every morning, the novel is waiting for you. As a poet writing fairly short lyric poems, you wake up in the morning, and there's often nothing waiting for you; you have to restart your engine every time.

Plimpton: Why didn't Coleridge dip into laudanum more than he did, so that he could have continued after being interrupted by the postman from Porlock?

Collins: I think he faked that whole Kubla Khan story. I don't believe that such a well-formed poem came out of an opium delirium. I think what's interesting is why Coleridge would make up such a story. It's not a story that Chaucer would have made up. The Romantics were the first poets to believe in spontaneity as a virtue, as a criterion for poetic composition. To compose spontaneously was a good thing, a movement against an artifice. Wordsworth said he composed "Tintern Abbey" in a carriage ride and jotted it down afterwards in a secretarial act. Jack Kerouac said that he just typed out *On the Road* on a scroll of architectural-drafting paper. I've seen what purports to be the original scroll and he has the name *Nietzsche* there spelled correctly. I don't think anyone spells *Nietzsche* correctly the first time. There are seven different ways to misspell that name, and I don't believe that you can take a bunch of Benzedrine, type away, and *Nietzsche* just comes out correctly. What's interesting about "Kubla Khan" is its claim to spontaneity; it shows you what a virtue spontaneity was—Coleridge pretending to be spontaneous when he was in fact an assiduous reviser. Yeats summarizes this whole thing in "Adam's Curse" when he writes: "A line will take us hours maybe, / Yet if it does not seem a moment's thought / Our stitching and unstitching has been naught."

Plimpton: Do you ever write formal poetry?

Collins: Well, in one sense—a loose sense—I consider all my poems to be formal. I try to write poems that are a series of clear, solid lines, to give each poem a stanzaic shape, and usually to organize poems around a beginning, middle, and end, or at least a distinct turn. I hope all that adds up to a certain degree of formality, an appearance of formality, anyway. The poem may not be wearing the official uniform of the sonnet, but still, its clothes are ironed and its buttons done up—except sometimes maybe the top one. You don't want the poem to arrive overdressed for the party. Like the tuxedo poems of some of the Edwardians and Georgians.

Plimpton: What about traditional genres?

Collins: I try my hand—sonnets now and then, even some Horatian-type odes written in college under the gaze of Jesuit Latin teachers. More recently, I actually invented a new genre without really meaning to. What happened was I wanted to write an intentionally bad formal poem, which would look like the result of an inept poet working over his head. The effect would be comic. Rather than write a terrible sonnet or villanelle (there are enough of those), I decided to make up a new form complete with its own rules. To add some silliness, I presented it as an obscure form begun by the troubadours, the boys who gave us many of the forms so popular as assignments in poetry workshops. You know, this week we'll write a villanelle, next week a sestina. Such an artificial way to proceed! I agree with Richard Wilbur who said that you shouldn't write a sonnet unless you have a sonnet-like thing to say.

Plimpton: So what was this new form?

Collins: The *paradelle*, which is like a fusion of parody and villanelle. The rules were an absurd mix of the dead easy and the nearly impossible.

I titled the poem "Paradelle for Susan" because I wanted a very American-sounding girl's name, and the footnote read: "The paradelle is one of the more demanding French fixed forms, first appearing in the *langue d'oc* love poetry of the eleventh century. It is a poem of four six-line stanzas in which the first and second lines, as well as the third and fourth lines of the first three stanzas, must be identical. The fifth and sixth lines, which traditionally resolve these stanzas, must use *all* the words from the preceding lines and *only* those words. Similarly, the final stanza must use *every* word from *all* the preceding stanzas and *only* those words." In the poem itself, the incompetent poet whose role I was playing—we should italicize *playing*—was able to repeat lines—bravo!—but could not manage to recycle all the words, so every stanza ended with a pile-up of remainder words, leftovers. Like, "And find the time, cross my shore, to with it is to." I sent the poem to the *American Scholar*. I knew the editor, Joseph Epstein, had a sense of literary humor. They published the poem, and that, I assumed, was that, until Epstein wrote to tell me about the mail they were getting. Subscribers were sending angry letters questioning the magazine's judgment for having published such a slovenly poem. How could the journal of the Phi Beta Kappa Society endorse such literary incompetence? One person said it was the worst paradelle he'd ever read. No kidding. Epstein invited me to respond to a typical letter. I didn't want to fess up and spoil all the fun, so I wrote a letter that asked for sympathy. The paradelle is an extremely difficult form, my defense ran. I did the best that I could. Then I began hearing rumors that the paradelle was being assigned as a workshop exercise. And now a young professor in Georgia is working on an anthology of paradelles! I agreed to write an introduction titled "A Brief History of the Paradelle" accounting for the disappearance of all the paradelles written between 1200 and 1998. My ultimate dream is to see the term *paradelle* in *The Princeton Encyclopedia of Poetry and Poetics*, but I've probably just blown my chances by taking you backstage.

Plimpton: Do you know Harry Mathews's work? We did a whole series. He's part of a society—the Oulipo—in Paris which does things of this nature; their great god is Georges Perec, who wrote a whole novel without using the letter *e*.

Collins: Forgeries and put-ons used to provide a fine subversive element, a counterweight to literary authority insofar as they questioned the whole idea of authorship. One bit of trickery I remember came from Rolfe Humphries. In the 1930s, *Poetry* magazine published a very serious-looking poem of his that turned out to be an acrostic. The initial letters of every line spelled out "Nicholas Murray Butler is a horse's ass." At play in the fields of literature.

Plimpton: How important is subject matter?

Collins: A little subject matter goes a long way. In fact I usually want to move the poem beyond its initial subject. Richard Hugo said, "Never write a poem about something that wants to have a poem written about it." This would eliminate the elegy, of course, and the ode for that matter, and the love sonnet, but I think once you step outside those forms, the poem can arise out of something very tiny, some little occasion. A poem about a mouse, for example. Or even three mice.

Plimpton: But as the newly appointed poet laureate, aren't you required to celebrate great events?

Collins: You must be confusing me with John Dryden. I think those days have passed, but commemorative poetry did have real significance when poets actually wielded power through their ability to flatter and satirize . . . and insult! They would have possessed something comparable to the power of a drama critic or gossip columnist. The power of Walter Winchell! In the bardic era of Irish poetry, poetic extortion was so rampant that St. Columba was called back from his monastic outpost in Iona to declare a limit on the number of bards that could practice in Ireland. I'm wondering how such a quota would go over in America today. My understanding of the American poet laureateship is that the post-holder is expected to raise poetry consciousness rather than knock off commemorative poems, though I recall that Brodsky wrote an odd preinaugural poem for Clinton in 1992. The idea of commemorating a wedding or a victory on the battlefield is surely a holdover from the British laureate tradition.

But poetry for me begins in secrecy, as far from the public eye as possible. Lines written in a diary with a little heart-shaped golden lock are the origins of poetry. Taking workshops, getting published, and giving readings are after-the-fact activities, a movement from that privacy into a public sphere. But the laureateship! A poet can hardly get more public than that. That's probably why Philip Larkin turned it down. Maybe Thomas Gray had a similar reason. I might add that commemorative or occasional poetry goes completely against the modern poetic grain because such poems must never lose sight of their subject, whether it's a coronation or the launching of a ship. I'm always trying to escape from the literal burdens of subject matter. Subject matter for me is just a gate of departure. A poem works best when it manages to transcend its subject or at least finds a safe place to hide from it.

Plimpton: Are your poems directly autobiographical?

Collins: I don't write about my life as a series of major autobiographical events. I write about events that are fairly trivial, like going for a walk and looking at a swan. I don't write about deaths in the family or divorce, which I haven't had. The Romantics were the ones who started talking about themselves in poetry, a fairly new thing for the times. The first line of Rousseau's *Confessions*, published in the 1770s, is something like, "I'm about to do something that has never been done before, will never be done again, and that is to tell the story of my life candidly." You have to go all the way back to St. Augustine to find another example of the self at the center. But autobiography has taken over poetry. It's become its consuming topic, and I think the autobiographical poem, driven sheerly by memory, accounts largely for the exploding popularity of poetry because it gives people a way of addressing their past, dealing with relatives or loved ones.

Plimpton: The New York School is full of that, isn't it? Kenneth Koch, Frank O'Hara.

Collins: But they value comedy, and they embrace trivia. The everyday is central: I had lunch with somebody, I did this, I did that. The autobiographical poetry I'm thinking about focuses on trauma or on anxiety produced by the family. The family was traditionally the domain of the novel, but it's become the domain of poetry now, and a lot of it, I think, is based on the presumption that people are interested in the families of others, though everyday experience tells us that they're not. Some people have to struggle to be interested in their *own* families, let alone the families of others. When you read many contemporary poets these days, you get a lot of information you might not want. A less presumptuous sense of an audience would correct some of this. I mean, writing a poem is an attention-getting act, so it might be worth asking whose attention are you getting and why?

Plimpton: Who's writing these poems?

Collins: Too many names to name. But a lot of contemporary poetry sounds like memoirs in lines. You know, Milton never wrote about his grandmother, Shelley never wrote about his dad. "Who cares?" would be the cry of the audience then, and I think "Who cares?" is my cry now. Maybe it's because I'm an only child and have no children, so I have a very thin sense of the family. But I do think that what used to be the subject of the novel, that is, the family, has invaded poetry. The confessional poets are another matter, because they really had something to confess—Anne Sexton and Robert Lowell had very interesting psychic lives. You can feel this strong sense of disclosure running through the poems like a wire; there's a high-wire of psychic tension. But not everybody is Anne Sexton or Sylvia Plath or Robert Lowell, and what passes off as a personal poem these days has become extremely impersonal. It has its own conventions and its own clichés, and I don't know if it will ever run into a dead end because people will never stop talking about themselves and their families.

Plimpton: Perhaps it's the easiest thing to write about.

Collins: It's very convenient subject matter. It's what occupies much of people's emotional and mental life, figuring out their place in the family and figuring out their relationships with other people. After all, the family has been called the original insane asylum. You just have to find your room.

Plimpton: In your workshop, do you talk about subjects the students should concern themselves with?

Collins: I try to convey a sense that the poem is an opportunity for travel, that poetry can make some progress into exciting imaginative territory. Many poems based on the idea of family or a loved one, which have a literal relationship to the poet's biography, never quite get off the ground; in other words, they're mired in these family issues, which limits the possibilities of some kind of transcendence. I think that the poem can sweep you up and take you at least beyond the limits of psychology.

Plimpton: Do you begin by teaching them a lot about structure? Do you make them learn what the various structures of poems are, rhyme schemes, etcetera?

Collins: Quite a bit. I might take a stanza from a poem of, maybe, Thomas Traherne, and we would scan it and find out its meter, and then I'd have the students write a stanza that would copy Traherne's meter exactly. As long as they're copying meter, their exercise doesn't even have to mean anything. In fact, I encourage them to write nonsense: The cat was putting on its hat; it doesn't even have to rhyme. But I don't think that teaches people how to be metrical, frankly; the lesson such exercises teach—and I give quite a few of them—concerns the degrees of difficulty in a poem. Maybe an analogy would be painting. I took painting lessons for a while, still-life painting. I can't really paint well at all, and I've since stopped doing it. But it taught me about the degrees of difficulty in still-life painting. My teacher used to put out the most unromantic objects. He didn't want to intimidate his students with a violin and a wine glass and a pear and some fresh strawberries, so he'd put out a tennis ball, some junk lying around the house. Simple to paint, simple objects, geometrical shapes like the cylinder of a toilet paper roll. But if I wasn't doing my work well, he would say, "You think this is hard—next time I'm going to have you paint a crystal bowl full of lightbulbs." I started to appreciate the bravura aspect of still-life painting, where you have a chandelier reflected in a mirror. You start to see that Vermeer is essentially bragging. So I try to encourage students to look at the challenge of formal poetry, to see, for example, that the fewer the end rhyme sounds, the more difficult the poem is. Frost has a poem called "The Rose Family." I think it's twelve or fourteen lines. It has just one rhyme: *rose, goes, suppose, knows.* He's bragging: I can write a fourteen-line poem with A-A-A-A-A-A. Can you?

Plimpton: What are the burdens of success?

Collins: Time. There are a lot of demands on your time. I used to have a lot of wool-gathering time, but now the phone rings, and there's lots of mail every day. I give almost forty readings a year. The image one has to present as a performer, as an interviewee and whatnot, is a very different self from the sensibility that actually creates the poems. You need to keep your center, the part that writes the poems, and not spin off into popularity. "Popular poet" is an oxymoron, although I think it's a vindication, in a way, for the models of clarity that I've tried to follow in these poems. I keep wondering why poetry seemed to go away and hide under various labels of modernism—it did, obviously, lose touch with the readership by turning in on itself.

Plimpton: Do you see a step up into something else?

Collins: For me?

Plimpton: Yes. I don't want to say another level, because you're up there now, but something vast that doesn't fit in any category.

Collins: It's one of the great curiosities. It's a double-edged sword when you consider the question of the growth of a poet, a writer, any artist, versus a distinctive way of expressing the self. There's an expectation that the artist must grow, must expand and change, and if you look at someone like Picasso, you see the evolution, these beautiful stages of outgrowing and developing. Yet there's also a strength in doing one thing well, subgenius, but sufficient. I would say Emily Dickinson writes the same poem over and over again. It's always in common meter, four beats, then three beats; she sings the same little tune over and over again, the tune of the nursery rhyme, the tune of the Protestant hymn, and she just sings this little song again and again, seventeen hundred times. But every poem is remarkably unique.

Plimpton: So that's why she stopped.

Collins: Well, I think she stopped for death.

Plimpton: For twenty years she didn't do anything.

Collins: She has a beautifully distinctive voice, because she learned to do this one thing well and to find variation in it. I think if you're stuck in a form, or if you're stuck in a voice, the challenge is to stay within the voice and keep finding variation within the voice and to have a voice or a form that is flexible enough that will accommodate new subjects, new thinking, new glimpses, new experiences. I don't envision any great creative breakthrough. My hope is to continue to do good work, which is to write good lines and good stanzas. Gasoline comes in gallons, cigarettes come in packs, and poetry comes in lines and stanzas. No matter what I'm thinking about when I'm writing a poem, no matter what is captivating my attention, all I'm really trying to do is write good lines and good stanzas.

Billy Collins with Henry Taylor

Henry Taylor / 2001

Henry Taylor, winner of the 1986 Pulitzer Prize in Poetry, interviewed Collins at the Lensic Performing Arts Center, Santa Fe, New Mexico, on September 26, 2001, as part of the Lannan Foundation's "Readings and Conversations" series. A reading preceded the interview. Printed with the permission of Henry Taylor and the Lannan Foundation.

Henry Taylor: What I want to do is massage a clichéd question just a little bit. The basic kernel of the question is "When did you start writing poems?" But I'm interested in the fact that you went all the way through graduate school in English, got a PhD, and then six or seven years after you got your doctorate, you had your first chapbook. Were you writing poems all through graduate school, or what?

Billy Collins: I was, but I wasn't very consistent or diligent about it. Plus, I was at once intimidated by actual poets and overly modest at the same time. I thought poets were gods, and now, of course, I know that they are. [Laughter] Writing for me was a covert activity. I kept doing it, and I went through a number of phases. I was kind of a proto-beatnik for a while, and I wrote a lot of bad Ferlinghetti and that kind of thing. I also went through a long, brooding, Romantic genius period, where I was really too sensitive to write anything. [Laughter] That lasted a few years. And Wallace Stevens cast a big shadow over me. I was smart enough about language that I could produce something that looked like a mediocre Wallace Stevens poem. But frankly, I was cheating. I really didn't know what I was writing about. I think if my poetry has any clarity now—or too much clarity, some might say—it's probably because I'm making up for earlier sins of my own dabbling into being obscure. Poetry is difficult to write. Randall Jarrell likened it to playing Pin the Tail on the Donkey, but he said for most poets, there's no tail and there's no donkey. [Laughter] There's just a blindfold. But my sense is that it's difficult to write; it *shouldn't* be difficult to read. If it's difficult to write and difficult to read, I don't think there's any hope for it. [applause]

Taylor: Bravo. When you wrote your dissertation ["The World's Ear: The Romantic Search for an Audience," alluded to during the reading], did it occur to you that you were going to find the kind of audience that you have found?

Collins: Oh, of course not. No, no. That's a good question. Everyone laughed when I said, "the search for an audience," but no, I was quite serious. I don't think anyone goes into writing poetry with the expectation of a large audience.

Taylor: I think it's worth pointing out that, though your poems have the clarity that you just mentioned—and they certainly do—there's no shortage of references to things that it is handy to have read if you want to get on with what's going on in the poem. I think of "Monday Morning," that wonderful, short combination of abbreviation and parody of "Sunday Morning" by Wallace Stevens. If you don't know Stevens's poem, "Monday Morning" is not meaningless, but it's not very weighty either.

Collins: Right. It's not worth reading. [Laughs]

Taylor: And you were talking about poems being Frankenstein monsters, assembled from spare parts of poems that you've exhumed here and there. That's how it works: we are trying to participate in a conversation.

Collins: It's a long historical conversation. To be a poet, in some *popular* understanding of the term, means to express your inner self and to give a verbal form to your individuality, but, in fact, it's not such an isolated activity. William Matthews says the poet is never alone because he's surrounded by all the voices in his head of previous poets. There is this cross-historical, achronological, nonsequential conversation going on, where Whitman is obviously speaking to Allen Ginsberg, but Allen Ginsberg is speaking back to Whitman. We read Whitman differently now that we know Ginsberg. And John Donne is talking to Marianne Moore, and she's talking back to Emily Dickinson. I think to step into this conversation means that you have to listen to it for a while to find out what's being talked about. And there is, unfortunately, the young poet who doesn't want to read poetry. Sometimes I ask them, "Who do you read?" "Well, I don't *read* poetry. I just want to *write* poetry." I always think of an analogy: if a student went to the Julliard School and wanted to play the piano, and the administrator or the admissions office person said, "Well, who do you listen to?" and the student said, "Well, I don't listen to music," they would call security. [Laughter] They would just press the little red button under the desk. But with writers you can get away with that. I think most of the references in my poems—"Sunday Morning" is kind of an exception—are not the token of entrance. You may have to know

Stevens to get into that poem, but usually it's just a little nod, quite like jazz musicians quoting songs in the middle of a solo.

Taylor: The new book, *Sailing Alone around the Room: New and Selected Poems*—outside of studies of medieval literature—is the only book I've experienced that mentions *langue d'oc* twice.

Collins: [Laughing] See I didn't notice that. I'm a recovering medievalist, yes. [Laughter] Before I switched over to Wordsworth and Coleridge, I went to a Jesuit school, so I had six years of Latin, two years of Greek. When I got to graduate school, I'd been living in the Middle Ages, essentially, the Middle Ages in Worcester, Massachusetts. [Laughter] So that's probably why.

Taylor: You're a very funny poet, but it's important to me that you're not *just* a funny poet, and I wonder how you feel about the proportion, whether you give that a lot of thought when you put a reading together. Do you take any pains to try to see to it that the audience doesn't go away thinking, "Well, that's a funny guy. That's all"?

Collins: I think so. I'm trying to manipulate the audience as much as possible, [Laughter] if anybody is still out there. It's dangerous because there's a huge gulf between writing a poem that might have something amusing or off-kilter in it and then getting up and performing it. If you read a poem, very rarely would you laugh out loud. You would smile, or you would have an internal sense of warmth that humor gives you. So in a reading it's a whole different thing. I do tend to try to balance it, but, for me, humor is more like a gate of departure. It's a way of getting into other dimensions, a kind of initial engagement. My friend Wordsworth really drove out humor and sex from poetry. If you think of the time before Wordsworth, poetry was quite funny. They didn't call Shakespeare's comedies "comedies" for nothing. Chaucer is hilarious, although satirists like Pope and Dryden are meant to make you ridicule someone. But with Wordsworth and Coleridge, sex and humor were replaced by landscape. [Laughter] So I'm at least trying to bring back some of the humor. Patrick Kavanagh, the Irish poet, says that tragedy is just comedy that hasn't been sufficiently developed. [Laughter]

Taylor: You remember what Mel Brooks says? "Tragedy is when I cut my finger. Comedy is when you fall into an open sewer and die." [Laughter] I wanted to ask you a little bit about the process of selection for the *New and Selected*. First, just a quick yes or no question: this does not mean the going out of print of earlier books, does it?

Collins: No. I hope they stay in print.

Taylor: It's impossible not to miss some. You have left behind poems that you must have been sorry to leave behind, along with the ones that maybe you were glad to. We all have those.

Collins: Well, it's the first time I've put together a book of poems from other books, a new and selected, so the experience was very new to me. Once you pick a pile of poems from your work that you're calling "new and selected," you leave behind a group that's called "old and neglected." I was saying the other day, it's like Noah not having enough room for all the animals. You're so sorry to leave some of these behind. I don't know exactly what the selection process was.

Taylor: Well, if you don't mind, I'm going to recite "Etymology."

Collins: Okay.

Taylor: They call Basque an orphan language.
Linguists do not know
what other languages gave it birth.

From the high window of the orphanage
it watches English walking alone to the cemetery
to visit the graves of its parents,
Latin and Anglo-Saxon.

Collins: I think that's quite a tribute. Sorry not to have that in the new book.

Taylor: But I still have it.

Collins: Very good. I think that's a typical—not that you asked—but a typical way of switching perspective in poetry. That is, for me, imaginatively refreshing, to tilt things to some angle and see them differently. There's a Turkish proverb I heard the other day, which is an example of switching perspective: "When the axe comes into the forest, the trees think, 'at least the handle is one of ours.'" [Laughter]

Taylor: Wow. That's great.

Collins: You get slightly dizzy when you hear something like that, a little disoriented.

Taylor: It's not completely foreign to think of some of the accidental things that turn your mind inside out momentarily. Back East where I work, if you're coming in from Dulles Airport, right after you've crossed the Beltway around Washington, there are a pair of highway signs that say, "All trucks must use next two exits."

Collins: [Laughing] Very challenging.

Taylor: I want to move into a realm that you touched on a couple of times in the course of the reading, having to do with traditional forms. In your poem "Sonnet," you mention that you're not going to play "the iambic bongos," and you're not going to string the rhymes around, "one for every station of the cross." And, in fact, you don't very often write formalist poetry. I understand that that's a matter of individual temperament and practice. Do you think about it, or is it just the way it goes for you?

Collins: I would say there are two kinds of form. There is a form that's imposed from without, as with the sonnet or the sestina, but there's also an internally imposed form. When I'm writing my poems, I'm *thinking* formally. I'm not fitting my poem into a preexisting form. It's like kind of laying the tracks while you're driving the locomotive. Whereas if you write a sonnet—I'm not saying it's easy—but the tracks have been kind of laid *for* you, and you are taking your train down a familiar pattern. I spend most of the time I revise—which is not that much, really, but I try to—thinking of form: tidying, neatening, balancing a line. So I'm always thinking as a formalist, but I'm not really following a pre-established form.

Taylor: I think that's certainly true. The great test that Valéry liked to put poems to was to look at them and see where he would make them better, by changing them in some way. I don't think your poems yield very much to that approach. And they do have their form, but it's the received forms that you've pretty much done without. One of the times you mention *langue d'oc*, though, you get to this idea. Do you want to read that?

Collins: You mean this paradelle?

Taylor: Yes.

Collins: Ok, well that's in here somewhere. Should I say anything about this, I wonder?

Taylor: Well, there's a note there at the bottom.

Collins: Well, that's true. [Laughs] You know my work better than I do. This is a form called the paradelle, and I should read the note first because it's not a very well-known form. "The paradelle is one of the more demanding French fixed forms, first appearing in the langue d'oc love poetry of the eleventh century. It is a poem of four six-line stanzas in which the first and second lines, as well as the third and fourth lines of the first three stanzas, must be identical. The fifth and sixth lines, which traditionally resolve these stanzas, must use *all* the words from the preceding lines and *only* those words. Similarly, the final stanza must use *every* word from *all* the preceding stanzas and *only* those words." [Laughter]

Taylor: It sounds hard.

Collins: It's very difficult. [Laughter] Much more difficult than the sonnet. This is my effort to write a paradelle. It's called "Paradelle for Susan." [Reads "Paradelle for Susan," laughter following each stanza] It's not great. [Laughter] That's why I don't write formal poetry. [Laughter]

Taylor: That poem was first published in *American Scholar*, and people wrote to the magazine in irritation that the editors would accept so amateurish and raggedy an attempt at traditional verse.

Collins: The editor, who did have a sense of humor, asked me if I wanted to reply. He picked a typical letter of complaint. The *American Scholar* is the journal of the Phi Beta Kappa Society, so this smart man had written in complaining that this was the worst paradelle he'd ever read. I wrote back, and I just said I did my best. [Laughter] I remember in the last paragraph I said something like, "the paradelle is a stern mistress," and I invited him to try his hand. But Henry Taylor has tried his hand at a paradelle, with much better results. We don't want it to seem too set up, but he just happens to have this.

Taylor: "Bring your paradelle," he said. [Laughter]

Collins: I did. "Don't forgot your paradelle."

Taylor: It's good advice. If you haven't got one, you better get one. This is called "Paradelle: Nocturne de la Ville."

Somewhat behind, rather than after, Villiers de l'Isle-Adam

An empty chair inhabits a troubled dream.
An empty chair inhabits a troubled dream.
Hoisted to light from wells of unknown depth,
Hoisted to light from wells of unknown depth.
Hoisted from an unknown chair to dream of light,
A troubled depth inhabits empty wells.

The lamp says he feels it's slow use his way.
The lamp says he feels it's slow use his way.
"Around the street here, I'm no drunk prisoner."
"Around the street here, I'm no drunk prisoner."
The drunk feels his slow way around the street lamp.
"It's no use," he says, "I'm a prisoner here."

Leaves fall from trees, moths fly to city lights.
Leaves fall from trees, moths fly to city lights.

On thin ice skaters flash across the dark.
On thin ice skaters flash across the dark.
Ice leaves the city to flash on fall trees;
thin skaters fly from moths across dark lights.

It's fall. The city around feels slow to light.
No thin trees fly, flash a chair from ice;
a hoisted lamp lights moths. Across the street
from here an empty drunk leaves skaters troubled;
his unknown prisoner inhabits depth of dream.
"I'm on the way to use dark wells," he says. [applause]

But, it's a trick. It sounds serious, and it has about it some of the whiffs of serious poetry, but it's still a trick.

Collins: I have to ask you a question. Yours is an excellent poem. Did you write yours backwards?

Taylor: I wrote one stanza of it backwards. That's all.

Collins: Okay. Because that's cheating. [Laughter] If I thought to do that, I would've written it backwards, because I could see it would be much easier.

Taylor: It was easy.

Collins: My problem was that it was like a Scrabble board with all vowels left at the end. I couldn't fit things together.

Taylor: George Starbuck, a wonderful, highly technical versifier, a light-verse writer who died a few years ago, told me once that he was working on a poem which consisted entirely of pairs of rhymed syllables, like *in-sin-cere ear*. He finally gave it up because what he turned into was a kind of mad scientist with little strips of DNA lying around him on slides, not being able to put them back together.

Collins: I was contacted by a professor from Georgia a while after this paradelle came out, and she wanted to do an anthology of paradelles. I said, "Good, this is great. I'll write an introduction." And then she asked all these poets in America to write paradelles, including Henry, and many of them did, and one of them said to her, "I think Collins just made this whole thing up." So she called me, and I finally had to confess that there was no such thing as a paradelle. I just made up the rules. But she soldiered ahead. [Laughter] I told her this is very postmodern, and it brings into question authorship and authenticity. What is form after all? But there are many people who have come up with very good paradelles. Mine was the first paradelle ever written, and the worst. I think things are going forward.

[Laughter] I've written my introduction, something called "The Brief History of the Paradelle," and I think it's going to be published somewhere. [*The Paradelle*, Red Hen Press, 2006]

Taylor: I think we need a few of the ones that she couldn't find. She began to notice that, although it was an eleventh-century form . . .

Collins: There were no examples.

Taylor: There were no examples. [Laughter]

Collins: At first, I told her that it was such a difficult form that very few poets even attempted it, and those that did produced such terrible results that they were discarded.

Taylor: When she first asked me about it, I went along. But then I called Billy on the phone and I said that I'd just talked to Theresa Welford, the editor. I said, "You haven't told her yet, have you?" [Laughter] I think it's no small thing to have added a form to our tradition.

Collins: It's making up for the fact that I can't write formal poetry, but at least I made up a whole new form.

Taylor: Fixed it so the rest of us have to. I want to thank you for being here. It's been a wonderful time.

Collins: Thank you for coming and talking to me. [Applause] Thank you.

The Poet and the Poem at the Library of Congress: An Interview with Billy Collins by Grace Cavalieri

Grace Cavalieri / 2001

This interview was conducted at the Library of Congress in December 2001 as part of the series "The Poet and the Poem," produced and hosted by poet Grace Cavalieri and broadcast via NPR satellite. In 2019, Cavalieri was named poet laureate of Maryland. Reprinted by permission of Grace Cavalieri.

Grace Cavalieri: This is *The Poet and the Poem*, from the Library of Congress. I'm Grace Cavalieri. Our guest today is Billy Collins, poet laureate of the United States. I'd first like to ask about the poem prefacing your book, *Picnic, Lightning*.

Billy Collins: This is a poem that's based on a quotation by William Butler Yeats. Yeats said that a poet never speaks directly as to someone at the breakfast table, and I have expressed my disagreement with him in this poem. [Reads "A Portrait of the Reader with a Bowl of Cereal"]

Cavalieri: Billy Collins is just officially inaugurated to be our eleventh poet laureate of the United States. I'm not going to ask what a poet laureate does because you are remarking how everyone wants to know this, even though my dentist did ask me yesterday. But maybe it would be good to know that the laureate is given a clean slate to do what he wants.

Collins: Well, the American poet laureate is very different from the British. Laureate, first of all, has a very antique ring to it. It sounds very British, and it kind of goes with ascots, and wearing spats, and carrying a walking stick or something like that. And people like John Dryden come to mind, or Tennyson who was poet laureate—I think he holds the record of forty-two years. Well in America we have a souped-up version of the British laureateship, in that the poet laureate here serves for only one year, and so we have a very quick turnover. I think the original British idea was that the poet laureate was attached to the royal household and wrote poems on the birth of an heir, or a wedding, or something like that. In America, as you say, the poet laureate can more or less write his or her own ticket. And the nebulous part of the job is that you are asked to define the job as you go along.

Cavalieri: I think that we could comment on what it means for a country to even have a post for poet laureate. I think that's the more important question.

Collins: Well, we don't have a prose laureate; we don't have a short story laureate, or a film director laureate . . . it's just poetry. It *does* say something about poetry, doesn't it? I'm not sure exactly what, but it's certainly a nod to the centrality, or the deep significance of what poetry is to perhaps any culture. I mean the fact that the Library of Congress since I think 1936 has had what they call a consultant in poetry, which then turned into the laureate in I think 1986. But the fact that the Library would want to install a poet in an office, so that he or she could be consulted about any poetry matters that come up certainly gives a sense of the significance of poetry to a culture.

Cavalieri: When you were not a poet laureate, which was for more years than you are, you must have had an impression of it, looking from Somers, New York. What did it look like they were doing here?

Collins: Oh it looked very far away. I viewed the laureateship, when I did, not with any kind of envy or desire to move in that direction, but as if looking at it through the wrong end of a telescope, tiny figures in the distance, doing I don't know what. I mean hanging around Washington and sitting on their laurels, maybe.

Cavalieri: Now you are one. Billy Collins. I'd like to hear about the poem you read last night, "Snow Day," and then talk about your personal agenda.

Collins: "Snow Day" is about that time when it snows so much that the day is declared by some "official" to be a snow day for schools, and then our lives change in [a] certain way.

Cavalieri: The audience last night laughed and cried out loud. The tears were coming out of my eyes last night because of the mournful humor of your voice as you made that litany of those nursery school names, some of them imagined, some real . . .

Collins: All of them are from a phone book! And I started writing that on a snow day, and they were closing schools, and that started the poem going. I kept listening to the radio, but, they were saying like PS 47, and Allentown

High School, so I went to the phone book and looked under daycare, and nursery schools, and I took all of them, even the Peas and Carrots Day School, I took them out of the phone book. They say that if you look in the phone book under "Beauty" you will find many, many listings, but if you look under "Truth," you will find nothing. But if you look under daycare, you'll find all those schools.

Cavalieri: We're in for quite a year here at the Library of Congress. I have to speak about last night. How many thousands were there? More than one thousand. Here we have this one room on the sixth floor of the Library of Congress Madison building. It was quite filled before the busloads tooled up to the door, and more people came in, and they came in, and they came in, and they broke down walls, not the students, the Library took down the walls, opening the room; and it was the most wonderful audience. Although it was a very responsive crowd, were you surprised at how the high schoolers were not quite sure they were allowed to laugh out loud? Did you get that feeling?

Collins: Yes.

Cavalieri: They were a little restrained.

Collins: I always get that feeling. Well, usually as high schoolers, they haven't been to many poetry readings, and certainly poetry, the sound of it, makes you feel a little like you're going to a chapel, or a serious, deadly serious cultural event, and you're supposed to be on your best behavior. People assume there's a kind of hushed etiquette about a poetry reading, which doesn't really need to be the case.

Cavalieri: It was a warm group though. Did you get anything back from them?

Collins: Oh sure. Usually when I give a reading, because some of the poems provoke laughter for some reason or other, I'm usually trying to modulate, I'm trying to mix serious poems with lighter poems, and I'm trying to create a mix of the two faucets. I don't want it to be just amusing, and I don't want it to be too much gravity and I would say that really is a guiding principle for the way I compose poetry. For me the perfect poem, and probably this is one of the things that makes me keep writing poems— is that maybe someday I'll write this perfect poem. I know I won't, but, the perfect poem for me would be a poem in which at any given point, the reader would have no idea whether the poem is serious or funny, and all of my poems are failures in the attempt to achieve that, because they either ere on the side of sentimentality and seriousness or on the side of amusement and lightness.

Cavalieri: That's actually not true at all. You have a mournful humor. Your humor is very tragic to me. It's a very lonely humor. In fact, even a listing of those nursery schools on a snowy day makes you have the ache of the light in the kitchens. I'm very interested in how tragedy is like comedy.

Collins: Well, I think it was an Irish writer who said that tragedy is just insufficiently developed comedy; and it was Nabokov who said—when he started teaching in America at Cornell—he was being falsely self-deprecatory—but he said, "I only know two things, I know that life is beautiful, and life is sad, and those are the two things I know." And I would add that life is funny. I think poetry is basically expressing, if poetry would express those things simultaneously. I think that's an aim for me: to express the beauty, the sadness, and the sheer ridiculousness of life at the same time.

Cavalieri: You do it many times, in many poems. Billy Collins, our poet laureate. He has several books, including *Picnic, Lightening*, University of Pittsburgh Press; *The Art of Drowning*, which was a Lenore Marshall Poetry Prize finalist; *Questions about Angels*; *Apple That Astonished Paris*; *Video Poems*, and *Poker Face*. The newest book is *Sailing Alone Around the Room*. Now *Poker Face* is little found. Is that still in print?

Collins: No, thankfully that has gone out of print years ago.

Cavalieri: 1977.

Collins: Yes, those are probably very rare. I have one copy myself, and if anybody out there does have a copy, if you send it to me, I'll pay you for it, and then I'll burn it.

Cavalieri: Is that right? That's how you feel?

Collins: Well, no, I consider those poems late juvenilia. They're poems I wouldn't read today and poems I think I developed from.

Cavalieri: Wallace Stevens's first little book is worth a fortune.

Collins: Well, thanks for the comparison.

Cavalieri: You have received many honors, including fellowships from the New York Foundation for the Arts, and the NEA; the Guggenheim; the Oscar Blumenthal Prize; the Bess Hokin Prize; the Frederick Bach Prize; and the Levinson Prize Awarded by *Poetry* magazine. Howard Nemerov used to say, "Bring them on!" He was very immodest about winning them. Billy Collins is a distinguished professor of English at Lehman College, City University of New York, where he's taught for the past thirty years. Are you going to keep teaching this year?

Collins: Yes, I'm still teaching. Still lifting the chalk.

Cavalieri: Working this around it?

Collins: Yes, so far, I can do both at once.

Cavalieri: You've arranged your schedule? Do people have to vie to get into your course?

Collins: Not really. I teach in the City University, and many of the students there don't know who I am, but I kind of like it like that. I can find some anonymity there and just concentrate on the teaching.

Cavalieri: And how many in the English Department.

Collins: Faculty members? It's quite large. I'd say maybe sixty or so.

Cavalieri: That's pretty impressive. And you teach creative writing?

Collins: Well, now I do. I taught composition for thirty years because in the city universities . . .

Cavalieri: You have to.

Collins: We teach an immigrant population, for many of whom English is an acquired language, and I'm not a bilingual expert, but I've been teaching English as a second language just by the nature of the student body that fills the classrooms. I teach creative writing workshops sometimes, but I also teach regular literature courses.

Cavalieri: How many courses do you teach? Two?

Collins: Usually three. Now I'm teaching two.

Cavalieri: Three's a lot.

Collins: Well, not to a coal miner it isn't.

Cavalieri: I know that William Matthews just taught one. You have to put your foot down!

Collins: We're going to have to do something about this.

Cavalieri: Right, now that you're poet laureate.

Collins: Well, maybe the president of my college is listening.

Cavalieri: I think he must be thrilled.

Collins: Or we can send him a tape.

Cavalieri: I know he's thrilled that you are the laureate. Tell us about the poem you wrote because you forgot your pencil.

Collins: Well this is a poem about something that writers are cautioned never to do, which is to leave home without your little notebook and a pen, just in case you are visited by the muse, and this is a case where I was caught without the implements, and it's called "Lines Lost among Trees." [Reads "Lines Lost among Trees"]

Cavalieri: Oh, that fantastic city. Phillip Levine has a wonderful poem, also about forgetting his lines. Do you know that one? And it's so poignant because those are the best lines you ever wrote. Are you sure?

Collins: Oh, those are the unwritten, unremembered, lost . . .

Cavalieri: They were the most marvelous . . .

Collins: Yes, the good ones.

Cavalieri: We talked about the high schoolers that were here last night, and you have your own wish to make poetry of significance in high schools. So tell everyone about that.

Collins: Well, what I've started to do as poet laureate is a program I've called Poetry 180, and 180 stands for the roughly 180 days of the school year, and it also signifies a kind of turning around, to poetry, you might say. The idea is to have a poem read every day in American high schools as part of the public announcements, so that at the end of the public announcements, that would be the best place I think, there would be a poem. And I'm choosing 180 poems, hand picking them. Poems that I think high schoolers will be able to get right away and that'll have some immediate resonance for them. The aim here is to make poetry for high school students a feature of daily life, and not just something to be studied, and that's why I want to encourage teachers to get with the program. And they can do that just by going to the Library of Congress website and they'll find the poems there early next year; that's 2002. But I'd like to discourage teachers from bringing the poems into the classroom and teaching them as they would the other poems in the curriculum. I really just want students to hear these poems and not have to study them, or write about them, or think about them in a public way. I just want them to simply take a poem in every day. My sense is, if a student hears a poem every day, there's probably one poem out there, at least one, for every student. All it takes is one poem to get you hooked.

Cavalieri: It follows, somewhat, in the national consciousness, where Pinsky put a poem on the *News Hour,* and, if you ask the regular Joe on the street—if he watches it—"Oh, yeah," he remembers that, but he may not recall the poem. The fact that it was there, that a poem was on the *News Hour* and is forever an indentation in our minds. You're following the idea that a poem can be read in a school over the PA system is not at all outrageous.

Collins: Right. Well, it'd be part of the public announcements, so you'd hear that the volleyball team has a practice at 4:30 or whatever; then you'd hear the poem. It's putting the poem in a kind of unexpected place. It's a little like poetry in motion, which puts poems on busses and subways, and as you said, a poem popping up on television. We expect to find poems in classrooms and anthologies, but I think when a poem ambushes us, and pops out from an unexpected place or time, it has more of an immediate effect on us.

Cavalieri: It will get some of the dust off of it too, in our minds. This is Billy Collins, and he is here to read you a poem. And I really hope you get to write one this year.

Collins: I'd be happy with one, probably.

Cavalieri: How many are you able to write a year?

Collins: Well, fewer now that I'm so busy doing this poet laureate work.

Cavalieri: Howard Nemerov said six a year was about right.

Collins: Six a year?

Cavalieri: And he did it all in a week.

Collins: He did it in one week and got it all over with.

Cavalieri: He had this energy that would just culminate, and he'd sit at the dining room table with the cats.

Collins: That's amazing. Well, it's kind of analogous to that idea that most married couples talk, on the average, fifteen minutes a week, and some of them just get it over with on Monday morning. Squeeze it all in. No, I'm more prolific than that. My writing is kind of spread out sporadically throughout the year. I've never really kept tabs or calculated the number, but I would say, a couple a month, maybe, or three or four a month.

Cavalieri: That would be a lot. You wind up liking all of them?

Collins: Well, if I don't like them, I just pitch them, so I do like all the ones that I finish.

Cavalieri: That's a nice thing to say. What is the latest poem you've finished?

Collins: It's called "The Death of the Hat." It starts out looking nostalgically back at that period of time in the twentieth century when men all wore hats, in cities at least. [Reads "The Death of the Hat"]

Cavalieri: Those mice of yours are in so many poems.

Collins: Mice are uncontrollable.

Cavalieri: But yet *yours* are not, that's the interesting thing. Mice are usually in poems because one can't imagine what they'll do. But *yours* carry matches, they wear little hats . . . they're so intelligent.

Collins: It's actually a little circus. Instead of a flea circus, it's [a] mouse circus that I'm running here. My poems are infested with mice, and I don't really know . . . there could be some childhood trauma attached to this, but I don't know why. I could put out a book of poems just called *The Mouse Poems*, I think.

Cavalieri: It is an extension of your consciousness. It is the twinkle in your eye comes out in the mouse. Which would lead us to my question about the poem you have with a mouse carrying a match.

Collins: That dangerous little mouse.

Cavalieri: What is the poem's title?

Collins: It's based on a bit of country advice, which is not to leave matches lying around. Well, the poem kind of explains that, and I learned this lesson from a friend of mine, who does live in the country, in Vermont. The poem is called "The Country."

Cavalieri: Billy Collins, poet laureate of the United States, is also a visiting professor at Sarah Lawrence.

Collins: Well, I do some of this kind of "hired gun" work. I taught at Columbia for a semester last year, and in the fall, I usually teach a course at Sarah Lawrence in the graduate writing program. So I do a little bit of that kind of "a stranger rides into town."

Cavalieri: Moonlighting.

Collins: Yes.

Cavalieri: Yes. And you live in Somers, New York, which is near the city.

Collins: It's in northern Westchester. It's about forty miles north of New York City.

Cavalieri: And when were you a Literary Lion?

Collins: That was in the nineteen nineties. It's basically an event to raise funds for the New York Public Library.

Cavalieri: It's very nice, though, to be named a Lion, I think. When you think of those big stone ones outside of the library.

Collins: They have names. I forget what their names are. It's like Patience and Prudence, or something. But, yes, once you're a Lion, you're always a Lion.

Cavalieri: Rita Dove said that that was one of the things she really was the proudest of. It meant a lot to her.

Collins: It's a very gala occasion. It's all black tie, and you have an escort who watches you all night. If you're left alone for a moment and not in conversation, this escort comes right over and makes small talk with you. When a real person comes and talks to you, the escort goes back to leaning against the wall. And they put a gold medal with a red ribbon around your neck so you look like an ambassador or something. It's quite a grand event.

Cavalieri: You're saying that with the same mix of respect, and humor . . . and irony. Respect and irony go together, I think. This is going to embarrass you, but that's my job. You are the most popular poet in America. Now, you have no way of knowing that, because there is just no data that we can assemble. But everyone says that you are the most popular poet in America. I don't know how that feels when you're alone in your bed, but it must mean something to you.

Collins: It's hard to calculate. The poems I write are basically for one person. I don't know who the person is, but I have an idea of speaking or whispering these poems to one listener, and I hope I'm aiming for a very intimate connection. When this one reader somehow multiplies into thousands of book buyers, there's a little bit of a gulf there, because I'm always speaking to the one, and then when they multiply, it's a bit surprising to me. So, I don't know why or how this has come about, . . . I'll be like Howard Nemerov, bring them on! I'm enjoying the ride!

Cavalieri: It's lots of fun. I see you have a handwritten poem on the table.

Collins: Well, this is a little poem based on something you hear on the radio every now and then, and the title is "Surprise."

Cavalieri: It's scribbled. It's a premier; I know it, because it's not even printed yet.

Collins: No, I haven't typed it up yet, it's a pretty new poem.

Cavalieri: When you speak with amusement, is there always a fear that people will smile at the next poem, and maybe reduce all of your poems to one idea. That's always the danger. I haven't seen it happen yet. I think maybe you can rise above that. We'll see.

Collins: It's the big risk, actually, because things are changing these days. Humor has had a very bad reputation in poetry ever since the early 19th century, when humor was affectively driven out of poetry by the English Romantic poets, I would say, and it's only now, I think, that humor is finding a way back into poetry from a ghetto where it was consigned, and that ghetto is called light verse. But there is a danger that if your work provokes humor, there's nothing to it.

Cavalieri: It lacks respectability.

Collins: Indeed. I mean, we've gotten used to connecting poetry not only with difficulty, but also with seriousness.

Cavalieri: But believing that something can be seen your way, with such conviction, can make you be the poet laureate of the United States, because Stafford has a poem about "what a muse is . . ." "The muse came to me and said, look at things your own way." And this has served you very well, and it may even change our attitude about the wisdom of humor, which had a time *honored* tradition. You are an expert in the Romantics. In fact, you've got your "phud," right? Your PhD in Romantic poetry?

Collins: I do, yes. I didn't start out being a poet. I was an academic, I got a PhD in English literature and wrote a dissertation on Wordsworth and Coleridge and began teaching in universities, and the poetry came quite late. I mean I really didn't get my first real book published until I was well into my forties.

Cavalieri: Sometimes I can see the light of the Romantics in your lines.

Collins: Well, the great romantic lyric, particularly those poems of Wordsworth and Coleridge that are poems of meditation were very influential. They're poems that begin with the speaker situated somewhere. There's always a sense of location, and it's usually, of course, in a landscape. My poems tend to be located in places too.

Cavalieri: In a hammock.

Collins: Yeah, it could be in a hammock, in the kitchen, or walking the dog around the lake, or something, but my feeling is that poetry is a form of travel literature, and I think we should end up at a different place at the end of the poem than the place we started. And if the poem is to transport us to another place, I feel it must start in some place. So I try to begin by orienting the reader, and you might say, toward the end of the poem, I wouldn't mind it really if the reader experienced a certain pleasurable level of disorientation.

Cavalieri: That is characteristic of the Romantics.

Collins: I think so. Those poems start with a set of simple observations; the poet kind of swiveling around and recording what he is taking in. And then there is a relaxation into a chain of memories and associations, and the poem begins to lift out of its original environment into areas of the imagination, and areas of psychology.

Cavalieri: I have to get this in. You are such a trickster. Do you know that I've taught the paradelle without knowing you were kidding? And got some fabulous poems. Describe a paradelle, please. I'll tell the audience: Billy Collins did a parody on a villanelle, but in his book, he did not reveal it was a parody, he just wrote a paradelle, I think, "for Susan, and, I was teaching a workshop in Italy, and so I . . . I think that's a good thing we could do tomorrow, *Everyone* will write a paradelle like Billy Collins. I get home, and the *Paris Review* reveals that I've been duped. It's a joke. So tell everyone what a paradelle is, and you will be surprised to learn it works as a serious form.

Collins: Well, I just made this up. I wanted to write an intentionally bad formal poem. I wanted to write a poem in which the poet couldn't handle the rules of a genre and botched it. And I thought, well, I could write a really bad sonnet or a bad villanelle, but I figured there's enough of those around, so I would just make up a new form, and I called it the paradelle, which is a kind of combination of a parody and villanelle, and then I made up this insane set of rules for it, and I tried to pass it off in a footnote as actually an old, fixed form from, I think, from the eleventh century, France. And the first rules are that the lines just repeat themselves. So that is almost, you know, kind of a numbskull sense of simplicity. But then the secondary set of rules asks you to use all and *only* the previous words, and it's a little hard to explain without looking at it, but it would be like having a really bad set of letters in a Scrabble game and being asked to write the Lord's Prayer with them.

Cavalieri: Well, everyone loved writing it. I know your own paradelle had kind of a funny last stanza. I thought it was a mess. But then I thought, well, you know, this might be language poetry.

Collins: The bad poet who wrote the paradelle can't fit in all the words, so all these remainder words, like *if* and *to* and *with*, are just kind of stuffed into the last few lines of the poem.

Cavalieri: At the end of the page, you should say, "Don't try this at home." So it was lots of fun. Billy Collins is our new laureate, and we're wearing him down, but we're still going to get information from him. You once spoke of writing a poem from the first lines of an existing poem.

Collins: I have a poem that takes off on another poem. It's called "Litany," and I use the first two lines of another poet to begin my poem. I found a poem by this poet who begins his poem by saying, "You are the bread and the knife; the crystal goblet and the wine," and I thought I would just restart his poem and produce a different version of it, and the title of my poem is "Litany." It's a takeoff on those poems where the woman is the moon and the stars, and it's kind of a parody of that kind of poetry.

Cavalieri: In "Litany" we have a little moment of still water, with the sound of the rain and the shooting star, because, in a way, in the midst of all the attention you're getting, I mean that's the way you must feel, really, as a poet. And that'd be great for a title of your new book, *The Bread and the Knife*. What *is* your title going to be? I see you have almost ten pages of new work here.

Collins: I don't know yet. I'm playing around with a number of titles. So I don't want to say one. Usually I just pick a title from a poem and paste it on the front of a book. I really don't think of titles as having to be a key to the whole book. I really think of titles as an interesting couple of words on the cover that will encourage people to open the book.

Cavalieri: The University of Pittsburgh Press has been really good to you over the years, and Random House will now pick up the banner for you. Do you have an editor?

Collins: Well I just lost my editor at Random House.

Cavalieri: What is the relationship between a poet and his editor?

Collins: We had a very friendly relationship, but I don't really need any editing.

Cavalieri: He doesn't change anything.

Collins: No, he doesn't. We did a *New and Selected Poems*, and he made a few suggestions about which poems he thought should be included.

Cavalieri: Were they good suggestions?

Collins: Yes, they were, but I don't need a line edit or anything. I don't want to compare myself to Nabokov, but Nabokov wrote to his publisher at one point and he said, "By *editor*, I assume you mean *proofreader*."

Cavalieri: And who could edit him anyway? Billy Collins is here, and on September 11, he had actually been inaugurated as poet laureate, although we hadn't had all the festivities yet. And he did have a chance to make one of the first public statements, which I read in the *New York Times*, about the purpose of poetry in a time of tragedy. I thought it was a really important remark. Do you remember how you framed that event and why poetry was called for? I know all of us got a lot of poetry. My email was glutted. And poetry was the preferred method of communication.

Collins: Well, the expression people have used is that, in this time of crisis, people have turned to poetry. The cynic in me feels that those people will probably be turning back away from poetry, because poetry is either part of your daily life, or it isn't. I think people turn to poetry in order to ritualize their grief. Poetry is a stabilizing force because it has form. It's a way of taking grief and turning into something sensible. Also, I think, poetry connects us to the past in very telling and dramatic ways. I think in that comment I said something that I still feel, which is that poetry is the only history of the human heart that we have. It's a history of human emotion. I mean, it's not a history of battles or treaties, but it's the history of human emotion. And when we feel overwhelmed with emotion, it's like looking at that history, and seeing that we're not alone.

Cavalieri: The words to say it. If we could just put it in words, that takes care of it.

Collins: Well, it stabilizes it to some degree.

Cavalieri: That's right. Music goes through us, but poetry becomes permanent, and then we can put it aside, once we've jelled it, maybe, with words. I know Brodsky said that our only record of human sensibilities, from earliest time, was the poetry that was. We have no other record of human sensibilities but through the poetry.

Collins: When you realize that the human sensibility is something that ties us all together, despite our individual eccentricities, and that, when you must take into account the sense that human beings have a thoroughly limited range of feeling—we feel separation, we feel joy, we feel grief, but there is a limited number of things we can feel. And history has recorded the way human beings have registered those feelings for thousands of years. So, to read poetry returns us to a community of feeling, and a history of feeling. And that, I think, acts as some consolation to our personal feelings. Because when we feel, when we are emotional, we feel alone, I think.

I could read a little poem that I wrote very quickly, actually. Well maybe you'd be able to tell this was written quickly. I'll let you decide that, but it's just about something I saw on a train quite recently, and I more or less just wrote the poem as I was observing what the poem describes, and the poem is called "Love." [Reads "Love"]

Cavalieri: I have to comment on the way you love God in your poetry. I love it.

Collins: I hope God loves it.

Cavalieri: It's in a lot of your work; it's in all the lines. I really love that. That is from your background. You're so reverent . . . in your incorrigible way.

Collins: I'm a bad altar boy.

Cavalieri: There is just so much belief at stake in your work. We must talk about the lovely Diane, when we speak of love . . . because, you know, literary gossip is important too. Billy Collins is married to this fantastic woman, Artemis, who is an architect? She is now about to be a furniture designer. She's a visual artist, and she is very charismatic. But I want to say how humbling it must be to be married to someone who knows calculus, physics, and the wind stress of buildings. This puts you in your place, doesn't it?

Collins: She knows real things like . . . she knows about concrete and I-beams.

Cavalieri: And does she wear a hard hat sometimes?

Collins: She carries a hard hat around in the trunk of her car, and . . . and stomps around these building sites, telling contractors what to do.

Cavalieri: She's a proper soulmate for you.

Collins: Yes, I take care of the, kind of, airy stuff, and she deals with making the roof not cave in. I feel competitive with her . . . because I'm really driven to write poems that will last longer than her buildings. "When all your buildings fall down, people will still be reading these poems!" Sounds like one of these Shakespeare boasts.

Cavalieri: She's going to be a great asset in Washington as well. You'll have to bring her every time you come. And we'll look for her furniture design, which is about to be launched. I think that is truly exiting. Will it have a name?

Collins: The Billy Collins Memorial Chair. No, I'll have to stay out of that.

Cavalieri: We're at the Library of Congress, and we have time for another poem.

Collins: Well, here's a poem that's called "Sonnet." It's a slightly more formal poem, and it mentions, maybe the first sonneteer, the Italian poet Petrarch, and also his, you might say girlfriend, Laura. [Reads "Sonnet"]

Cavalieri: How do you describe your education? From the beginning. Holy Cross College . . .

Collins: "Jesuit," would be, probably, the one-word explanation. I went through the full metal jacket of Catholic education.

Cavalieri: From kindergarten?

Collins: Well I did lapse there. I went to a public kindergarten. And then, I don't know why, but then from the first grade on, I was in Catholic school. And all this culminated with four years of Jesuits at Holy Cross College.

Cavalieri: Yes. Well the incense has left but I still get the essence of it in your writing.

Collins: That education can certainly get an amazingly vivid set of religious images.

Cavalieri: And imagery!

Collins: And you also get a taste for Latin, the sound of words without understanding what the words are, because as altar boys (now, altar people) memorize the Latin, presumably without having much of a clue of what it means. And so you memorize syllables. And you're memorizing these sounds.

Cavalieri: The music.

Collins: You're memorizing the music of the language without understanding it, and it's similar to the pleasure you can get out of listening to a poem in a language you don't understand.

Cavalieri: If our children go to Catholic school, there's no guarantee they'll be poets, is there?

Collins: But there are examples, like Gerard Manley Hopkins. It doesn't *prevent* poetry.

Cavalieri: Nothing prevents poetry in a room with Billy Collins. He has launched a website, which will be available in January 2002. We will hope that all of the teachers call the Library of Congress and find out more about it. The site is www.loc.gov/poetry. That will give you the first image, and then you go to the home page, and punch that up, I guess, and just follow the directions from there.

Collins: And what you'd be looking for is the program called Poetry 180.

Cavalieri: That's the title.

Collins: And I think if you go to the homepage, you'll be directed to Poetry 180.

Cavalieri: And even if there's a search mechanism, you may be able to write in Poetry 180. As you leave us today, what poem shall we remember?

Collins: A poem is called "Forgetfulness." Something that happens to us all. [Reads "Forgetfulness"]

Billy Collins, Bringing Poetry to the Public

Dave Weich / 2004

Dave Weich of Powell's Bookstore in Portland, Oregon, interviewed Collins during the Portland Arts and Lecture Series in January 2004, during which Collins's reading sold out all 2,700 seats of the Arlene Schnitzer Concert Hall. First published at Powells.com (https://www.powells.com/post/interviews/billy-collins-bringing-poetry-to-the-public), the interview is used by permission.

Dave Weich: It's been fun the last few weeks reading your poems, particularly jumping around from book to book, which isn't always possible when I'm reading journalism or novels.

Billy Collins: I don't think anybody reads a book of poetry front to back. Editors and reviewers, only. I don't think anybody else does. When you put a book together and arrange it, there's a lot of anxiety and turmoil about what order the poems should be in. I find this, teaching MFA students: they're all concerned about the order. It doesn't make any difference whatsoever. It's total vanity because it's not the way people read. I always tell them there are two ways to organize a manuscript. First is preparing the manuscript to send to an editor. In that case, you totally front-load it—take your fifteen best poems and put them right up front. Then if the manuscript gets accepted, the poet can say to the editor, "By the way, I thought of a different organization," and you can mess around and orchestrate and try to make some symphonic-looking book.

Weich: But I noticed in *Sailing Alone around the Room*—and this is a collection, so these aren't even poems that originally appeared together— there are interesting progressions. For example, there's "Shoveling Snow with Buddha," then "Snow," then "Japan" comes next. First the outside snow scene; then the falling snow as it appears from inside the speaker's home, set to different types of music; and finally a meditation on a poem whose meaning changes every time it's spoken, which hints at similar questions of art and context.

Collins: Well, you're performing literary criticism now. I mean, that's not something that would ever occur to me.

Weich: But someone made a conscious decision to put the poems in that order, right?

Collins: I did, but I usually don't arrange them so logically.

I have a rather intuitive way of putting a book together. What I do is, I find the biggest room in the house, and I put all the poems out on the floor, in any kind of order. Then I walk around and, almost as if feeling your way through a Ouija board, I try to sense *Maybe this poem wants to be over there with that poem . . .* They start falling into groupings. But there wouldn't be groupings with Oriental influence, death, family? I'm not sure what they have in common, but I kind of intuit that they enjoy the company of each other.

Weich: "Japan" imagines a haiku whose meaning changes each time a man recites it.

Collins: It turns into an erotic poem in the darkness. I need these simple structures to build on. A lot of my poems either have historical sequences or other kinds of chronological grids where I'm locating myself in time. I like to feel oriented, and I like to orient the reader at the beginning of a poem. *Where we are* and *when we are*—those are two basic pieces of information. If you went through my poems, you would see in the beginning of them there are often time-space coordinates in one way or another. We start out with some kind of orientation. One way to mark the progress of the poem is that we leave these known coordinates and move off into some terra incognita, a place that is attracting our desire to get disoriented, to get lost.

Weich: "Bar Time" is like that. It starts off with a well-known concept. Anyone who's ever spent too much time in bars knows about bar time.

Collins: It's common knowledge.

Weich: But the poem takes that common knowledge through a series of logical steps and winds up in a fairly surreal place. What's interesting is the very logical progress into fantasy.

Collins: I think that's true. There's a lot of stepping logically, but the progress is usually toward something that is beyond my sense of logic. My poems tend to have rhetorical structures; what I mean by that is they tend to have a beginning, a middle, and an end. There tends to be an opening, as if you were reading the opening chapter of a novel. They sound like I'm initiating something, or I'm making a move. By the end of the poem, I want to feel disoriented and unsure of where I am. I want to feel a little dazed or surprised, as if I've found a way to slip into some other dimension or just slip from the binds of logic into some imaginatively more free area.

Weich: Does that progress reflect the process of writing?

Collins: Yes. I think I need handholds as I go. It's like laying your own railroad tracks in front of you in order to go forward. I'm also very conscious of guiding the reader through the poem. I feel like I'm giving the reader a tour of a house that I'm in the process of constructing. I feel kind of Virgillian, if that's not too pretentious a word, in that I'm leading the reader somewhere. Not to a many-circled hell, but to some much more modest place.

Weich: Often you address the reader directly. The first poem in *Nine Horses* is called "Night Letter to the Reader." There's a congeniality in the tone and the style that's somewhat unusual.

Collins: Are you saying I'm the Miss Congeniality of poetry?

Weich: I guess I'm saying that it might be worth entering yourself in the competition if you're so inclined.

Collins: Well, that's a good word for it. *Reader-friendly, hospitable, congenial, welcoming?*

Someone wrote an article in the *Hudson Review*, I think—his name escapes me, but he was talking about poetic manners as another way to describe these extremes of highly accessible poetry and very difficult, demanding poetry. His feeling was that in a lot of cases the poetry that seemed to be making serious conceptual, cerebral, and linguistic demands on the reader was in fact nothing more than a display of bad manners, that in fact the reader was not being paid much attention to. He kept up this kind of Emily Post metaphor and talked about various kinds of poetic rudeness. I assented to all that he was saying. I feel that I'm trying to be well mannered, at least in the beginning of the poem. I was talking about these coordinates, knowing where you are and when you are: *it's Wednesday and I'm looking out at this lawn*, or something common like that. I like the poem to get a little ahead of me and a little ahead of the reader, but I'm incapable of engineering any kind of poetic travel to some unknown or interesting place if I don't have a starting place. That's why I always tend to begin a poem with something fairly clear or a piece of common knowledge, like "Bar Time" or the song "Three Blind Mice," something we all know, some little common ground that becomes the grounding wire.

Weich: What's most interesting to you about poetry?

Collins: I think what's interesting to me is not so much movements or the state of American poetry or post-postmodernism, but actual poems and how they work, how they maneuver. That's my fascination, I think: how a poem gets from one place to another.

When I teach poetry, instead of asking, "What does a poem mean?" I try to substitute the question of "How does a poem operate?" or "How does it get from one place to another?" We look at poems as a series of pivots or shifts or maneuvers, slipstreaming one idea into another, the way a poem is groping toward its own destination. The reason I'm saying this, I guess, is that this is what preoccupies me in the process of composition. That's basically what poetry is to a poet, I think: the act of composition. It's not the act of literary criticism or the act of figuring out where your poetry belongs in some broader context.

In composition, I'm trying to do a number of things. I'm trying to write good lines. I do think a poem is a series of lines. You'll probably find a lot of weak lines in these books, but I try not to go forward until I have what I think is a line. We used to measure lines metrically, so a line would simply be *ba-ding, ba-ding, ba-ding, ba-ding*. That would be a tetrameter line. Once you turn off that iambic metronome, you have an open-ended question: What's a line, if it isn't four or five beats? There's something that makes up a good line. I'm not sure what it is, but maybe you could say that each line is doing its job; it's making its little contribution, it's not slacking off. In composition, I guess it goes without saying, but I'm working one line at a time.

The other thing that's going on is, I'm trying to see if this poem has a destination that I have been put on Earth to discover. I'm like the first person to go on this little journey. Whether the poem is going to find some branch to land on is a driving curiosity. Some poems don't go anywhere, and I just get rid of them.

Weich: Do you abandon many poems?

Collins: Quite a few. There are quite a few false starts. I used to try to force them, and they just got worse and worse, like a painter that tries to fix a painting in the wrong way and paints too much until it all turns to mud. I need a clean line that I'm following. If I find a clean line from the beginning of the poem, this line of energy, this spinal direction, and I sense that the poem starts to go forward down this line of energy? But if there's any blockage, or if it turns into a backwater where the energy isn't working, and you have to go back and rethink it, basically at that point I just give it up.

I think I've written enough so that I can sense at the beginning of the poem its potential; I can feel this energy moving forward, and I'm trying to stay ahead of it, but I believe the waste basket is a writer's best friend. That's one of the troubles with so many writing programs today: they're all based on revision. Someone said, "You can't teach someone to write, but you can teach them to rewrite"—or at least you can *make* them rewrite. What else is there to do? You discuss this poem, then everyone makes suggestions, and either the young poet ignores the suggestions, or they follow some of them, and if they follow some of them, they're doing this revision. Then they come back, and of course it's not perfect, so they revise again. The drudgery of revision is threatening to replace any kind of compositional spontaneity that young poets might trust in. Then again, it takes a while just to figure out a way to do it; it takes a lot of this drudge work to get there.

Weich: You were talking a moment ago about more demanding poetry. I don't pretend to know much about painting, but a lot of modernist poems, filled with obscure references and supported by inches and inches of footnotes, put me in the mind of abstract art. The typical abstract painting isn't looking to travel, I don't expect a narrative, but as a viewer I can't find a way in. In their own way, some of those poems give a lay reader no grounding at all.

Collins: Well, painting is instantaneous: it happens to you as soon as you look at it. It's not linear, so you're not missing a reference here, then a reference later on, and you're not asked to connect the dots as you would be reading Eliot's *Waste Land*. The analogy reminds me of that book by Tom Wolfe [*The Painted Word*] about modern painting, where he says that for the first time in the history of painting, painting doesn't make sense unless you read the theory behind it. Art criticism and art theory begin to intervene; you have to go to school in some way to appreciate cubism or abstract expressionism. The analogy holds up there, doesn't it? Just as with Eliot you'd want to read *The Golden Bough* or Jessie Weston, texts that help you read the second text. You don't need a text to understand Robert Burns, for example—you just need Robert Burns. (And a Scottish glossary. Someone said, "He was a great poet, but a terrible typist.") But that's the analogy there, needing to read Clement Greenberg in order to understand Ellsworth Kelly; you have to read Jessie Weston to understand T. S. Eliot.

I'm a professor of English, and I've spent most of my life teaching poetry and literature. There are plenty of references and allusions in my poetry—it's really quite literary in some ways—but the reader is never required to pick up any of these references to gain admission into the little theater of the poem. If you pick them up you get bonus points, fifty extra Poetry Bonus Points, but if you don't you still get full credit.

Weich: You note in your introduction to *Poetry 180* that "textbooks and anthologies often lag behind the times." I went to a particularly old-fashioned university, so I was somewhat shocked to discover the joys of contemporary literature after graduation.

Collins: The poems taught in schools tend to be lagging behind fifty or a hundred years. One reason is that anthologies change so slowly. The popular anthologies tend to have gatekeepers that are very reluctant to let a rabble of contemporary poets come in, some ragtag group of poets, because they want to give history a little time to sort things out and get a sense of who's going to last. Otherwise, they'll have to take the poet out, and that becomes embarrassing. If the end of your anthology is full of poets that are being admitted then tossed out for the next edition, it doesn't fulfill the anthologizer's role of being a controller or a harbinger of posterity. One of my ambitions as poet laureate, as you know from reading that introduction, was to bring high school students a quick exposure to very contemporary poetry. I don't think they hear those voices in the classroom. And as I said in there, even if the teacher is kind of hip—and the teacher might be a poet herself and will read a poem by Stephen Dunn or Mary Oliver or Sharon Olds occasionally—unless they just want to Xerox their life away, which they're doing anyway, they're still limited to the anthologies the schools approve of. Teachers in high schools don't usually control those choices. How old is "The Red Wheelbarrow"? Was that written in 1920-something? [Editor's note: 1923.] That's still thought of as kind of a groovy, wild, contemporary, minimalist poem, but it's pretty old. To use an analogy from my own experience, when I was in college, or in graduate school, in the sixties, it would mean reading Edwardian poetry or late Victorian poetry like Swinburne as being up-to-date.

Weich: Do you draw inspiration from other modes of design, other structural forms? You write a lot about music, for example.

Collins: I think it's much more basic than that for me. It's probably my years with the Jesuits, learning about Aristotelian rhetoric, things having beginnings, middles, and endings. Also, reading Elizabethan and metaphysical poetry, in particular, Herbert or Donne, there's always a very clear sense of logical development, in the course of which you have all this sparky leaping around, the deployment of incredibly imaginative images and conceits. Marvel's "To His Coy Mistress" is a great template. *If we had world enough, but we don't, so therefore?* It's a very clear, syllogistic organization. I think I'm copying those models more than something I would intuit in music or the structure of the blues. But the sonnet is like the blues; and the popular song is similar to some poetic forms, going out and then having a subdominant chord and some kind of modulation and return. These structures, some of them I think are very underlying.

Weich: I ask because I once took a course on postmodern literature in which, before the professor assigned any fiction, we read a book about postmodern architecture. To see the applications in another form, particularly a visual one, illustrated the underlying principles better than any literary criticism could have.

Collins: A lot of postmodernism tries to defy symmetry, but I think the pleasures of symmetry are irreplaceable. One simple analogy is the pleasure of massage. Massage is always symmetrical. It's one thing to have someone run their hands all over your body in some chaotic way, which is fine after you've had a couple bottles of wine, but one of the pleasures besides the sensual pleasure of having your muscles taken care of is that what is done on the left side will be done on the right side. You can anticipate that. As the left side is being massaged, the right side waits in anticipation; then it is satisfied. You go back and forth: hands and shoulders? That's such a basic pleasure, which would carry from massage into aesthetics and poetics. Modernism seemed to try to get away from symmetry, and broader historical sociocultural reasons were given: Nietzsche said, "God is dead"; Einstein turned physics upside-down; two World Wars? *The world cannot waltz anymore; it can't pretend to have symmetry because it's leaning toward chaos.* That sounds good on the blackboard, but I question the pleasure of listening to chaotic music, walking out of it saying, "That reflects our times, therefore I got real pleasure out of it."

Weich: You mention in *Poetry 180* that a reader should be able to derive pleasure from one reading of the poems. That represents a fairly basic split right there: between those who would write to provide pleasure and those who would, as you say, represent our times. But the canvas on which you're working, at least on the surface, doesn't beg questions about current affairs, for instance. More often the speaker is simply standing on his lawn or in his kitchen, thinking.

Collins: My poetry is suburban, it's domestic, it's middle class, and it's sort of unashamedly that, but I hope there's enough imaginative play in there that it's not simply poems about barbequing.

I'm a professor. I've been an academic most of my life. I enjoy a great deal of what used to be called "domestic tranquility." But also, besides those biographical facts, what I'm also doing with this creature on the lawn, as you mention, or the fellow looking out the window at the lawn or the bird feeder, I'm picking up an eighteenth-century or early nineteenth-century English figure: the stroller, or the walker, the Wordsworthian fellow who has all the time in the world, this leisurely sense of time, this luxury of being very preoccupied with your own thoughts and having a certain degree of delight in landscape and environment. I'm taking that romantic stroller, that fellow who sits on a wayside bench and falls into a meditation, basically taking him out of the early nineteenth century and putting him in an American context.

Weich: There's often a flirtatiousness in your poems, a confidence at play not unlike seduction.

Collins: It's an attempt to achieve intimacy. You could look at some of the strategies as seductive devices. They're meant to seduce the reader into being interested. They're meant to form a kind of temporary companionship with the reader, without being presumptuous, without presuming that a reader would be interested in my inner turmoil just because it's my inner turmoil. I don't think people read poetry because they're interested in the poet. I think they read poetry because they're interested in themselves. That's why I read poetry. I read poetry to discover things about myself, not so much to discover things about Emily Dickinson. My consciousness and my thought processes have a lot to do with the content of these poems, but I'm always careful not to foist my problems or personal turmoil onto a reader in a psychoanalytic way. I presume that they're not interested.

Weich: Have you been reading anything particularly good lately?

Collins: I've been reading George Herbert some more. And I've been reading a lot of William Matthews because his collected poems just came out, called *Search Party*. I've been reading a lot of those and realizing again how good he is.

Weich: What did you take out of being Poet Laureate?

Collins: Well, I did perceive it as having a civic and communal American cultural dimension, and that's why I did *Poetry 180*. I also started a poetry channel on Delta Airlines. If you fly Delta, you can look in the in-flight magazine where it has music and comedy and business talk; now there's a poetry channel with jazz and poetry, a parfait. The poems are contemporary, like the poems in *Poetry 180*—in fact, some are the same poems. I believe poetry belongs in unexpected places—in elevators and on buses and subways. That's a good way to get it out of the classroom, out of the hands of academics and to bring poetry into public spaces. I thought airline audio would be a good thing to do. That and *Poetry 180* were basically my legacy, if you want to use that word.

But you do get to see how people react to you differently, which is odd. You get treated with a sudden deference on the part of people who are hosting you. Instead of just meeting a couple of English professors when I'd visit a college, I'd start meeting trustees and the president and donors and other people who are philanthropically connected to the college. You realize that this title has some shine to it and that people are going to trade off that title to raise funds. At that point, I become a little more detached from myself, even more than usual. You become aware of the overlay on your ordinary social image, which I don't put much stock in to begin with. It only increased my sense of having these two selves. The outer self, the self that had the title, was getting so much attention that I found myself walking around with this dark little secret, that I wasn't really the poet laureate; I was really just me.

Weich: Do you see your poetry changing? Are your interests changing in terms of subject matter or style or tone?

Collins: Not too much. I'm not really interested in developing very much. I'm just trying to find new things to write about. I'm not interested too much in stylistic development. I just want more topics or more imaginative passages to follow. I think I've found some kind of style to write in, and I'd be perfectly content to keep writing that way, advancing the same persona, staying within this tonal range that I've established. I think development is overrated. Emily Dickinson never developed.

A Brisk Walk:
Billy Collins in Conversation

Joel Whitney / 2006

This interview appeared in *Guernica: A Magazine of Art and Politics* in 2006. It is reprinted with the permission of Joel Whitney.

Joel Whitney: What was your childhood like?

Billy Collins: I would say it was a fairly happy childhood. But they say he who says that is just better at repressing things. In fact, I think Howard Nemerov . . . or somebody said that you didn't need to suffer extraordinarily to be a writer because adolescence itself is suffering enough. But factually, I was an only child, a very late child, born to parents who were both thirty-nine at the time, which was very late back then. That kind of confirmed my sense of being the center of the universe, which I guess every child feels—children and poets both tend to feel. What else? I went to a lot of Catholic schooling. I went to kindergarten in a public school, and then I went immediately into Catholic first grade and stayed there—not in first grade but Catholic institutions—all the way through college—I went to a Jesuit college—and finally returned to secular education not until I went to graduate school at the University of California. That's a quick ride through my childhood.

Whitney: When and how did you get into poetry—when did you write your first poem?

Collins: I had this early memory. You know how sometimes you just have a memory of looking up and seeing a face looking over your crib and then remember nothing until tenth grade?—I have one of these early memories where I'm in the back of my parents' car, a place I loved to spend a lot of time as an only child, not having to fight with venomous siblings over the only toy. And we were driving up the East River Drive—I was born and raised in New York City. And I saw a sailboat tacking its way up the East River. And I immediately had a literary response to it. I mean, I could have been seven—I don't know. Whenever you're able to make letters, maybe a little older. But I wrote something down. I don't remember what I wrote, but I remember writing it. It was my first observational poem, observational poems being where the poet says, "I saw something and I felt something about it."

And that's when it began, and it continued. I mean, it's kind of a long story, but it continued through the throes of adolescence. And in that period, I was writing kind of covert, dark, wounded, misunderstood—I would say Gothic—poetry. Bad, you know—terrible. And then I suddenly came under the influence of, first of all, people like Karl Shapiro and Howard Nemerov and Reed Whittemore and a lot of other contemporary poets that I was exposed to only because for some complicated reasons my father used to bring *Poetry* magazine home. And so I got to hear not just school voices, like William Cullen Bryant and John Greenleaf Whittier and all these extremely dead guys, but the voice of living poets that rang with speech and sounded like talk. And that was my first exposure to I guess what modern poetry was.

And then there was just a series of influences. I was influenced by the Beats because I actually just began to commit adolescence around 1955, when "Howl" and *Rebel without a Cause* and a lot of other new things were popping up. (Again, I'm trying to give you a finite version of this career.) And then I came under the sway of Wallace Stevens when I was in college and graduate school and basically set as a life goal the ambition of writing third-rate Wallace Stevens. I thought I would be completely content if I was recognized at some later point in my life as a third-rate Wallace Stevens.

Whitney: You once told an interviewer that if you're a novelist you have to invent dozens, sometimes hundreds of characters. If you're a poet you have to invent just one. So I guess you're an advocate of efficiency—

Collins: Or laziness.

Whitney: Or laziness. To what degree is that one character you?

Collins: Well, to back up a little bit first—there's this pet phrase about writing that is bandied around particularly in workshops about "finding your own voice as a poet," which I suppose means that you come out from under the direct influence of other poets and have perhaps found a way to combine those influences so that it appears to be your own voice. But I think you could also put it a different way. You, quote, find your voice, unquote, when you are able to invent this one character who resembles you, obviously, and probably is more like you than anyone else on earth, but is not the equivalent to you.

It is like a fictional character in that it has a very distinctive voice, a voice that seems to be able to accommodate and express an attitude that you are comfortable staying with but an attitude that is flexible enough to cover a number of situations. The character I invented, if I had to describe him, is probably an updating of a character you find strolling through the pages of English Romantic poetry. He is a daydreamer, obviously unemployed, plenty of time on his hands, spends a lot of time by himself, and has an unhealthy fascination with his thinking process, his own speculations and fantasies. So he is not a really new character. He is kind of a remodeling of this earlier Romantic character, the poet who would find himself daydreaming on a wayside bench somewhere.

Whitney: He's also been described as "affable, congenial, polite, welcoming." You've spoken pretty consistently for accessible poetry. Is difficulty your biggest gripe, is difficulty the "trouble with poetry"?

Collins: I think there are kinds of difficulty. Some difficulty is warranted, and other difficulty I think is gratuitous. And I think I can tell the difference. There are certainly very difficult poets that I really enjoy reading. I could mention six or seven, but I'll mention John Ashbery and Jorie Graham. I find their difficulty enjoyable. More often than not in poetry I find difficulty to be gratuitous and show-offy and camouflaging, experimental to a kind of insane degree—a difficulty which really ignores the possibility of having a sensible reader.

So that kind of difficulty is one trouble with poetry. And the second trouble with poetry—and I'm going to stop the list at two—is the presence of presumptuousness in poetry, the sense you get in a poem that the poet takes for granted an interest on the reader's part in the poet's autobiographical life, in the poet's memories, problems, difficulties, and even minor perceptions. I try to presume that no one is interested in me. And I think experience bears that out. No one's interested in the experiences of a stranger—let's put it that way. And then you have difficulty combined with presumptuousness, which is the most dire trouble with poetry.

Whitney: You say that you were once a perpetrator of some of these more troublesome aspects of poetry. Tell me about this shift from difficult poetry to more accessible poetry. Was it sudden, was it gradual, was it just a matter of changing influences as you suggested earlier?

Collins: Particularly when I thought of myself as a Wallace Stevens acolyte, I wrote very difficult poetry, and I was really guilty of not knowing what I was talking about. I was going for a kind of clever verbal effect. I was trying to sound linguistically or verbally interesting. I had a sense, I guess, from just reading a lot of poetry of how a poem would start and how it would end, but really I didn't know what I was doing. It had very little connection to my life. I was committing these acts of literature—there was no wiring that was connected to thought, feeling, or experience—it was purely literary. And I think I kind of bought into the assumption that poetry had to be extremely gloomy and incomprehensible, or nearly so. And when I wrote, I took on the role of the despondent and difficult to understand person, whereas in life, I was easy to understand, to the point of being simpleminded maybe.

The change came I would say when I began to dare to be clear because I think clarity is the real risk in poetry because you are exposed. You're out in the open field. You're actually saying things that are comprehensible, and it's easy to criticize something you can understand. But I think when I transitioned to a poetry that was clearer, it really was about shifting influences. I started moving away from poets like Wallace Stevens and Hart Crane and started reading poets like, again, Karl Shapiro, Howard Nemerov, Philip Larkin, and the British poets who were imported through that important anthology put together by Alvarez—and those would include Thom Gunn and Ted Hughes. And I think these poets gave me assurance that there were other ways to write besides the rather involuted style of high modernism whose high priests were Pound, Eliot and Stevens, and Crane perhaps.

Whitney: One of your habits is to mock poetry, to knock it off its altar. Was that something that you became conscious of early on, that poetry could use some mocking as Americans simultaneously are mystified by and disdainful of poetry, maybe even a little patronizing toward it?

Collins: I think I was not able to dare to do that until I had a few books under my belt and I had some kind of little reputation. I felt at some point that I had nothing to lose, and [Laughs] maybe I was wrong. I think, you know, there's always these little autobiographical secrets behind things. I think I was really attacking my earlier self, and this kind of pretentious figure. I just think that the world of workshops—I've written a poem that is a parody of workshop talk, I've written a poem that is a kind of parody of a garrulous poet at a poetry reading who spends an inordinate amount of time explaining the poem before reading it, I've written a number of satirical poems about other poets . . . I have a poem coming out in the next humor issue of *Poetry* magazine, which is not going to make me any friends because it's a sort of a parody of, well, Irish poetry generally, but more specifically you'll recognize maybe [Seamus] Heaney's style in it perhaps—I love Heaney's work, but there are excesses that I'm trying to satirize. The literary world is so full of pretension, and there's such an enormous gap between how seriously poets take themselves and how widely they're ignored by everybody else. So I appointed myself the poet who's going to feel free to take potshots at the whole enterprise.

Whitney: You said in one interview that "one way to mark the progress of the poem is that we leave these known coordinates and move off into some terra incognita, a place that is attracting our desire to get disoriented, to get lost." So getting lost but avoiding confusion—is that the game?

Collins: That's a better way to put it than I can think of. Because by clarity I don't mean that we're always in kind of a simple area where everything is clear and comforting and understood. Clarity is certainly a way toward disorientation because if the reader isn't grounded, if the reader is disoriented in the beginning of the poem, then the reader can't be led astray or disoriented later. So yes, I see the progress typical in some of my poems as starting with something simple and moving into something more demanding. This is certainly the pattern of weird poetry. Coleridge is an example; we start with someone sitting in a backyard, and we go off into these levels of airy speculation. Frost is a good example. We start by coming across a divided road in the woods, and we're talking a couple of lines later about decision making and the road of life and the rest of it—I think I'm just following what is a common pattern of lyric poetry and, for that matter, it's a common pattern of songs. Singers know that you start kind of soft and you go out bigger.

Whitney: Are poems easy for you to make?

Collins: Poems are not easy to start, and they're not easy to finish. There's a great pleasure in—I wouldn't say ease, but maybe kind of a fascinated ease that accompanies the actual writing of the poem. I find it very difficult to get started. There are just long gaps where I can't find a point of insertion. I can't find a good opening line, or I can't find a mood that I want to write into. But once I do, once a line falls out of the air, or I get a little inkling of a subject and I recognize that, it's like the sense that a game has started. Part of writing is discovering the rules of the game and then deciding whether to follow the rules or to break them. The great thing about the game of poetry is that it's always your turn—I guess that goes back to my being an only child. So once it's under way, there is a sense of flow. Usually, the poems are written in one sitting. There's always a groping towards some satisfying ending. But I'd say the hardest part is not writing. Once the writing starts, it's too pleasurable to think of it as a difficulty.

Whitney: Who are you speaking to in your poems?

Collins: I'm speaking to someone I'm trying to get to fall in love with me. I'm trying to speak intimately to one person. That should be clear. I'm not speaking to an audience. I'm not writing for the podium. I'm just writing, trying to write in a fairly quiet tone to one other reader who is by herself, or himself, and I'm trying to interrupt some silence in their life, which is utterance. I don't really have a picture of this person. But as soon as I start to write, I'm trying to be aware that a reader just might well pick up this poem, a stranger. So when I'm writing—and I think that this is important for all writers—I'm trying to be a writer and a reader back and forth. I write two lines or three lines. I will immediately stop and turn into a reader instead of a writer, and I'll read those lines as if I had never seen them before and as if I had never written them. If they still make sense, and if they still have good cadence, and if there's something interesting going on there, then I'll go forward, turn back into the writer, and write another two or three or six lines, and then go back and bring the reader out and see what he thinks of it.

Whitney: You were made poet laureate in 2001, an interesting year to be foisted into this role as the public poet of the country. You told the *New York Times*, "In times of crisis it's interesting that people don't turn to the novel or say, 'We should all go out to a movie,' or 'Ballet would help us.' It's always poetry. What we want to hear is a human voice speaking directly in our ear." But don't they turn to all of these, don't they also turn, say, to iPods?

Collins: I hope not. I think that—if you bring up technology—I know people who are working on this now, and I think that within a year or two you will find iPoetry, which is an interesting phrase because poetry is always about the "I." You'll find iPoetry. You'll find that you can download poetry, that you can stuff your iPod with recorded poetry. So just to answer the question that way, I think that poetry is going to catch up with that technology quite soon.

Whitney: Have you ever been tempted to tackle politics in your poems?

Collins: I think when I was in my Lawrence Ferlinghetti wanna-be period . . . I wrote some poems in high school—and no, you're not going to see them—which are diatribes against conformity and capitalism. They had this kind of ranting rhetoric, crying out against social ills. But I am glad I got them out of my system.

Whitney: You said I'm not going to see them? Does that mean they still exist?

Collins: [Laughs] I shouldn't even have said that. No, they've been destroyed.

Whitney: How important is humor to your poetry?

Collins: I think it's vital. It's odd to me because many people say we live in these awful times, and we need culture and art especially in times like these, in these dire times. Well, first of all, I don't think these times are more dire than other times. People who say that just need to go back and read Herodotus, read any book of history, read a biography of Attila the Hun. If people are going to wring their hands over these troubled times, I would think that humor should be indispensable. I find it strange that—at least in my take on it—the people who are the most alarmed about the dire times we live in are the ones who seem to be humorless, in their taste for poetry anyway. Humor is just an ingredient. It's always been in poetry. It kind of dropped out of poetry I think during the nineteenth and up to the mid-twentieth century. But it's found its way back. And it's simply an ingredient. It's one of the humors—if you will—of the human spirit, as well as grief and loneliness and whatever other emotional notes we are able to flag on ourselves. I don't see why it needs to be questioned. You could just as easily ask, "Why is there so much seriousness in poetry?"

Whitney: Last couple of questions. True or false: Billy Collins's poems are prose vignettes cut into verse?

Collins: Well, false because I write one line at a time. I'm a line maker. I think that's what makes poets different from prose writers. That's the main way. We think, not just in sentences the way prose writers do but also in lines. So we're doing these two things at the same time. When I'm constructing a poem, I'm trying to write one good line after another, one solid line after another. You know a lot of the lines—some hold up better as lines than others. But I'm not thinking of just writing a paragraph and then chopping it up. I'm very conscious of the fact that every line should have a cadence to it. It should contribute to the progress of the poem. And that the ending of the line is a way of turning the reader's attention back into the interior of the poem. So, in other words, false.

Whitney: True or false: you perhaps more than any poet living today have challenged the cliché that poetry necessitates poverty?

Collins: [he laughs for a long time] True.

Whitney: Last question.

Collins: You keep saying that.

Whitney: For real this time, I promise. Do you think that your poems will last? Do you care?

Collins: There's just no telling. I don't know. I always think [W. S.] Merwin's poems will last of anyone writing today. If I had to bet on posterity, I would bet Merwin. My poems could easily evaporate. So I don't know. If you find yourself as a writer thinking about posterity you should probably go out for a brisk walk or something.

Brick by Brick—A Conversation with Billy Collins

Adam Johnston / 2007

A science professor at Weber State University in Ogden, Utah, Adam Johnston teaches courses in general physics and science education. He interviewed Collins in November 2007 during the Fall Author Event hosted by the Ogden School Foundation. The interview, which originally appeared in *Weber: The Contemporary West* 28, no. 1, Fall 2008, is reprinted with the permission of Adam Johnston.

As I write this introduction to my meeting with Collins, I'm tempted to repeat the phrasing that Collins himself uses in his poem "Taking Off Emily Dickinson's Clothes":

[Lines 13–19 of "Taking Off Emily Dickinson's Clothes quoted]

My meeting with Mr. Collins was much different, of course. Yet, you will want to know that his entrance was announced not by his physical presence, but by the clearing of his throat I heard first. When listening to a Collins reading, whether on tape or in person, this simple audible preparation is to me as characteristic of my favorite poet as standing by an open window would be characteristic of Dickinson. We would sit by an open window, Collins comfortably in a sweater, and me in a typical buttoned shirt—I restrained myself from rolling up the sleeves for once, since, after all, this was an interview with a former US poet laureate.

So there he was, standing before me, relaxed and comfortable as we arranged chairs in the hotel lobby. "So, you're in physics?" he asked me. Perhaps he thought I was a gimmick, a ruse, and he followed with, "What is 'surface tension'?" Here I had been preparing to switch myself from physics teacher or education researcher to a literary role, and now I was thrown back to explaining forces between molecules and their arrangements in a fluid. Satisfied and, it seemed, amused, Collins exclaimed, "You really are in physics, aren't you?"

This dissonance, a science teacher interviewing a poet, seemed to be a theme that others asked me after having heard me introduce Collins at the Fall Author Event for the Ogden School Foundation later that evening. "How does someone in physics become interested in poetry?" they pondered. There's a long story, but each time I try to explain this I quickly realize that there really isn't an explanation, at least not a very linear and logical one. And, I want to proclaim, there doesn't need to be. I'm not particularly well read, but I like to read, and I like verse. Why should the poets be the only ones reading poetry?

Billy Collins's work speaks quite clearly to this. He writes, I suppose, to first please himself and his senses, but also to a very local reader. One gets the sense while either reading or listening to his work that the words are not being written for any particular group, but for an individual—even a physics teacher—sitting next to Collins or perhaps looking over his shoulder as he scratches out lines, in his own words, "brick by brick" on his notepad. The title and first lines of his poems open a welcome door and offer an easy hors d'oeuvre, but the conversation and flavors become more complex once inside.

My meeting with Billy Collins was delightful and incomparable to anything else I do. While I started with my first question on my prepared list, Collins was able to allow the conversation to flow easily. After opening with "What is poetry?" I let him steer the conversation wherever it needed to be. So, we ventured from physics to poetry to education, and when he wondered out loud where else we could possibly go, I tossed into the ring "global warming." And he quite willingly tackled this as well, just as aptly as he was able to switch over to jazz and Thelonious Monk.

Adam Johnston: Can you explain for us what poetry is, especially since you seem to scoff at traditional forms and do your own thing? It confuses us.

Billy Collins: Well, I don't necessarily scoff at—I mean, I make fun of a lot of things in poetry, not just traditional forms. I take the poetry very seriously, but at the same time I realize there are people who take it too seriously and themselves too seriously. And so I like to kind of shoot up the saloon occasionally and write parodies and take a kind of irreverent attitude toward the whole enterprise. I mean, writing poetry is the most egotistical of any art because it's the lyric—the lyric poem is all about the "I." It's all about the self and there's a presumptuousness there. And the presumption is that someone else is interested in your private life or your internal, interior life—your interiority, as they call it today. Well, we know from real life that no one is interested in your internal life except maybe your wife in a good mood . . .

Johnston: . . . on a good day.

Collins: . . . and a few friends on a good day. So why should strangers be interested in your internal life? So that's one kind of presumption that I tend to try to counter in my poetry. Well, but to get back to your question—I guess I could put it this way: it's like saying, "What is religion?" or "What is physics?" This is not my first camping trip, but most of the questions that you get in an interview, I could sit in a room for five hundred years, and they would never occur to me. It would never occur to me to ask these questions about myself. And I don't think about the future of American poetry, I don't think about "What is poetry?" I do as a teacher, you know, because you have to get up and talk about it. But here's one answer. It's all provisional, these answers, but one answer would be that poetry is what occurs, or what comes into play, when the limits of prose have been exhausted. So prose continues to a certain point and has certain expressive capabilities, right? But if you imagine a point at which you have said everything you can in prose, and there is still something else to say that can't be expressed in prose, at that point poetry comes into existence; this is another demonstration of its superiority to prose. That point I'll be making frequently during the interview.

Johnston: [Laughter] I see. So where does music fit in? Does that trump poetry, or are we just in a whole different ballpark?

Collins: Yeah, music trumps everything. I mean, all art aspires to the condition of music—according to Walter Pater, I think. Well, the overlap between poetry and music is that most poets write with their ear as well as their mind, and they also write with their sense of rhythm, too. So, I'm always writing with my ear. I'm trying to keep a beat, make sounds come together in an agreeable way, and make sense. And it's a matter of doing some things at the same time. It's similar to driving a car when you're doing three or four things at the same time. You're not thinking of them as individual acts; they're orchestrated into some behavior pattern. Music, for me, is in my poetry; I think I try to make my poetry musical. And I think there's probably more form in my poetry than you're suggesting. I mean, I make fun of traditional forms like the sonnet—playful—and I've invented this form called the "paradelle," which is sort of a parody on formal poetry. But as soon as I begin a poem, I am thinking about form. I'm thinking, first of all, about stanzas. You know, I started a poem on the airplane today, and it wanted to be in three-line stanzas, it seems. So that's the way it is now.

That might change. It might tell me later that it's not happy being that way. But it started out with a three-line stanza, and from that point on I put on this little formal jacket, and I assign myself the task of now writing a series of three-line stanzas that are not just this thing chopped into three lines. Each stanza has a kind of integrity, or each stanza's a unit. So you're thinking in terms of the line—making a good line. You know, "No line must sleep," Charles Olson says. Every line should be a little aware of itself. You're then aware of making these boxes—these things they make boxes—and you're aware, at least I'm aware, of having a kind of conceptual run of the poem—where it's going somewhere. But I don't move forward until I write a good line—until I can stand on that line. And until I'm sure a reader can take that line in well, and then I go on to the next line. Very much brick by brick.

Johnston: So, I wanted to ask you about the writing process itself. Using that line-by-line, brick-by-brick method, do you get to the end and feel finished? You don't have to try out the piece somewhere?

Collins: Not anymore because I've learned how to do it. You know, I've been doing it for a long time. So, I mean, this is the poem here [showing the poem on a notepad]—it starts there, and it ends here, and it's in three-line stanzas. And these little things will change—right, these little words, here [pointing at words], or this might change, but the overall structure isn't going to change. It goes from here to here, and that's not going to change. So that means the conceptual run of the poem—dot, dot to dot, you know, and step, step, step, the end—that doesn't change. That's done in the first sitting *always* because that's the movement of the thing.

Johnston: So, you'll never get to a poem a month or a year or five years down the road and tweak it?

Collins: Oh, no. Well, maybe, occasionally you'll read one of your poems out loud, and you'll need maybe an extra syllable or some tiny thing. But almost never, no. Well, and you also, you know, have to learn not to send poems out before they're cooked. I mean, if you send out hastily, "Marry in haste, regret at leisure," especially in terms of a book. I mean, my publisher has to tear a manuscript from my hands because I don't want to let go of it because I'm not sure if it's right, you know. Eventually, I get tired of pulling, and he wins the tug of war.

Johnston: [Laughs] Let me ask you a bit about you as a teacher and your view of education. The Poetry 180 Project probably has an explicit view of what poetry is for in society and what maybe education is for? What do you see either for the role of education itself or for the role of poetry within that educational setting?

Collins: Well, again sitting in this imaginary room for five hundred years, I can't imagine saying [Laughs], "Hmm, what about the role of education in America?" However, to answer your question: Poetry 180 was meant as a supplement to the teaching of poetry. These are poems that are not, should not be taught. These are poems that have, I feel, a transparency or an invitational quality to them that does not require rereading or study. That doesn't mean you can't get some extra pleasure through rereading, but ideally, I was telling high school teachers to not quiz their students on these poems. Just read them and shut up and let them hear the poem. It was meant as a supplement, a complement to the classroom teaching poetry. It was also meant to bring students up to date in terms of contemporary poetry.

Johnston: You've made a similar comment about William Carlos Williams's "The Red Wheelbarrow" as being viewed as contemporary, when really it's quite old.

Collins: Yeah! And that's sold as a modernist poem, but it's as old as your granny. And you know, textbooks and teachers are always lagging behind. I mean, high school teachers—I don't see how they have time to breathe, let alone keep up with poetry. So I'm certainly not blaming them. I mean, it's a task in itself and not necessarily a pleasant one to read a lot of contemporary poetry. I was there, you know, so I spent hours, hundreds of hours, just going through poetry books and anthologies to pick out the best that would give a good sampling of what teachers probably don't have time to keep up with or find and what students, therefore, are missing because they're not going to go out and find. Unless they're exceptionally curious, they're not going to go out and look for what's going on in the world of contemporary poetry. And, you know, the Poetry Project was put into place as a declaration that interpretation is one of the pleasures—an intellectual pleasure, putting your mind against a difficult poem. It was saying that there are poems that you can ingest without the interpretation of a teacher. What are we going to do when we get out of school? Does that mean, since there's no more teacher, there's no more poetry? The teacher does not necessarily have to stand like the minister or the priest between you and God. There can be a direct link there. So that's the idea of Poetry 180—being a slight corrective, offering more of a balance. In other words, it's not competing with classroom teaching. I mean, I got a PhD in English literature. So, if I didn't like explication, I really shouldn't have been taking that major.

Johnston: So, for you, yourself as a teacher, what's your view of yourself? What's your role within a classroom when you're in your own classroom?

Collins: Well, in teaching literature or in teaching creative writing? Or either?

Johnston: If there's a difference that would be interesting to hear, too.

Collins: Well, the difference is, if you're teaching literature, you're teaching the poems of actual poets, whereas, if you're teaching creative writing, then you're teaching the work of poets who happen to be in your classroom. So, there's a clear difference there . . . [Laughter] between the sophomore and William Wordsworth.

Johnston: Right, so for the sophomore, where do you start?

Collins: Well, with exercises. I try to tell them that literature is derivative, that you can't just go off and try to be original. That's a very adolescent idea, you know, that "I'm not going to read anything because it will compromise my genius." The only way to learn how to write is to read, and you do that. And so, I have them try to do exercises based on other poems. So, we'll take a poem by William Carlos Williams or a poem by Thomas Hardy, and we'll do a kind of a version of it. We'll say there are four or five guidelines to follow. Let's say this poem is called "November." You have to use a month in your title, and you know it has to be in four-lined stanzas or something. So, I put them into formally restrictive situations and ask them to perform within those boundaries. The other function in creative writing is to try to act as sort of a dating service, so that you can match up students with the right poets to read. So, I would read your work and I would say, "Have you read Kenneth Koch?" or "Have you read John Ashbery?" And, if you said yes, I would say, "Oh, so that's how you sound like that!" [Laughter]

But, if you said no, then I would say, "Well, then, you need to read these poets right away because you're drifting into their lane and, you know, you should probably get further—not steer away from them—but get further influenced by them." So, it's kind of matchmaking. And sometimes it doesn't work. Sometimes you'll say, "You should read Thomas Hardy." And the student comes back and just says, "Hardy stinks," or, "He leaves me cold." And that's okay, I was a bad matchmaker then. It just means I need to get a better client list of poets so I can hook them up.

Johnston: So, do students ever read that which you find to be similar to their own writing and decide they need a different style or they don't want to be that particular poet?

Collins: No, not as frequently as you'd want. I think the reason is that influence is so slow in the course of a semester. There are certain poets I've read, and right away I wanted to write like them or incorporate, you know, that into my style. But I think in the usual case it's much more creative and gradual. And they might come back to those poets. You know, teaching is very mysterious because you don't know what students are writing down, or you don't know if they're text messaging or taking notes. At the end of the class, it's like the end of a telethon; if everyone was to write down what they think they thought you taught, well, you'd have a lot of different versions.

Johnston: I once asked students to write down the question they had at the end of each class and incorporated this in a study. And it turned out the questions they were thinking about and the things that I wanted them . . . well, it was a terrifying study. I should never do that again.

Collins: No, and it kind of reminds you that maybe the only real, true teaching strategy that works is repetition—that people need to hear things more than once before it makes sense. And when students really learn something, they learn it when—by some accident—something you've said is corroborated in the real world or by another teacher or by a friend or a parent or something. They'll say, "Yeah, I just heard—you were just talking about this and someone else just mentioned that." Well, why did you need this other person to validate me? It shows that students are either inattentive or skeptical about what's being said in the classroom. [Laughs] You know, like, "I heard on the radio that thing you were talking about, or that poet you mentioned was on television." And that's okay. It just means that repetition actually works. The mind loves repetition; it loves repetition more than anything. That's why we're such slow learners, because the mind really doesn't like new information. I think of the mind as fairly lazy, and new information is disturbing to the mind.

Johnston: It fights with the stuff that's already in there.

Collins: Yes, it resists new information. What it wants is a confirmation of what it already knows; it wants constant reassurance that what it knows is not only true but sufficient. So, you come along with some new idea about surface tension or something crazy [Laughs] and they resist. That's why teaching is hard—that's why learning is hard. That's why it takes us so long to get out of college and graduate school. That's the invention of night school.

Johnston: [Laughter] I've been teaching this science education course this year, and we've been addressing exactly these issues, and I've been using, especially, your piece "Introduction to Poetry." They are undergraduates who are going to teach science. So this very thing that you're describing actually comes up—the resistance of the mind to take on something new because it's either lazy or so well built up with all its ideas.

Collins: Yeah, it just wants repetition. You see people in photographs or films on assembly lines and people with these repetitive jobs assembling something, and there's always kind of this instant sympathy for these people—that they have this arduous and repetitive and boring job, and probably it is. There is a mind-numbing and mind-grinding aspect to it, but I think for a lot of people it is really sort of liberating, that your mind is totally free. Most of them, I think, are in a state of daydreaming. And it probably includes some English teachers [Laughs] who are teaching, you know, "I Wandered Lonely as a Cloud" for the fifty-fifth time. Their mind's going to wander too while teaching. You know, that thing about the English teacher who dreamed he was teaching a class and woke up to find that he was? [Laughter] Yeah, that's the guy we're talking about. Okay we've covered poetry, education, science, what now?

Johnston: We'll just solve global warming.

Collins: Well, here's what Thomas Friedman said about global warming. The reason we're not solving it, and we're not going to solve it without policy—radical policy—is that there are two things: the enemy is invisible—you can't see pollution. You can see smog and what not, but you can't see it. And where all these cars are driving around, it's not all smoky or anything. So, you can't see it. Second, the reason we would change our entire lifestyles is for people who have not yet been born—because we're fine! I mean, we're going to get along fine in our lifetimes, more or less, but it's for our grandchildren—for the unborn. So, if ever there was an equation that resulted in apathy, that's one of them. I mean, an invisible enemy that poses no immediate threat, and we're supposed to change our whole lives for people who will be born in 2070?

Johnston: It's a difficult sell.

Collins: It's a really difficult sell, a really difficult sell. And he said, "This is not a green revolution." He said, "In a revolution, people get hurt." This is a green brunch, or something, a green bridal shower—it's not a revolution. You go out and buy a Prius and buy a low-intensity light bulb . . .

Johnston: There's no bloodshed.

Collins: You'll feel good about yourself, but essentially, it's not doing anything. You need government. Stern revolutionary government policy, you know, forty miles a gallon or whatever. Anyway, so that takes care of global warming.

Johnston: Sure, well, we can check that off the list.

Collins: How about modern photography? Do you want my views on that?

Johnston: [Laughter] I wanted to ask you about Thelonious Monk, and maybe music in general, but I'm also a fan of Monk. I like the imagery, and he shows up in a lot of your work.

Collins: Well, the first and most important thing about Thelonious Monk is to know how to spell his first name. It's I-O-U-S, not U-S. How do you have it?

Johnston: I forgot the "o" in this copy [as part of a set of interview questions I had, embarrassingly, sent previously] but have spelled it correctly in other places.

Collins: That's number one. Well, you leave out the "I-O," and he leaves out all these notes. It is notes and spaces. I mean, it is so spare and angular. It's just amazing that here's the piano and that someone can come along and get out of this piano an entirely new sound that's unmistakable. You can hear two notes, or one chord, and you know it's him. And, one thing that gives me no pleasure is listening to Thelonious Monk covers because I just don't think anyone could cover him. They can't cover him. It just sounds like bad Thelonious Monk. Not just Thelonious Monk on a bad day, but just, you know, like really trying to be Thelonious Monk and obviously not being Thelonious Monk. I don't know how to, you know . . . describing music is really difficult.

Johnston: You're a poet—if anyone's going to do it, it needs to be you.

Collins: Well, I've written about it, but the actual description of what the music is is difficult. There's this book called *Coltrane* by Ben Ratliff, who's the *New York Times* jazz critic. It's not a biography of Coltrane; it's subtitled *The Story of Sound*, and it's the story of how his sound developed.[4] And Ratliff can, with very energetic prose, actually describe music; he can describe solos. And he is talking about solos I know. He's saying, "Coltrane's solo on 'Straight, No Chaser'" and I've listened to that seven hundred times. He's the best at it. I mean, I listen to a lot of jazz, but Monk is difficult to describe. Maybe I could make something up. [Laughs] Maybe it's the fact that he—and Miles Davis does this too—does leave out so much, and when he comes in, it's often at an unexpected place from a bizarre angle. And I think if there is an analogy—I don't know if I'm forcing it for the sake of the interview—poetry is known for leaving a lot out, too. Poetry is a kind of clearing away of everything that's irrelevant, whereas in prose, there's more room to add things. One thing I've told my poetry students is that revision should always be taking away. Always be taking away. No, don't add a new stanza. Don't stuff a stanza in the middle, because you lose this organic flow. So knowing what to leave out is very important, and Monk obviously bases much of his music on those silent spots. What do you like about him? How would you describe him?

Johnston: I'm trying to figure him out. I see the chord charts, and, I mean, it's—you play the piano?

Collins: Some, not well. Do you play too?

Johnston: Yeah, I'm . . . well; I'm not Thelonious Monk, but I'm fascinated because I just can't comprehend what would be going through his head or his spirit to come up with what he's come up with. And, here, we were listening to Coltrane and Monk—the recent Library of Congress findings and hearing them together—it seems so brilliant, but I can't understand how that comes out of something.

Collins: Well, I guess it's knowledge, too. It's experiencing . . . what do they do when something's in orbit and they fly out of orbit?

Johnston: Slingshot.

Collins: It's just like a slingshot where you slip the bounds of gravity or something. But the orbiting, in this case, would be practicing.

Johnston: The repetition.

Collins: Yes, the repetition and practicing. There are a lot of scales involved in jazz. I took someone to a jazz club once, which was kind of a mistake. And he said, "It's just like scales." Well, it is. He [Monk] was very reticent. Someone asked him, how do you get that sound, and he said, "Put the sixth in the left hand." He used the left hand to hit the sixth note. I've tried that, but it didn't really work.

Johnston: [Laughter] *You'll have to fall back on poetry, after all.*

Collins: [Laughter] It's a little too simple, yeah. But I also think of jazz as a kind of violence that it does to ordinary music, a kind of fracturing. I mean, there's some sweet jazz. But edgy players like Coltrane, and Miles Davis, and Thelonious Monk, and Charlie Parker—they're taking these standards, like "Satin Doll" and "The Way you Look Tonight," and using them as trampolines into this stratospheric kind of soloing. And in a way, it's doing some violence to the music, particularly in the case of Monk. I mean, the discordance. We've learned from Monk. Early on he sounded very discordant. Ornette Coleman sounded very jangly. I used to listen to *The Shape of Jazz to Come* in college—his first album, I think—and everyone on the floor of the dormitory would be screaming to turn that stuff off.

Johnston: Because of the dissonance?

Collins: It was very, very discordant. He still sounds great today, but we've gotten kind of used to it. I mean, Monk's discordance has become, and Monk's become, just his sound. Whitmore Sells was once talking about the difference between classical music and jazz, and he said jazz is based on improvisation and surprise, and the only time you're surprised in classical music is when somebody screws up, when somebody makes a mistake. In jazz, on the other hand, if you make a mistake, you just repeat the mistake and the mistake becomes the new thing. So I've speculated that jazz arrived at that improvisation, really arose out of boredom. You know, earlier musicians essentially played dance music, played the same songs night after night and no one was listening; they were dancing. People were using the music as an accompaniment or a reason to dance. And having played the same songs—the same American songbook year after year, night after night, out of boredom—they started fooling around making little riffs, adding notes that weren't there, and the people stopped dancing and started listening. That was the moment in jazz when it goes from dance music to listening music.

Johnston: Would it be too forced to make parallels between what you do as a poet and what Thelonious Monk does as a jazz musician?

Collins: Yeah, it's ludicrous. Because poetry (pointing to the poem on his notepad) is not improvisation, right? There's no eraser on a saxophone, no? Jazz is actual improvisation. This is not improvisation. You go back, and you correct. Maybe the idea of all of this correction is to try to sound spontaneous. But it's a very artificial way of trying to make it sound spontaneous. Whereas in improvisation, it pretty much is composition on the spot. So, the difference is there's no net in improvisation exactly.

Johnston: You're not going to get out before us tonight and improv a poem.

Collins: No, I'm going to read some new poems. I'm going to read some poems I've read fifty times. Yeah, that's the big difference. I think there's this sense that, well, jazz is cool, and poetry is cool, so there's this kind of connection. The audiences for the two—both of them react to some degree. Whenever I see people making a kind of facile, self-congratulatory connection like that, I want to break it. I want to talk against the connection. I'm very against mixed media anyway. I don't like drawings with my poems. I don't like if you have a poem about a flower and you have a picture of a flower next to it. I mean, give me a break.

Johnston: So what do you think of the set of animations on the Internet (https://www.bcactionpoet.org/) that go along . . .

Collins: No that's different [Laughs], that's really different. I don't know—I really like those. That was done for the Sundance Channel. They were using them as kind of filler actually between programs, and they commissioned J. Walter Thompson to find some animators to do this. I participated myself. I went in a studio and read the poems, and they drew these animations, which I more or less approved. Yeah, I worked with them; I cooperated with them. That sort of contradicts what I just said, but . . .

Johnston: I have it on tape now.

Collins: [Laughter] But I think it's good to get poetry in kind of unexpected places like that. Like on YouTube, or people talk about iPoetry. Maybe you just download it onto your iPod, or on the subway and stuff like that.

Johnston: I did want to ask you maybe finally—since you mentioned never being able to imagine the questions you get in an interview—what should we ask you? What questions would you like to answer?

Collins: I suppose it is questions about individual poems. I mean, that's what I'm thinking about as a poet is writing individual poems. I'm not thinking about the history of American poetry or the future of American poetry or the difference between slam poetry and lyric poetry—these things never enter my mind. It would never occur to me to have a thought about any of that stuff. So I suppose I like a question about, well, how did this poem get started and how does it get from one place to another, something like that. That's where I feel I'm, you know, most at home. It's like some guy cutting fish in a fish market and you going up to him and asking what he thinks about the international fish market laws, and Japan, and dolphins. He's just trying to clean the fish the best he can.

Johnston: So, with "The Lanyard," when you wrote that were you really "ricocheting slowly . . . off the walls" and finding the "L" in the dictionary . . . ?

Collins: I was, yeah. And I call that "backing up the poem." In other words, you start the poem with the back-story to the poem. And that's another kind of antipresumptuousness, or that's another technique, I think, that puts a check on some of the presumptuousness of poetry. If you begin the poem by talking about the occasion for the poem, then it seems like the reader is brought into the beginnings of it, and you're not getting ahead of the reader right away. When you open up a dictionary, there are bold faced words at the top of the page. In fact, I flipped the dictionary, and "lanyard" was the header word and that's how it really caught my eye. And I just recognized that as having potential.

Johnston: Thank you. With that, let me help you save your voice for the rest of the evening.

The Pleasures of Disorientation:
A Conversation with Billy Collins

Arlo Haskell / 2009

This interview first appeared in *Littoral: The Journal of the Key West Literary Seminar*. It is reprinted with the permission of Arlo Haskell.

Arlo Haskell: Which poets do you read again and again, and why? Which poet did you read last?

Billy Collins: My reading of poetry is very random at this point because I am not so much studying a particular poet as I am cruising the pages of poetry books and literary magazines looking for a poem, or even a passage, striking enough to urge me to write my own poem. What inspires poetry is poetry. So I read others not to steal but to find gates of departure for my own flights. Of course, some poets provide these more reliably than others. A few of the ones I return to often are Ron Padgett, Charles Simic, Clive James, Yiannis Ritsos, and Wislawa Szymborska. They all make me jealous, often enough to try to show them who's boss by writing a better poem than any of them. This always fails, but at least something gets written. Did I mention John Donne and Emily Dickinson? They make me furious.

Haskell: Did your time as United States poet laureate change how you think about poetry and the audience for it? How so?

Collins: My overall view of American poetry and its audience did not really change during my tenure as poet laureate. I knew that the audience for poetry was relatively small but that there were many readers out there who had been driven away from poetry and were ready to find a way back. Something I did not realize then was the readiness of high school students to respond fully to poetry if they were exposed to the right kind of poetry. I suppose what I am really doing here is endorsing the Poetry 180 program that I put in place at first for high schoolers. I had no idea I would hear from so many teachers who found that Poetry 180 made poetry come alive for their students, some of whom actually demanded to hear more poems. For me, making the poems available on the Library of Congress website was setting out the water; I had no idea so many horses would come to drink. And I mean "horses" in the best sense of the word!

Haskell: One pleasure of your poetry is the way it cuts through the ceremoniousness of capital-'L' Literature. In *Ballistics*, for example, you spoof well-known lines of poets including Wallace Stevens and Robert Frost. How much should younger readers and writers respect established literary elders like these, and how much should they try to have a more irreverent experience?

Collins: I wouldn't advise coming right out of the box and ridiculing your betters. But if you think you have learned enough from a teacher, you seize the opportunity to signal their current uselessness. Any poet I have parodied or poked fun at—O'Hara, Frost, Stevens—I have been in awe of at one point. But for every poem I have that pokes fun at a poet or poetry itself, I have at least another poem that pokes fun at me. I am critical of poetry because I often suspect its intentions, and I am leery of the easy elevation of poetry into an empyrean condition. The clay feet of every artistic endeavor need to be kept in mind.

Haskell: I tend to think that what sets poetry apart from prose is a certain density of language, making it relatively difficult to decipher. Your poetry, on the other hand, is praised for being easy to read and readily accessible. What do you hope a reader will find in your work the third or fourth time around?

Collins: "Transparency" has become a popular word recently in all sorts of areas, usually in the sense of revealing secrets. A good poem, no matter how plain the language, will always have a little secret it is not telling us; and that, it could be said, is what makes poetry different from prose. What both genres have in common is diction and syntax. I tend to use a simple diction (few trips to the dictionary) and straightforward syntax (I write in sentences). But as the poem moves ahead, I am trying to nudge it into somewhat mysterious or at least hypothetical territory. The experience of reading the poem should contain a feeling of shifting (or being shifted) from the familiar to the strange, from coziness to disorientation. To reread the poem would be to re-experience that shift. In just about every poem of mine, we know exactly where we are in the opening lines, but I would argue that explaining where we are at the end would present more of a challenge.

Haskell: At the end of your poem "Evasive Maneuvers," you look up *gastropod* in the dictionary and then hide in the woods, as if fleeing from the definition's certainty. This reminds me of John Keats's praise for "being in uncertainties, mysteries, doubts without any irritable reaching after fact and reason." What is it about mystery and disorientation that is so appealing?

Collins: For disorientation to be a pleasure—an odd concept in the age of the GPS—one has to feel relieved to let go of the helmet of opinions we tend to wear every day. Keats thought poets should have no character, so that they could become other characters and make intimate connections with the world that lies beyond the self, which would include, in his case, nightingales and Grecian urns. T. S. Eliot thought the poet should be lacking in "personality," perhaps for similar reasons. I write to give myself pleasure, and that includes not knowing exactly where I am at the end of a poem. It reminds me now of that Chet Baker song "Let's Get Lost." When you wake up in a strange bed, often you don't know where you are for a couple of seconds. Surely, that is not a pleasure for everyone, but it is for some. How refreshing to take a little break from always knowing where we are, or least fooling ourselves into thinking so.

"A Poem Should Not *Mean* but *Move*": Billy Collins Speaks with AP Literature Students

Charleston School of the Arts / 2010

This interview was conducted on October 15, 2010, via conference call between John Cusatis's AP English literature class at the School of the Arts (SOA) in Charleston, SC, and Billy Collins, who spoke from his home in Central Florida. Interviewers were Cusatis, SOA creative writing instructor Rene Miles, and the following students: Jordan Baer, Colleen Brennan, Mary Lee Carter, Austin Cope, Stephanie Hardy, Free Kopsak, DeVante Lee, Rachel Riddle, and Madison Smith. First printed in *Dictionary of Literary Biography 374: Twenty-First-Century American Poets, Second Series*, edited by John Cusatis © 2014 Gale, a part of Cengage, Inc. Reproduced by permission. www.cengage.com/permissions.

School of the Arts: Hello, Professor Collins.

Billy Collins: How are you?

SOA: Good, how are you today?

Collins: Pretty good.

SOA: We've got ten AP English literature students here from School of the Arts studying contemporary poetry who will be asking you questions, and several creative writing students and their teachers are listening in. We were wondering if you might have something nearby that you could read to us? Maybe something you're working on?

Collins: Yes. I've got all sorts of stuff I could read to you. Well, I wrote a poem this morning I could read to you?

SOA: That would be great.

Collins: It's a little poem. I'm afraid I write too many poems about writing, but often there just seems to be nothing to write about. But that never stopped me from writing. It's called "A Start."

"A Start"

After a long silence,
A stillness in the rooms of this house
And the notebook open blankly on the desktop,
The pen begins to move again, at last,
Slowly at first, like an engine
Of a long train straining, yanking
The whole train forward,
Then, gaining momentum, it moves
On the rails of its own writing
Until all the boxcars follow easily,
Even merrily, across the prairie of the page.

SOA: [Applause] Thank you very much for sharing that.

Collins: I've never gotten applause over the telephone before.

SOA: We're honored to be the first to hear it. I like the use of train rails to suggest the order and direction in the lines. It calls to mind the beginning of your poem "Winter Syntax" but with a much different extended metaphor.

Collins: Yes, the basic thing, I think, that poets do, a basic job description, is to look for new metaphors to say old things. I think I was reading something about a train, and there are trains that go through the town I live in. And you analogize starting to write again to this train that starts to pull all the cars. When I said, "it moves / On the rails of its own writing," I probably got that from Frost's essay ["The Figure a Poem Makes"], where he says that the poem is like an ice cube you put on a hot pan, and it slides around on its own liquid. So the poem is riding on its own acoustics. It's really just plugging in trains and poetry writing, trying to see if those two can go together. About 77 percent of the work of writing poetry is in engineering metaphors.

SOA: Yes, we frequently discuss whether a particular poem is *made*, or if it's more of an organic thing that *grows* and develops on a natural course once the poet starts writing it.

Collins: Well, I try to write everything in one sitting. This poem, frankly, took fifteen minutes or so. But it could take two or three hours, or more. But I try to write the first thing in one sitting, all the way through to the end because I *want* it to be an experience, an organic one if possible. I don't want it to seem like I wrote the first part one day and then the next part a week from Thursday. I want there to be a kind of energy or a spine through the whole thing. For that to take place for the reader, I think that it has to first take place in my composition. So I pretty much sit with the poem until it's done. When I go back, the revisions are for clearing up places and making it sound better, making little corrections. But the whole gist of the thing, the rhetorical run from beginning to middle to end, that is almost always done in one session.

SOA: In "Introduction to Poetry" you question the tendency in students to want to tie a poem to a chair and beat it with a hose "to find out what it really means." What elements of a poem do you feel students should concentrate on to increase their understanding and appreciation of poetry?

Collins: Well that's a good question, and I answer it with metaphors earlier on in that same poem when I say that I want them to hold the poem "up to the light / like a color slide." I want them to just look at the poem as a visual thing. Also, the poem has a physical shape to it, unlike a short story or a novel, which are set in continuous print. The poem displaces silence on the page. Prose is a constant, you could say relentless, flow of sentences. I also ask students in that poem to "press an ear against its hive," which, of course, means listening to the music of the poem. I think there are many pleasures to be derived from poetry besides the pleasure of figuring out its meaning. In some poems the meaning is just there, completely obvious, and in other poems the meaning is too mysterious to ever be articulated except by reading the poem again. And I can mention a couple more poetry pleasures: the pleasure of metaphor, which is the pleasure of seeing two things you wouldn't think of inhabiting the same part of your brain and experiencing the connection between them, like writing poetry and a freight train starting out from a dead stop. Often, if it is the right kind of metaphor—mine is not a great example—you kind of feel the synapses opening up in your head. And then there's just the pleasure of rhythm, the pleasure of sound, the pleasure of whatever imaginative travel is involved. But these things are a little harder to talk about in a class. It's a little easier to talk about meaning, so often that's what gets talked about.

SOA: Do you feel that some people overanalyze your poems?

Collins: I think any analysis of my poems could amount to overanalysis. [Laughter] I know my poems are taught, and I'm thankful for that, but I don't know what there is to say about them really. Archibald MacLeish said, "A poem should not mean / But be." In other words, let's not analyze; let's just let it be. But the way I look at poetry is that a poem should not *mean* but *move*. I'm interested in the poem being a little bit of imaginative travel that moves from the simple to the complex. To follow that movement could be one way of looking at the poem. But I think that my poems would be very easy to overanalyze. When you are studying poetry early on, you haven't read enough of it yet to know how hard to analyze. You can't analyze all poets or books with the same degree of critical pressure. If you push on a Robert Frost poem, things will be revealed. If you push on a poem by another poet, your fingers may go right through the poem. There's not enough resistance there. Whereas a poem by T. S. Eliot could take half a semester to unpack. You've got to know how much to press on a poem without destroying it. It's a little like friends. With some friends you can have a deep conversation. Other friends you have a more superficial one, and that's fine. It's the same with getting to know poets.

SOA: One poet we have studied, Robinson Jeffers, felt strongly that poetry was more earnest than prose and far more suitable for the expression of important ideas. Do you make a similar distinction, and why have you chosen to express yourself almost exclusively in verse?

Collins: Well, the answer to the second question is, I don't know how to do the other thing very well. [Laughter] No, I really don't. Types of writing are as different as musical instruments, whether it's sports journalism, poetry, short fiction, or creative nonfiction. I think they are as different as the violin is to the trumpet or the oboe. I think the members of the band might agree with me. Just because you can play one instrument well doesn't mean you can switch over to a different instrument. And what I learned to play was the instrument of poetry. I certainly agree with any comment that places poetry on the higher level. [Laughs] I think it *is* the highest, and certainly the most ancient form of written expression. Historically speaking, the novel is a teenager. I'm not saying I'm the best example of this, but poetry offers the possibility of the most creative and imaginative freedom. Also, poetry can present emotion in ways that can be more intense than looser forms, like the novel, are capable of. So, poetry is superior to prose. Period. I have an ongoing argument about poetry and fiction with a friend of mine who is a novelist. Last time I saw her, I said, "Look, think of it this way: poetry is a bird and prose is a potato."

SOA: [Laughter] Poetry is a bird and prose is a potato.

Collins: That's it. Put that on the blackboard. [Laughter]

SOA: In what ways, if any, did becoming U.S. poet laureate change your writing?

Collins: Well, it ended my writing. [Laughter] For a while, at least. The office can put a halt to one's writing because of all the attention from the media. Interviews and public appearances can pull a writer out from the privacy of writing into the public discourse of talking about writing. To write poetry you have to have a taste for solitude. You really have to enjoy being alone. In fact, your writing is an intensification of being alone. So you're dragged out of that little area where you enjoyed being alone and into the public, so I got very little writing done during my two years as laureate. I started to suspect, in my latent paranoia, that the poet laureateship was a government plot. The idea is to locate a poet who is doing pretty well and appoint him poet laureate, and that will silence him. [Laughter] I do have something of a public image largely because of all that exposure, but when I write I return to that privacy space, which has no connection to the laureateship or the public or the auditorium.

SOA: Some of your poems focus on idioms and popular expressions, and in your poem "Bathtub Families" you write that "language is better than reality." Can you comment on this affection for language?

Collins: When you say "idioms," are you thinking of things like "Oh, My God!"?

SOA: Yes, that's another poem I'm thinking of.

Collins: I have a poem that's coming out in a book next year [*Horoscopes for the Dead*], and it's spoken in the voice of a young woman. The poem begins, "When he told me he expected me to pay for dinner, / I was like give me a break." [Laughter] It goes on to say that she's "not the exact equivalent of give me a break." She's "just similar to give me a break." [Laughter] I hear these kinds of tics in the language, and it's fun to respond to them. I don't really believe language is better than reality. [Laughter] It's like the Frost poem where he says, "Good fences make good neighbors." Of course, this quote is taken out of context. It's really a bad neighbor that's saying that. It's not something Frost is endorsing in the poem, no more than I really mean that language is better than reality. One of the things about poetry is you can make outrageous claims. In that way you're not just being honest. Sincerity in poetry is very overrated. I have more fun playing with language than I do working to sound sincere.

SOA: You write about childhood in your poems often. How has your own childhood influenced your poems? When we read "On Turning Ten" and "The History Teacher," for example, are we hearing your own recollections in some cases, or are they purely imaginative?

Collins: No one escapes their own childhood. We're all really children dressed in a kind of costume called adulthood. What's worse, we can't escape adolescence, and one of the earmarks of that strange period of time is that we feel grossly misunderstood by everybody. I'm afraid that bad news is that this feeling continues throughout the rest of your life. You will always feel misunderstood. The difference is that you care about it less as you get older. Reaching full maturation means you just don't give a feather about what anybody thinks about you. But you're always misunderstood. It is just a matter of how much you care about it. I was an only child, so I have no trouble with getting attention from other people. I think "only children" often have a kind of artistic sense because they spend so much time alone— as I was saying about the taste for solitude—in the hiding places and in the private games of childhood. Someone said that if you think you had a happy childhood you're just repressing all the sad information. But as far as I can remember, I had a pretty happy childhood.

SOA: In your poem "Nostalgia" you write, "Even this morning would be an improvement over the present." And in many poems you chronicle the passage of better days. Do you see poetry as a sort of antidote to the passage of time?

Collins: That is a very good question. Yes, poetry is sort of a reminder that time passes. Probably at some point in your instruction, your teacher, John, has written the words "carpe diem" on the black board. That is one of the oldest themes in poetry, the idea that you want to carpe your diems because you don't have all that many diems left. [Laughter] So carpe away. Time and poetry are very connected, and carpe diem poetry tends to be a reminder that time is running out. We shouldn't just walk around presuming that we are immortal in some degree. Many poems can be boiled down (though I don't recommend cooking poems) to this same message. Life is beautiful, but it will end. "Nothing more terrible, nothing more true" as Philip Larkin put it.

SOA: A few of your poems such as "Plight of the Troubadour," "The Death of Allegory," and "American Sonnet," look back fondly on largely forgotten ways of expression. To what degree, if any, do you think our culture is stagnant or dynamic compared to earlier times?

Collins: Oh, well that's a little essay. [Laughter] I'm an English major. I just stayed in school until they threw me out, and to do that they gave you this PhD. [Laughter] So a lot of my poems are English major poems. That reference to the Middle Ages and the troubadours, and the other poems you were mentioning, tend to acknowledge that I'm writing in a certain historical line. Every poet has a line of poets in back of him or her informing them, and I see no reason not to acknowledge that. As far as our times go, I think everything's getting worse. And you'll think it's pretty old fashioned when I say things like this, but I think the amount of time we spend in front of screens, whatever that screen happens to be, will potentially ruin us. I'm really kind of anti-Facebook. *In* your Face-book. I just think it's an amazing waste of time. There are good things about it, connecting to family and that, but most of the content is deeply insignificant. It's not so much that it's trivial in its content, such as "We're going out for pizza now." But what kills me is all of the people who feel the need to make a comment: "Oh, you're going out for pizza? That's great!" or "Too bad I'm not going out for pizza," or "Pizza LOL." [Laughter] Everybody has to kind of chime in, as if, if they didn't chime in, they wouldn't exist. I think social networks like Facebook give people a kind of virtual identity, and they have to keep up with that. If they don't react to your going out for pizza, they think they cease to exist. One's virtual identity must be announced relentlessly.

SOA: Alright, well thank you. And in my defense, I would like to profess my own strong, strong distaste for "LOL."

Collins: Good. I'm convinced that no one has ever written "LOL" while they were laughing out loud. [Laughter]

SOA: In *Poetry 180* you include mostly living poets, but your poetry is filled with allusions to great poets of the past such as Shelley and Proust. Can you name a few of the poets of the past that you think we should not ignore, and maybe comment on a few in the present whose work you think is likely to endure?

Collins: Well, it's such a vast door you open there. I'll just choose two. Samuel Taylor Coleridge, I've learned a lot from him. He has two kinds of poems: his mystery poems, which are very popular, "Kubla Khan" and "The Ancient Mariner," for example, and his conversation poems, like "Frost at Midnight" and "This Lime-Tree Bower My Prison." Maybe John will present one of those to you this semester. I find the second kind exciting because they begin in very domestic settings, like a backyard or by the hearth, but then they lift off into some very exciting conceptual and imaginative zones. As far as contemporary poets, frankly, I would say about 83 percent of contemporary poems are not worth reading, but the other 17 percent is vital in its importance. I would recommend that John bring in a poem for you by Charles Simic. He's one of the best examples of creating mystery with a very simple vocabulary. He uses very few modifiers too, and when he writes something like "Brooms," it evokes the whole history and symbolic significance of the broom, but he does all this with subtlety. And at the end of his short poems, he disappears.

SOA: We are preparing to participate in the Poetry Out Loud competition. Do you think a poem is greatly enhanced by reading it out loud? And to what extent does sound influence your writing of a poem?

Collins: Well it depends on the reader. Are song lyrics better when they're sung or just written on the page? A good singer will do a good job, and a bad singer won't. Bad readers of poetry will do harm to the poem, but a good reader of poetry will let us hear the sounds that the poet has embedded in the poem. I write with my ear as much as I write with my mind. I'm always trying to make the poem sound right. That doesn't mean I'm trying to make the sound mellifluous or poetic, or use beautiful, lilting language. I use pretty plain language, but I'm still trying to make it sound good. I'm going to bring sounds together that are close to each other. I think of the poem as being a little acoustic arena, like a little sonic closet in which all these sounds are echoing off each other. Any good poet realizes that you are not just writing down thoughts and emotions and observations; you're making a little song. You are creating a little bit of music. I guess the reason Poetry Out Loud is competitive, with state and national competitions, is that some people do it better than others. It's like dancing or playing ping-pong. [Laughter] We are not all equally blessed with these talents.

SOA: Allusions to the works of great thinkers, such as Aristotle and Jean Paul Sartre, figure into your poems. Especially considering your Catholic upbringing, are there particular thinkers—philosophers, psychologists, or others—who have helped shape your outlook?

Collins: Freud was very important. Reading his book *Civilization and Its Discontents* gave me a way of looking at things. When I was in college, existential philosophy was very important, so I was reading Jean Paul Sartre and Albert Camus and others. One identifies so strongly with these formative books and thinkers, and as you grow up you lose direct contact with the early influences that you've read. But at some point, you may find you've assimilated them, so they are part of your thinking or part of the perceptual apparatus with which you see the world. And I'm sure my Catholicism has played a big part, certainly in terms of language. When I was about ten or eleven, I studied to be an altar boy, and I had to memorize all the Latin responses to the Mass. Well, I knew only a few words in Latin, just like the other boys—this was before they had altar girls—so we memorized the Latin syllable by syllable. We didn't know what we were saying. I still say the prayers. They're still in my head. But I think it was like reading poetry in a foreign language. I didn't understand it, but there was a music to the syllables. It's very hard to look back at your past and say, "Oh, this influenced me seventeen percent, and this another percent." It all turns into a kind of soup. I would say certainly Freud and a French philosopher named Gaston Bachelard, were both very influential.

SOA: Your poems read easily, and the language flows naturally, yet a closer look reveals careful attention to style. How do you maintain the organic nature of the poem while still being conscious of craft?

Collins: I think the best way to answer that is, and this sounds a little obvious, but I really write line by line. Charles Olson, the poet, said, "No line must sleep." Every line has to be wakeful, aware of the lines around it or aware of its contribution to the poem. The line is very, very important. You probably studied this in class, or it was at least mentioned: poetry comes in lines. There's a reason why it doesn't go out to the end of the page. That reason changes with time, but the main reason is that it comes in these units, and the basic unit is the line. I'm trying to write one good line after another, and I want the lines to be contributing something syntactically or contributing an image. I test every line before I go on to the next line. You said I make it look easy or it reads naturally, and the reason it does that is that I put a lot of attention into making one good line after another. I work to make the poem sound natural, so the reader doesn't have to do the work.

SOA: The voice in your poetry is so distinct and so refreshing. Since we have a few young writers in the room today, what advice can you offer them about developing a voice in their poetry?

Collins: Okay, well that's a good question. I have a good answer for it. [Laughter] The expression "finding your voice" is one you'll hear often. Unavoidably, you will hear it if you study writing, and there is something wrong with the way it is posed, I think. "Finding your voice" seems to imply a kind of inward gazing, an introspection, as if your voice in poetry is sort of tied up with your own sense of authenticity as a person. It is almost as if you have to decide whether you're one of the elect or not by careful self-examination of your content. I think that mystifies the process. It clouds it over. I think your voice is not lying within you somewhere, in some pocket of yourself that you need to access. Your voice in poetry has an external source, and the source of the voice is basically the poetry books in the library. You form a voice through reading, and through borrowing tonal effects or stylistic mannerisms from other poets. So if you read any poet who seems to have a distinctive voice, that poet has formed that voice through the borrowings and influences of other poets. He or she has just combined those influences in such a smooth way that you can't recognize the sources. The poet may go through a process of slavish imitation, but then he or she, if they are lucky, ends up internalizing these effects. So the way to find your voice is not to sit around, kind of gazing into yourself, it's going to the library, or going to the bookstore, or going online and reading tons of poetry. Edward Hirsch says one of the paradoxes at the center of the writing life is that that the only path to originality is through imitation.

SOA: Right. We encourage our creative writers to imitate the writers they read, so they can learn what ideas and techniques they want to hold on to and incorporate into their own work.

Collins: I think students who do well at writing poetry are the same students who are able to do voices, imitate people on television, imitate cartoon characters. There's a certain kind of malleable personality, like Keats's negative capability. You can become all these other things. And I think that's sort of an unacknowledged ability for people who want to write, because writing is role-playing. And he who plays roles easily has a lot of facility in that.

SOA: I sometimes have students in AP literature class write parodies of literary works as a way of delineating a writer's most distinctive traits. But what you said reminds me of a quote from the novelist Colum McCann, whom we spoke to recently: "We get our voices from the voices of others."

Collins: Yes, many of us are saying the same thing. Did your students read *Let the Great World Spin*?

SOA: Over the summer, they read another of McCann's novels, *This Side of Brightness*, but we will read *Let the Great World Spin* in the spring. Last year's class enjoyed it very much.

Collins: It's an amazing book.

SOA: I agree.

Collins: Incidentally, John, I've really enjoyed your CD [*April Days*]. Do your students know about this other life you have?

SOA: [Laughs] Yes, a few of our vocalists and strings majors have recorded or performed live with me. I'm lucky to recruit them while they are still affordable. But that's a great compliment, considering your taste in music. I appreciate it.

Collins: Sure.

SOA: This has been really helpful and a lot of fun. We have a large photo of you superimposed on the smart board, so it's as if you're in the room with us.

Collins: I really enjoyed talking with everybody today. I think it's a great idea. If you can't bring a lot of authors right to the classroom, why not just call them up? But why not use Skype next time?

SOA: We've thought about that, and you are right. We need to begin doing that.

Collins: Yes, you should try that.

SOA: I also wanted to let you know that during this unit on contemporary poetry, each student is required to discover a poet whom he or she will study independently, and I send them to your anthologies, *Poetry 180* and *180 More*, to discover these poets. Those books have made a big difference, and I know Rene uses the Poetry 180 website daily in her creative writing poetry workshops.

Collins: Perfect. I think that's exactly the way it should be done. I think the thing about *Poetry 180*, or any anthology, is to lead you to other poets. You flip through the book. You're not required to like every poem, but if you come across a poem you really like, and you see that the author's name is Galway Kinnell, then the perfect thing is to go out and get a book of Galway Kinnell's. Use the anthology as a reference book to find poets—a gateway—and go into them more deeply on your own.

SOA: As we wrap this up, I'd like to say that when I heard you read this summer at Keystone College in Pennsylvania, I really enjoyed the selection of haiku. Can we end with a haiku? Do you have one around?

Collins: I don't. I'm stuck in this room on this phone tied to the wall. [Laughter]

SOA: That was almost a haiku in itself. [Laughter] How about the one about the sushi bar?

Collins: Oh, I can do that one:

Mid-winter evening,
alone at a sushi bar—
just me and this eel.

SOA: [Applause and laughter] Thank you.

Collins: Good to talk to all you students, thanks for your questions.

SOA: Great talking to you, and we are looking forward to your reading in Charleston in January.

Collins: Come on up and say, "Hi."

SOA: We will. Take care.

Wordsworth's Heir

Margaret Renkl / 2010

Margaret Renkl: You were named poet laureate shortly before 9/11, and, if I remember right, you were suddenly getting calls from the media—like the *News Hour* and *Time* and *Newsweek*—because they wanted you to recommend some poems they could print or read on the air that would speak to the experience of the attacks. Am I remembering this accurately?

Collins: Yes. The timing was either perfect or awful, depending on your point of view. But I was appointed poet laureate just a few months before September 11. I was pretty much swamped with not just interview requests but, as you said, recommendations—like, "What should we be reading now?" It was very revealing, and yet not unfamiliar, that people would turn to poetry and not, for example, movies or the ballet when in times of national uncertainty. I guess that was the mood of the country—it was the mood of intense uncertainty—and poetry has always had not just a consoling aspect to it but a steadying influence on people. I think the reason poetry can be consoling is that it reminds us that we're not alone, that whatever emotion we're experiencing is really nothing new. It might feel overwhelming to us, but [then we read] a poem written in 1767, and this person seems to be going through a very similar crisis. So by bringing us into this kind of community of historical suffering, poetry reminds us that we're not alone.

But also, poetry has formal properties—rhyme and meter, but there are others that are substitutes for those two—and [those] formal properties have a kind of steadying sound to them. Unlike a short story, a poem has rhythmic comfort. It's short, sometimes memorizable, and you can carry it in your purse or your pocket; it's transferable. So I'm not surprised that people wanted to read the poems. And there's one thing I'll just add to that. One of the reactions to 9/11 was people saying, "We were going to get married a year and a half from now but we decided to move it up to next week." Or, "We were going to take our family to Paris in a year, [but] we're going to do stuff now because we are reminded that life is not a guarantee." This is the oldest message in poetry. It's called carpe diem. You can't get out of high school without seeing it on a blackboard at least once. And anyone who has the slightest interest in poetry knows that that is the crucial message of poetry. Of course, you're supposed to live for the moment. Of course, you're supposed to live engaged with life more immediately because you are reminded here of your mortality. Poets did not need a terrorist attack to remind them of their mortality.

Renkl: We don't have in this country the expectation, as the British have, that our poets laureate should write occasional verse, but you wrote a 9/11 poem yourself—"The Names"—and delivered it to a rare joint session of Congress. Do you remember why you did?

Collins: I remember clearly. If the British poet laureate is a member of the royal household, then the American poet laureate is really an employee of the Library of Congress. And we are not obliged in any way to write on the events of national importance, but I was responding to a pressure that was put on me by Congress—and by Congress I mean probably the public relations office of Congress—because they called me and asked me to do that. I initially told them I didn't think I'd be able to because that's not the kind of poetry I write. But eventually I realized two things: I could use the form of the elegy, and just write about the victims of 9/11, the fatalities. And, also, I could use the alphabet and kind of step, as from one stone to the other, through the alphabet. Reciting a name for each letter, and the alphabet would steady me.

Renkl: As poet laureate, you launched the Poetry 180 initiative, in which you urged schoolteachers to read the poems to students without discussing them or assigning work related to the readings. I was thinking about that when my fourteen-year-old was at the table last night griping about poetry. This is a child we thought was almost a poetic savant—always making up rhymes and playing with language, like singing "Swing Low Sweet Cherry Pie" to the tune of "Swing Low, Sweet Chariot." Any theories about what happened to him?

Collins: How old was he when he was changing "chariot" to "cherry pie"?

Renkl: Four, probably.

Collins: Well, he seems very typical. He seems to represent a pattern of how people's sense of poetry develops and then is ruined. I think we're all natural poets. Children, as you know, love that kind of stuff. They love chariot and cherry pie. It's really part of rhyming. Those words don't rhyme exactly, but they're cousin words—they sound similar, right? And to substitute words that sound similar and usurp the whole meaning of the verse and take it from its religious [meaning] to nonsense is such a delight because it appeals to the subversive sense of children. And the other basic pleasure is just rhyme. Children are delighted and astounded to discover at some point in their life that the thing that they used to eat their cereal with sounds almost exactly like that big white thing in the sky at night—moon-spoon. It feels good on their lips and it connects these two wildly different things, and that's one of the very primal pleasures of poetry. But there are others, too. So, what's your son's name?

Renkl: That son's name is Henry.

Collins: I have such respect for the teachers, who are caught between students and parents and administrators and test preparation. But what happens is, the teaching of poetry seems to be weighted very heavily on the side of interpretation. So it might be that he just heard this poem by Edgar Allen Poe, and the teacher says, "Henry, what do you think that means?" Or, "What do you think that stands for?" It turns into a kind of interrogation, and it associates poetry with anxiety. And teachers don't mean to do it, but there's only one dominant way to teach, and that's the school of interpretation. You can't very well, at the age of fourteen, sit around the classroom and talk about cherry pie—it isn't going to go anywhere as a serious subject, and it's not preparing children for the explication that might come up on the test. So boys and girls often have the natural pleasures of poetry beaten out of them by the time they get out of high school. Two reasons why: forceful emphasis on interpretation and using poems that are very dated—poems that were written a hundred years ago.

Poetry 180 was meant to alleviate those two things—first, by offering students poems that were super-contemporary, so they could hear the voices of contemporary sounds. And, secondly, the warning was, "Do not interpret these poems; just let the students hear them." No quiz; no midterm; just hear the poem. I was hoping—and, really, confidently believing—that no matter how recalcitrant the student was, or how resistant to poetry, that one of those poems would probably stick because they're funny, and they're clever, and they can pretty much be gotten in one hearing. Obviously, I'm not going to go in there and change the teaching of poetry, but the hope was that I would present an alternative way to present poetry. And I've got to tell you quite modestly, if I had a nickel for every high school teacher who came up and thanked me after a reading, I would have a lot of nickels. It seems that the program and the subsequent anthologies really work in the practical world.

Renkl: You recently told an audience at Cornell, "The trouble with poetry is its availability: you can pick up a twenty-nine-cent pen and express yourself. Self-expression is overrated. If I were Emperor of Poetry, I would make everyone learn to play the trumpet before they could write poetry, just to make it difficult." It's a little surprising to hear that a writer whose work is routinely described as "accessible" longs for a way to make writing poems more difficult.

Collins: These are two very different uses of "accessibility." What I'm accused of by critics is that my poems are accessible—that anyone can read them with a certain degree of comprehension. I'm not trying to make my poems inconvenient to read. You can get into them and understand them pretty quickly. What I meant in the comment at Cornell was the means of writing poetry are too accessible. In other words, if you were to play the cello, you'd have to obviously go to school and buy a cello and practice. Even oil painting or ballet requires lessons; you wouldn't just get up there and start jumping around in a tutu. And you wouldn't just pick up the trumpet and just blare into it. But with poetry, people think you just pick up a pen and start writing down how sad you are in the middle of the night and add some autumn leaves, and you've got a poem. The training in poetry—the training for a musical instrument—is hours and hours of practice. Malcolm Gladwell recently said [*Outliers: The Story of Success*, 2008] that to be really, really good at something, let's say the violin, requires 10,000 hours minimum—ten thousand hours! When I read that book of Gladwell's, I thought, "Yeah, I'm of a certain age, and I've easily spent 10,000 hours reading, writing, and teaching poetry." The training in poetry is reading. Reading, reading, reading. Reading from Chaucer on. Reading the Spanish poets. Reading John Donne. Reading, reading, reading. Memorizing ten Emily Dickinson poems. That's the training. If you pay ten dollars to go to a piano concert or a string quartet, and you sat down on the twelfth row, and they started playing, and after a few seconds, it was very clear that they were very, very bad—just terrible: wrong notes, confused—you would walk out and get your money back. However, most of us will sit in a terrible poetry reading and not understand a word that's said and just take it. I don't know why we do that. That's what I meant. Those are two very different deployments of the word "accessible."

Renkl: I found an old interview you did with the *New York Times*, where you said, "As I'm writing, I'm always reader conscious. I have one reader in mind, someone who is in the room with me, and who I'm talking to, and I want to make sure I don't talk too fast, or too glibly. Usually I try to create a hospitable tone at the beginning of a poem. Stepping from the title to the first lines is like stepping into a canoe. A lot of things can go wrong." Can you describe the reader you're imagining as you write?

Collins: I can't really pretend to be someone else. If I could, if I had that capacity, I'd probably write fiction because that involves a degree of empathy where you can imagine yourself to be someone else. But I lack that form of empathy, and the only person I really think I understand is myself. So my reader is probably me. But as I'm writing, I'm switching from writer to reader, writer-reader, writer-reader. I keep going back and forth. I'm really checking for comprehensibility. And then, at some point, I'm asking the reader for more—not making it easy for the reader to follow. My sense of my own poetry—which doesn't apply to all poetry—is that I start very clearly and end up in some kind of fog, some kind of hypothetical *Alice in Wonderland*. They start very simply—I'm looking out the window or taking the dog for a walk—and they end up in some conditional make-believe area. The end of the poem would be inaccessible if it were not for the beginning of the poem.

Renkl: Critics, too, have noted your tendency to begin by describing something very ordinary, and in very conversational language, only to take a turn for the distinctly original and unexpected at the end. When you sit down to write a poem, do you have some idea where it's going from the beginning?

Collins: Yes, well almost never. You can look ahead just a little bit, just enough to kind of keep going. The metaphor of driving at night might apply: your headlights throw light ahead of you to keep driving, but they don't show you much more than that. I would say that the best poems I've written are the ones where I'm really surprised at the ending. I don't know how I got there, but I am really surprised and delighted. It's almost as if the ending of the poem is not just a conclusion, but it's a new discovery of some revelation that is only possible because of the words above it. It's like the poem is the only path to get to this place. The one way to get there. In some cases, I'm not going anywhere, and then I stop writing.

Renkl: *Entertainment Weekly* once called you "the best buggy-whip maker of the 21st century." Any response?

Collins: What does it mean, exactly?

Renkl: I think it means that *Entertainment Weekly* believes you're really good at an art that's now completely irrelevant.

Collins: That's probably right. It doesn't mean that I'm old-fashioned; it just means that people don't use buggy whips anymore. We talked about

Henry, whose very basic delight in word play—with chariot and cherry pie—went through a kind of ruination. At some point it advances from being a simple pleasure—like the pleasure of a bowl of pasta or something that delivers the pleasure immediately—to a pleasure that requires study. That requires reading a lot of poetry. Most people don't have that devotion. It's a minority sport. It's not something that everybody plays. And the irony is that poetry really tries to talk to everybody because poetry does deal with these very basic human emotions, and because poetry values subjectivity. It lights up inner parts of you—your appreciation of nature, your conscience, your desire for love. All these areas of your interior are being sparked by a poem, and so one might say, "Why doesn't everybody read it? It sounds pretty good." But most people don't. It doesn't play any part in most people's lives. All you have to do is say to somebody next to you on an airplane that you're a poet. You get some pretty strange reactions.

Renkl: And yet, even before you were appointed poet laureate, the *New York Times* called you "the most popular poet in America."

Collins: I don't know why I became popular. To tell you the truth, it's basically NPR.

Renkl: Your buddy Garrison Keillor?

Collins: And my buddy Terry Gross. They had a lot to do with the audience for my work. It's just an incredibly powerful medium, radio. And perfectly suited to poetry. Now instead of reading to twenty-five people at the local women's club, you're reading to three million people when you're reading on *A Prairie Home Companion* or *Fresh Air*. And very few poets get that chance.

Renkl: Readers coming to your work for the first time—through radio, or even at your public appearance in Nashville—might be surprised to encounter so much wit, and even outright humor, in your poems. Do you ever find that people in your audiences, especially when you read to students, are shy about laughing at the funny parts?

Collins: They are at first, but they're relieved to be able to. And then for some people it's like giggling in church. But I think it usually comes as a relief to people. And of course, the other audience—the people who know my work and who read other poets—know that humor has reclaimed its place in poetry. There's an anthology that just came out this year called *Seriously Funny*, and it's a collection of maybe forty poets who write humorous poems that are not silly. They use humor to get into serious stuff.

Renkl: You mentioned that the initial experience of poetry is pleasure and that to get beyond that experience requires some study and some effort.

Didn't Wordsworth say that the point of poetry is pleasure? What would you say is the point of poetry?

Collins: It can't really exist as a communicative medium without pleasure. I wrote a dissertation on Wordsworth, so I have an unfair advantage here: Wordsworth mentions pleasure over fifty times. In his essay "A Preface to *Lyrical Ballads*," he just keeps chiming this note of giving pleasure. Indeed, that's why I write it, and that's why I read it. I myself wrote an article called "Poetry, Pleasure, and the Hedonist Reader." I don't read to be edified, to increase the capacity of my soul, although if those things happen as byproducts, that's great. I read for pleasure, verbal pleasure, and the kind of pleasure that you get from "Swing Low, Sweet Cherry Pie." I find that very pleasurable. I'll probably be laughing about it for days. Either you think that's really funny, or you don't. And if you don't, probably something that takes language as seriously as poetry is not for you. No, it has to begin with pleasure. Verbal pleasure or imagery, which is another kind of pleasure. The pleasure of metaphor—there can be far-fetched connections between things, and that's a mental pleasure for a lot of people. For a lot of people, it really isn't. And that's probably why poetry, even though we did say it speaks to the human soul, is not for everybody.

Renkl: Have you ever seen that YouTube video of a tiny kid reciting your poem, "Litany"?

Collins: I've not only seen it, I'm addicted to watching it. I think the kid is so astonishing. I don't know if I should say this, but I've seen it about twenty times. It was brought to my attention back in May, I think, and there were something like 500 hits at the time, and now there are—I haven't checked recently—but there were about 300,000 last time I looked. I'm actually in touch with the child and his mother. They live in Arizona, and I'm going to go there to read next month, I think, and we're going to get together. That child does not read—he's three years old—yet he says things like "speaking of the plentiful imagery of the world."

Renkl: He seems to illustrate your point that we're born for poetry.

Collins: Well, I think we all are.

Interview with Billy Collins

Andy Kuhn / 2014

This interview appeared in *How a Poem Can Happen: Conversations with Twenty-One Extraordinary Poets* by Andy Kuhn, Red Spruce Press, 2017, 45–51. Reprinted by permission of Andy Kuhn. All Rights Reserved.

Andy Kuhn: You have been involved with the Katonah Poetry Series for a long time, happily for all of us. Can you say a little about how that came about and how the series and your engagement with it have changed over the years?

Billy Collins: My then wife and I moved into an old mid-nineteenth-century house in northern Westchester in 1989. We had been living in Scarsdale, and like many people in that part of the county, we never ventured to the north. So the scene was very new to us. Then one day I found in a local paper that William Matthews was going to be reading at the Katonah library the following Sunday. That's how I discovered the series, then run by its founder, Robert Phillips. I was amazed that some of the top poets in the country would be coming to my local library. When Phillips accepted a job offer from the University of Houston, he left a career in advertising and asked me if I would take over as director. A natural born shirker of official responsibilities, I hesitated. But in the end, I promised to bring the series into its twentieth year—in two years' time—but I ended up at the helm for I think fifteen years. Now the reins are in the capable hands of others who are kind enough to consult me on their choice of poets.

Kuhn: Your poems accommodate readers in ways that readers of poetry have learned they cannot take for granted with other poets. You tell us where we are, in time, space, weather; you describe things in such a way that we can readily picture them; you respect conventions of grammar and punctuation; you tend not to use jargon or vocabulary that would require most of us to fire up the browser (unless you're kidding, which does happen). Beyond that, you have spoken about the poem as a sort of conversation with the reader, and the conversational tone you take is another way you engage us. At this point, it is what we expect in a Billy Collins poem. But did you always write this way? If not, how did your poetic values and voice evolve?

Collins: Well, you just pretty much described the style of a Billy Collins poem, if we can say there is such a thing. But those features did not become visible until later in my writing, when I came under a helpful set of influences. It seems we are all born with about 200 bad poems in us. Some people have the good sense to die with them intact and unexpressed. Others, who want to write, have to exorcise the bad ones, and the only way to do that is write them out. Early on, I thought poetry had to be mysterious, so I wrote mysteriously. Now I feel that a good poem is a mix of the clear and the mysterious. It's crucial to grasp the difference. I would say most bad poems either are mysterious about something that should be clear (like you're on a sailboat) or clear about something that will always remain mysterious (like the soul).

Kuhn: Your commitment to readability, and your hostility to obscurantism, has earned you some critical brickbats from people who seem to mistake simplicity of address, for instance, for simple-mindedness. Despite the mild and bemused persona in most of your poems, you've given at least as good as you've got, both in interviews (the *Paris Review* one springs to mind) and in poetry. The title poem of *Ballistics* concludes with a fantasy about shooting up a recent volume by "someone of whom I was not fond." In it, you mention "the poems about his childhood // and the ones about the dreary state of the world." Was it always a bad idea to build a poem around these topics, or has it become a worse idea recently? If so, why is that?

Collins: In that poem I wanted "poems about his childhood" to represent narrowly autobiographical poetry and "ones about the dreary state of the world" to represent broadly and explicitly political poetry, both of which have imaginative limits. As for the critical opinion that my poems are too simple, my response is: go "problematize" them. After all, that's what keeps a lot of critics busy these days.

Kuhn: You are, it's safe to say, the most famous and successful poet in America today, if not of all time. Yet you didn't publish your first collection until you were forty. Were you passionately devoted to poetry from early on, or did it creep up on you?

Collins: Like Kay Ryan I was afraid to be that embarrassing thing known as a poet, yet at the same time, I wanted nothing more than to be one. An odd bind. I was writing all along beginning in high school right through graduate school (PhD in English of all things) and into my teaching career.

Frankly, it just took me a long time to figure out a way of writing that made me happy. I later learned that these poems made other people happy too. Who would have guessed?

Kuhn: Is it weird to be both a poet and a celebrity? Rock musicians end up writing a lot of songs about being rock musicians; writers like Norman Mailer, who became celebrated early, end up wrestling, sometimes interestingly and sometimes not, with issues of fame. Poets in the last fifty years haven't had to deal with this much. Do you find that the fact of your fame creates any extra static or complication, any sense that you have to intentionally set it aside when you sit down with yourself to write?

Collins: It's just time consuming, like managing a little business. Seamus Heaney said that you have to learn "how to survive your success." It drags you from the private place where you write (think of how children like hiding places) into the world. I like Bob Fosse's take on success: "You spend half of your life struggling to be famous, and the other half hiding in a closet." Then there's Yeats's calling himself "A sixty-year-old smiling public man." Sorry if I'm hiding behind a fence of quotations.

Kuhn: You have spoken of your poetic persona or avatar as that of the *flaneur*, which is an evocative French term. My friends at Wikipedia tell us this about the *flaneur*: "Flâneur (from the French noun *flâneur*), means 'stroller,' 'lounger,' 'saunterer,' or 'loafer.' *Flânerie* refers to the act of strolling, with all of its accompanying associations. The *flâneur* was, first of all, a literary type from nineteenth-century France, essential to any picture of the streets of Paris. It carried a set of rich associations: the man of leisure, the idler, the urban explorer, the connoisseur of the street."

Were you a *flaneur* before you ever heard of the term, or were you won over to this stance after having read about it? Do you have any literary heroes who were or are *flaneurs*?

Collins: Before my acquaintance with flaneuring (not a word, by the way) I was attracted to that figure in English Romantic poetry who wanders through the countryside—unlike the urban *flaneur*—often falling into a reverie then writing a poem that is a mix of landscape and thought. He's a stroller, a dawdler, head in the clouds. My persona is really a modernized version of that character drawn primarily from Wordsworth and Coleridge. He is by nature a daydreamer whose favorite toys are his thoughts. Not content to leave the natural world alone, he uses its scenes as launching pads for imaginative flights. By the way, the *flaneur* tradition was recently revived in a terrific book by Teju Cole titled *Open City*.

Kuhn: Some of your work does involve strolls through European landscapes and cityscapes, but many more of your poems start in a room, and in narrative terms, stay there. The narrator shares with the *flaneur* an intentional lack of intention, but there's a subtle tension there at the outset, which I have come to experience as the question, *How is he going to get out of it this time?* There's a Houdini-like aspect to your poems, which so often start in a state of confinement (more comfortable, certainly, than locked up in a chest) or a determinedly banal situation (walking the dog, eating in a restaurant) and progress to an escape, however momentary, or imaginative, or rhetorical. Often humor provides a leg up, and the whole exercise feels like a bit of a lark. But even then, there is a sense of something significant at stake, which often turns out to be, in some form or fashion, dealing with death. What is it about poetry that so many of its paths lead to "the Big D," as it is never, ever called? And how have you come to deal with it in these particular ways?

Collins: I am beginning to wish my responses were as articulate and insightful as your questions! I find that starting with something mundane manages to include the reader and put pressure on me to find a way out of the mundane. You don't want to board a plane in Miami then land in Miami a few hours—or lines—later. So the poem has to "escape" its initial confinement. There are lots of doors leading into bigger rooms, but the two big ones for poets are clearly marked "LOVE" and "DEATH." The shadow of mortality falls across the page and would darken it completely if the possibility of love were not available.

Kuhn: There's a kind of abstemiousness or austerity about the poetic limits you have set for yourself. You decline to make many of the usual claims poets often try to make on a reader's attention: a tone of high moral seriousness; grisly or shocking narrative material; displays of dazzling technique with difficult forms (except, again, when you're joking around); elaborate sonic or rhythmic effects; extremes of emotional intensity. You also refrain from making large claims on the readers' time. Stanzas are mostly short—three lines, typically—and your longest poems don't run much more than about forty lines. Do you have lockers full of notebooks with rhymed fantasy epic poems teeming with characters, or sonnet cycles about your childhood, or multipart allusive cantos referring to obscure historical events in a variety of languages? Any deconstructive tone poems in there? But seriously, do you ever get a yen to try something completely different? Do you think you might catch a lot of grief if you did, like Dylan going electric at the Newport Folk Festival?

Collins: No secret lockers. What you see is what you get. And I'm not really interested in developing because I still find in my persona an agreeable voice and a lasting source of curiosity. He still has a lot to explore. If I could only think of it! If a poet is lucky and smart enough to create a lasting persona, a kind of vocal character, then he or she can ride that persona into the grave. Writing poetry for me is not like trying on different costumes. A lot of that went on before I knew what I was doing. See aforementioned late bloomer.

Kuhn: Poetry was originally a spoken art, and you have delivered more poetry, aloud, in your own voice, than anyone around. Your appearances on *Prairie Home Companion* had over four million listeners; recently on *The Colbert Report* over a million people heard you, and Stephen Colbert read alternating stanzas. But you also have a heavy schedule of live readings all over the country. Is there something about hearing poetry aloud, particularly as read by the poet, for which there is really no substitute?

Collins: Well, in some cases, the listener wishes there *were* a substitute! Not every poet knows how to make friends with the microphone or the audience. When I compose a poem, I never read it aloud to myself or the cat. But I know exactly how it will sound when I read it for the first time from a stage because I hear every syllable as I am writing. I hear it in silence. I write with the ear. Much of my fiddling with a poem after its initial run is aimed at making the poem sound better.

Kuhn: Looking back at the list of the poets who have read for the series (http://katonahpoetry.com/history/), can you name a few whose work had an influence on your own, or with whom you had a particularly good time when they came to town?

Collins: It's a truly impressive list of poets, and because influences wash over one from all sides, it's hard to isolate a few. But I learned from Katha Politt how clear, simple diction can keep emotion under control. Immense debts to James Tate and the late Paul Violi for their larky humor, and to William Matthews for showing me you include in poems your taste and your learning. Violi, it should be said, was one of the most faithful attendees of the poetry series before his untimely death.

Kuhn: We are very much looking forward to your reading and appreciate enormously how much you've done and continue to do for the Series.

A Conversation with Billy Collins

Daniel Menaker / 2014

This interview was conducted on May 13, 2014, at the John F. Kennedy Presidential Library and Museum in Boston, Massachusetts, by writer and longtime fiction editor at the *New Yorker* Daniel Menaker. It is printed with the permission of Daniel Menaker and the John F. Kennedy Library Foundation.

Daniel Menaker: Such a pleasure. I'm not going to ask you what your favorite color is, but I am going to ask you how you write your poems, which is very close to the first question.

Collins: Well, to talk about your composition practices, I can respond. It's a little awkward though. If you ever buy a puppy and you bring the puppy home, and then usually a younger person will show the puppy its reflection in the mirror: "Look at you, look at how cute you are, look." Dogs have no interest in the mirror; they're interested in smells. Parakeets would be interested in mirrors, but . . . That's just a metaphor for getting an author to talk about his own writing.

Menaker: Never mind.

Collins: I start with a little something, something very small, like just the idea of not touring Italy and then usually the first line or two sets the tone, in which case that's the tone of someone very unsuccessfully trying to convince themselves of the joys of being local.

Menaker: You convinced me!

Collins: Well, sort of like the Wallace Shawn character in *My Dinner with Andre*, who doesn't need to go to Italy or around the world to have all these marvelous, tiny experiences. So usually the title and the first line are kind of a key signature that just set the tone. And then I try to start with something that's kind of ordinary because if I do that, I'll get bored, and then I'll have to push the poem in a more interesting direction, if only to keep myself interested. More, I can't tell you.

Menaker: The thing about not having to go to Italy—I noticed in the poems that you read and also in working with you over the years, which was a great privilege—that a lot of your work, and even in the poems you read this evening, mostly from the new poems, have a negative kind of tone. They are not touring Italy, or there's no Venice outside the window, or it's a kind of clearing away. Are you aware of the fact that you . . .

Collins: No, I'm not. Do tell. [Laughter] It's fascinating.

Menaker: Suffice it to say you do it. It's really interesting. There's a kind of almost willed minimalism, a kind of exclusion of fanciness, of putting on airs. And that is one of the things that I think gets your audience to respond.

Collins: Well, in that way, yes. You have to leave a lot out. You really have to leave poetry out in a kind of more old-fashioned sense of what poetry is. Or in a more common sense that fulfills people's expectations, that they're going to now experience this thing called poetry. I try to write in a very plainspoken way. And I try to start very straightforwardly and then get a little more complicated as I go along.

One of my favorite analogies for the poem is it's like an eye chart. So there's this big E in the beginning that everybody pretty much can see, we hope. And then the letters get smaller as you go along, and you reach in the doctor's office a point of illegibility. And I don't want the poem to be incomprehensible, but I think I want to make more demands on the reader later than earlier. I think a lot of reasons I stopped reading poems—and that's something that we could even discuss—is that, I don't know about you, but I don't finish reading very many poems. I mean, there are just a lot of deal breakers there. And one deal breaker would be starting in Oz. Tom mentioned I like to start in Kansas and travel with the reader to Oz, but if a poem starts in Oz or in Wonderland with a croquet game with flamingos in the first line, it's just . . . I'd like to be taken there, but I don't want to just suddenly be thrust into this paracosm, or whatever.

I conduct some workshops, and I sometimes tell students, "You think your poem ends with the last lines that you so carefully and overly carefully crafted, perhaps, but your poem actually ends where the reader stops reading. [Laughter] And that's usually somewhat before the last lines."

I'll bet if I throw a question at you as a former editor—and editor today, but a long career in editing—and I tell my students that when editors are reading manuscripts of poetry, they're not looking for particularly great literature or mind-blowing imagery; they're looking for a reason to stop reading, so they can get on to the next manuscript. Because there's a pile of them, right?

Menaker: Yes, and you usually find a reason quite quickly. It happens very quickly. And the poets that I have worked with have the same sort of approach that you do—Virginia Hamilton Adair, Deborah Garrison—they primarily and premierly (if that's an adverb) have a way of making you go on. Robert Frost is another fine example. And there are classical examples, too.

Collins: Does it happen with fiction, in your view, as quickly?

Menaker: Well, I think, as with most readers, you'd like to be, as they say, hooked at the start. You're a master of that in your poetry. And you can see the evidence here; people come to hear you, which is pretty unusual. And I think it's precisely because you have a sense of getting interest and keeping it and then, as you say, becoming a little more complicated later on. But you've built the foundation so that the dome that you didn't see when you were traveling around Westchester . . .

Collins: Well, I think I'm careful about not getting ahead of the reader, early anyway. I like to put demands on the reader that the reader needs to kind of see that something odd is going on and they need to pay a little more attention as a kind of maneuver or a head fake somewhere in the poem. But I don't want to get the reader early on; I want to start, like dance class, we start on the same foot and then we move ahead.

Menaker: I had another honor of being at the Alice Munro symposium in Ottawa a couple of days ago, and I worked with her, too, at the *New Yorker*. I remember that she once said to me that trying to do something serious in a way that will capture an audience's attention is a little bit like being a juggler or an entertainer on stage. You keep the bowling pins going in different permutations, and at the same time you're trying to tell the audience something, communicate something serious. I think that aspect of a little bit of show business is common to all great poets. Like the poem you just read about the poet and the reader never having met, but they're together anyway and you're speaking to them, and you don't want them to walk out of the room.

Collins: I got that from Borges, who is more known for his fiction but did write poetry. In the introduction to his book of poems, he said, "I'm sorry that I wrote these down. You probably would have eventually. It just so happened to be me instead of you." [Laughter] That sort of makes you wonder. But he's bluffing and being ridiculously humble. But he's sort of proposing an ideal world in which we're all poets and eventually, like the monkeys eventually writing *Hamlet*, that eventually we would write all the poems in the world. But "eventually" means forever in this case.

Menaker: In these poems that you've read and in other work of yours,— in this particular set of new poems in this book—there seems to be a little bit of a thread of Catholicism. I don't know if you realize that.

Collins: Well, I had sixteen years, a full metal jacket of Catholic education. [Laughter] It's not surprising. I have a much earlier poem called "Questions about Angels," which begins being about that question of how many angels can dance on the head of a pin, a question made up to mock the kind of scholastic, analytic theology that was popular in the Middle Ages and at Holy Cross in the 1960s. [Laughter] Even more popular in western Massachusetts than it was in the Middle Ages. In the end of the poem I say, well, maybe it's just one angel, and maybe she's "dancing alone in her stocking feet, / a small jazz combo working in the background. / She sways like a branch in the wind, her beautiful / eyes closed, and the tall thin bassist leans over / to glance at his watch, because she has been dancing / forever, and now it is very late, even for musicians." [Laughter] So I secularize her, and that was sort of a revolt. I think it's a subtle revolt against the rigors of my Catholic education.

Menaker: I just wonder; there is an absence of religiosity in these poems, not that there should be a presence. But it's coupled with, to me anyway, a sense of loneliness. Many of the poems seem to me to be lonely. Are you cognizant of that?

Collins: Oh, yes. Well, there are two things there. I'm always alone in my poems. I was talking about deal breakers or when I cut out of a poem, and there are a couple of words themselves that'll stop me from going any further. One of them would be that whole—well, like *Grandpa* or *Dad*. I'm just gone. I just turn the page. [Laughter] Or *Mom*. Just write a memoir or write a novel or a short story. There's nobody in my poems. That's the reason you're detecting loneliness. Occasionally, I write about my parents, but they're dead. When I wrote about them, they were dead. And if it's a love poem, there's some love interest there. But I want to be alone with the reader, see? And the more people you have in your poem, the less alone you are with the reader. And that's why I appear to be lonely. I'm not really lonely. I'm not that alone.

Menaker: Good.

Collins: But let me get back to the first part of your question, which is the lack of religiosity.

Menaker: Yes, that was. They were sort of a pair of questions.

Collins: That's my persona. He is very much satisfied with the world around him, and he's one of these characters who's ready to be delighted, always. He's not always delighted, but he's always ready to be delighted.

Menaker: Well, he keeps missing the azaleas.

Collins: Right. And I think if he had a theology—I don't think he has one—but if he had a theology, it would be that there was a creator of some kind, but there's no afterlife. And that the creator would say to the earthlings, "You want an afterlife, too? [Laughter] Isn't this glorious enough? And doesn't the transitoriness of it make the gloriousness even more glorious?" He would say, "I'm the eternal one around here, not you." Anyway, pretty much he would be locked into earthly experience, but would have a sense of some creationist beginning.

Menaker: There's the spiritual question, which you've just answered, and then there's the concomitant sort of alone-with-the-reader-ism. And it's also often that your poems are very domestic. They're not always. But they often have to do with a cup of tea or looking out the window. And I wonder whether that's some kind of conscious decision or just the things you want to write about. In other words, how aware are you of the kind of general setting of your work?

Collins: Basically, that's learned. That's a literary influence. And the influence is a group of poems by the Romantic poet Samuel Taylor Coleridge, whose poems are divided into these two critically convenient categories: the mystery poems that we're more familiar with like "Kubla Khan" and "The Ancient Mariner" and "Christabel." I was interested in those when I was younger, but I'm not interested in them now. What I'm interested in is what's called the conversation poems, poems like "This Lime-Tree Bower My Prison," "The Nightingale," "The Eolian Harp." There are about six of them, and they all start in a domestic setting. Coleridge is in a living room—"Frost at Midnight" is another one—a fire is going, his child is in his crib, he's in the backyard. And then the poem takes off, and it rises into dizzying heights of speculation and meditation on what is nature, what is friendship, what is love, that sort of thing. And I really learned that from him. To put it into technical terms, the domestic setting is sort of a launching pad for speculation. Because the poem will eventually go down and end, or in and down, or whatever. [Laughter] Because it starts out looking out the window or having a cup of tea, surrounded by crockery or something, and then at some point the poem will take its dive into the subjective. I really learned that from reading those Coleridge poems over and over again.

Menaker: William Blake did it in one line, "a world in a grain of sand." That's the kind of thing where you find everything in simply what's at hand, in small things.

Collins: Although Blake never talks about sitting in an Adirondack chair. [Laughter]

Menaker: No, they didn't have Adirondack chairs.

Collins: Oh, that's right, silly me.

Menaker: They had sand. They had a lot of sand. No Adirondack chairs. I knew this was going to deteriorate. [Laughter] Before we started, I asked if you would walk us through a poem. And I really think that it would be fun and interesting to do that.

Collins: Yes, because I think of them as little journeys in a way. I've taught in colleges since I got out of graduate school, basically. This is a long answer, but I'll shorten it. At some point, I realized that the way I was teaching poetry was completely opposed to the way I compose poetry. I taught poetry in a fairly traditional way, where you'd do explication: what does the poem mean? Whereas, when I wrote, I never thought about "What does this poem mean?" It would be a silly question; it would distract from writing. Or what's the theme? None of these questions would occur to me. What I was thinking about when I was writing was getting the poem through itself, making progress through itself to a point where you have a satisfying ending. And a satisfying ending means: I don't want to say anymore; you don't want to hear anymore. We'll all be happy; it's over at the right point. So I started teaching like that. I started not so much talking about what does the poem mean, but how does the poem go, like mapping the poem. How does it move through itself like that? Anyway, I'm kind of conscious when I'm writing that I'm pushing the poem forward and trying to make some progress.

Menaker: It's interesting that you also . . . Actually, go ahead, I'll wait.

Collins: It is interesting. [Laughter] But still.

Menaker: It will be.

Collins: [Laughter] It will be even more interesting later.

Menaker: To be honest, it will be interesting when I remember what I was about to ask you. [Laughter]

Collins: Now, that would be interesting.

Menaker: It'll be interesting that I remember . . .

Collins: Yes, that's what I mean.

Menaker: . . . by itself. Where are we?

Collins: This is a poem I'm going to walk you through.

Menaker: I know, but which one?

Collins: Oh, "The Suggestion Box," 197.

Menaker: I think that's a great idea for a poem.

Collins: I'm going to read the poem. So this is a poem; it's about something that poets get and novelists don't get it, playwrights don't get it. Poets get this all the time. So just stop doing it. Oh, I haven't told you what it is yet. Wait a minute. So. [Reads "The Suggestion Box"] [Laughter] [applause] So you have to be a little crazy to write these poems. The one thing about this is it responds to an irritant. It's annoying when people say, "You could write a poem about that." They're always wrong. [Laughter] And they're wrong for the same reason—it's just too big. Like, if they see the building's on fire with fire trucks, "You could write a poem." Well, no, it's too much action. You could write a movie about that. Anyway, so I thought I'd respond to it by mocking that intrusive and unwanted and always erroneous habit that people have. And I decided to order it chronologically in a day. So it started in the coffee shop. The next stanza is later in the morning, then in the afternoon. And then later I wondered that evening by the shore of a lake. So we've gone through the whole day. And the implication there is the day is just peppered with these suggestions. And then finally these ducks come to my rescue. In all of these poems, I never know the ending before I start. I've probably written maybe two poems where I kind of had a clear view of the ending. So I don't know how I'm going to get out of the poem, and that's what poets are thinking about. They're not thinking about, "This is about love or death." They're thinking, "How am I going to get out of this thing and get on with the rest of my life?" [Laughter]

But somehow I was standing by the lake shore. I wanted to just get the speaker out of the diurnal habit of conversation and be alone by a lake, that sort of romantic position of the poet. And then happily these two ducks pulled out, and the female looked over, and then she made the suggestion. I don't know why she's talking in an Irish brogue. [Laughter] I have no idea. I just thought she quacked with a bit of a brogue.

Menaker: If she were a male mallard, she'd have a green head, so he could have a brogue. But the female has no . . .

Collins: I see. It's a good thing you write memoirs. [Laughter]

Menaker: Okay, now he's started, I can tell.

Collins: So there's not much to it, really.

Menaker: You talk about getting out of a poem as if it were sort of getting through a jail sentence or getting through an ordeal of some kind. I mean, it sounds as if it were almost painful, like the irritant itself.

Collins: No, it's all pleasure, it's all self-entertaining, really.

Menaker: No sweat?

Collins: Well, there's an anxiety about how to end it because you know it can end, I wouldn't say badly and in a bad way, but you just might not be able to resolve it in some way. Clearly, to have a duck talking at you is not a resolution of anything. [Laughter]

Menaker: It could be a sign of something serious.

Collins: Well, I wouldn't say, "Therefore, in conclusion, this duck came out." [Laughter]

Menaker: Actually, that's pretty good. I want to tell you that being Collins's editor consisted of his taking a comma maybe every seventh poem or agreeing that a comma should come out and that was about it. It was for that reason a huge joy. I didn't have to do anything. [Laughter]

Collins: Yet, we had long telephone conversations.

Menaker: We did, we did. One more question: You talked about a persona that you had, which is I think the first time I've heard you say that—although for all I know you've said it again and again—but as if it were a different person. And I want to know whether this shade, this ghost over here, how close he is to you and how true he is to you.

Collins: Well, he's an improvement over me [Laughter], that's for sure. I envy him. He doesn't have any family obligations. [Laughter] He doesn't go to work. He just wanders around the house and falls into these speculations, and he has very little capacity for misery. There's very little anguish going on there at all. He's a projection. He's basically a voice; I mean, a persona is a set of vocal mannerisms. And writing these poems is really a form of role playing. The whole idea of romantic sincerity is kind of played out for a lot of people. And I don't mean that the poems are coldly ironic. I don't feel that my persona has to live up to a kind of criterion of sincerity. I have a poem called "Fishing on the Susquehanna in July" that starts out, "I have never been fishing on the Susquehanna / . . . // Not in July or any month / have I had the pleasure—if it is a pleasure—/ of fishing on the Susquehanna." [Laughter] I like to keep the reader a little off balance. But my persona, he's a way of talking and he's also a way of looking at things.

Menaker: Sometimes he seems to come closer to you, and sometimes a little bit further.

Collins: We have a lot in common. [Laughter] More than anyone. But a lot of the stuff in my life is sort of rinsed away. And by stuff, I really mean autobiographical baggage. I'm not an autobiographical poet. I write from personal experience, but by autobiography I mean my past. I'm not burdening you with traumas or anguish or sadnesses or loss or memories, not in a literal way. I hope there's sadness in my poems, and I hope there's the right amount of melancholy, because that's part of the human experience. But my persona is someone who's there. The poem opens, and he's looking out a window, and there's an apple tree, and he starts thinking about death, and that's enough. But he's not bringing a lot of autobiographical or sociological baggage into the scene. He's not trying to lift that up and convey it to the reader. He's more just present in the moment.

Menaker: There's a plane flying overhead, and also you said before we started, it's always good to end with a good answer. And I think you just did that. So I wonder if there are questions from the audience. I certainly hope so and urge you to use one of the two mics that are here.

Collins: Whenever a plane flies over, it's time for audience questions. [Laughter]

Menaker: This is an old tradition.

Collins: You're so mysterious. You're a mystic.

Menaker: No, it started with Coleridge.

Audience Member: Thank you. I want to thank the Kennedy Library and you all for helping us with this great gift tonight. There's a wonderful book about authors' favorite first poems that influenced them, from "Flanders Fields" to "Corsons Inlet." You talked about Coleridge. But as a young person, what was the poem that touched you, that had you fall in love with poetry?

Collins: There were a lot. My mother was a great reciter of poetry. She had a lot of poetry in her conversation. And so when I was young, I could hear that my mother had two different ways of talking. It was like AM and FM or something. [Laughter] I was born an NPR toddler because I liked FM better. And when I got to school, I realized this FM was called poetry. But the poem that really got me going is a poem by John Donne. If you're going to be a writer, the most important emotion you can really have is jealousy. And this was the first poem that made me jealous. It's a poem called "The Flea," a widely known poem. It's a seduction poem and he says, "Look at this little flea. It bit me, and now it bites you. Mark but this flea, and mark in this, how little that which thou deniest me is." He goes on like that. It's a playful argument of seduction, and it manages to be very sexy and very funny at the same time. I guess I read that in high school or maybe a little later. And I didn't know, I thought funny and sexy were forever separate categories of human experience. [Laughter] And here the two were shuffled together in this amazing way.

Menaker: When did you start writing poetry?

Collins: I think as a teenager. I remember when I was about nine or something, I asked my mother for a pencil because I was in the back of my parents' car and I'm an only child, still *am* an only child [Laughter], and for all the only children out there, you know that one of the joys of that isolation is that you have the back seat to yourself. There's no territorial squabbles or fighting over toys; it's just your area. And you can go from one window to the other. [Laughter]

But we were driving on the East Side Highway and there was a sailboat sailing up the East River, and I apparently had a literary reaction to this at the age of seven or eight or nine, and I wrote something down. I don't know what it was.

Audience Member: It's an honor and a delight. I want to say I'm reading right now *Sailing Alone around the Room*, and you're my type of poet. You're very light touch, but with a touch, a little bang.

Collins: Thank you.

Audience Member: And I just wanted to mention the two poems so far, I haven't gotten through this . . .

Collins: Take your time.

Audience Member: . . . that I like the best are about writing. One is "Advice to Writers." And let me see if I have—I lost the other place. It's about having people try to understand a poem. Do you want me to look for that?

Collins: No, that's okay. I know the poem you're talking about. [Laughter] It's a poem called "Introduction to Poetry," where I just suggest some other approaches to poetry besides tying it up to a chair and beating it with a hose. [Laughter]

Audience Member: I wanted to ask one question. You've answered some of it, and I guess that's on the mind of everybody. It's really kind of brave to decide to be a poet, and I wondered was that a conscious decision at nine or seven, that you liked to write.

Collins: I can answer that. It wasn't really a conscious decision. I don't think it ever is. I hate to drag in some of the other authors, but here are two authors responses to your question "When did you decide to become a writer?" John Updike said it was like being swallowed by a hobby. It was like doing a little tinkering with something, and then it overcomes your life. And the second guy is Patrick Cavanaugh, the Irish poet, who said you begin by fooling around with words, and at some point, it becomes your life. So it's something very gradual. But fooling around with words and being a hobbyist are very important. You don't start out by deciding this is your mission in life, I don't think. You start out with a rather perversely intense interest or curiosity about language, and then it takes over. Thank you.

Audience Member: Mr. Collins, Boston is about to appoint a new poet laureate sometime in the fall. And having been America's poet laureate twice, I was wondering if you had any friendly advice for this new laureate.

Collins: Do you have a laureate now, or is this your first one?

Audience Member: This will be our second one.

Collins: Well, there are a lot of them around these days, aren't there? [Laughter] I mean, my real thoughts about it? I think there should be one. No, I think it's good to have a lightning rod. I guess the main thing about being poet laureate is to try not to be dragged too much into the public light and to continue to write your poems. Writing is a very solitary act, and that's one of the reasons I got into it, or one of the attractions was it was not just something you did by yourself, but it brought out your ability to be yourself or be alone. And being poet laureate does mean a lot of media stuff, and it puts you over on the more public side of the brain. I guess my only advice was advice I got from a poet, from Robert Hass, which was don't let them drag you out of your cave. Be able to find your way back to that place where the poems start.

Menaker: And yet, here you are.

Collins: Here I is. [Laughter]

Audience Member: An (a) and (b) question. You have managed to do something quite unusual, which is to be highly regarded by poetic critics. Some people call them serious poetic critics. At the same time, you've won the affection, approbation, popularity almost, one might say, of many of us who may not be that. I'm curious if there has ever been the instance where, as always happens in the arts, someone has written something that is very strongly critical, and I'm curious how you feel or felt about that experience. What did you do? Did you feel simply that it's of no importance to me, or that I really should think about it, or maybe I want to change? That's the (a). And the (b) is: Is there some goal, some poetic vision that you have, some aim, to put it more simply, that you really could articulate and let us know about?

Collins: Well (a), I've gotten some good critical responses and some bad ones. Let me say this: I think there are four kinds of reviews. A good review for the right reason; a bad review for the right reason; a good review for the wrong reason; a bad review for the wrong reason. And I'd rather get a bad review for the right reasons than a good review for the wrong reasons. I'd rather be understood and not liked than be misunderstood and loved. [Laughter] But the usual criticism is that the poems are, I'd say they'd say, underconceptualized. And my response is most of these critics are specialized in a rather heady form of criticism. So my response is, well, just problematize them. [Laughter] You seem to be good at that anyway, so surely you can make them more difficult. Just tie some knots in them that don't belong there.

And disappointing or not, I really never thought of having a mission. I'm very grateful for all the luck and attention and book sales and the amount of readers I have. I don't know how it all happened, really. But there it is and I'm very grateful for it. But I never intended anything. And I never think of any of this, except when I'm there. I really—it sounds a little too Boy Scout-ish and sincere—but I'm really just trying to write one good poem after another, because I'm in it for myself. As I said, these poems are immensely gratifying. They're immensely self-entertaining. And I love writing them; I love writing a good poem. I feel good, I feel a kind of afterglow for 48 hours after I've written something that I think is pretty good. So no mission state-ment, really.

Audience Member: Your poem that has affected me the most and most deeply is "Workshop." And particularly in the way that it ends up, it's sort of metapoetical enjoyment at the level of the mouse and its own little home. And when I first read it—and actually many, many times I've read it—it never fails to touch me with a sort of sweet vulnerability. Then, as I read more of your poems, I kept noticing mice in your poems. In a way I thought, "Oh, gee." The times that went on, I felt a little bit less excited because he already did the mouse. Can you just talk to us about the mice?

Collins: I think if you write poems long enough, or any genre, certain obsessions begin to come to light that even you're not aware of. And I had a book come out some years ago called *Nine Horses* and a friend of mine said, "You should have called it *Nine Mice*." It's a real theme, it's a very serious theme. I think it's a combination of cartoons, of being obsessed with cartoons when I was a child and loving the mice. And also living in a mouse-infested 1865 house in New York, bless their hearts. [Laughter] I don't know, they seem to be just the right size for an animal. [Laughter] That's a real theme.

Audience Member: Thank you.

Collins: Thank you.

Menaker: I'm not sure how we are for time, but maybe a couple more?

Collins: I think we're good.

Audience Member: I want to make a statement more than ask a ques-tion, but I do have a question as well. And that is: I just want to thank you so much, Billy, for what you do, I think, is give us some sort of enjoyable access to something that we don't think about or experience all that often. I know something about Jungian psychology. It seems to me that you get to those images somehow in such a delightful way. And every poem that you've read tonight I'm familiar with, and I just appreciate it so much.

Collins: Thank you.

Audience Member: It's a great talent, and I really appreciate it. My question is: What is it about the word *cicada*?

Menaker: Well, the cicada and the mice are best friends, I think.

Collins: We were talking about these deal breakers, like Mom and Pop and Granddad's hammer, and stuff like that. I once wrote an article called, "My Grandfather's Tool Box: The Limits of Memory-Driven Poetry." And all my grandparents were dead before I was born, so I never had a grandfather, let alone one with a tool box. But it was about these fetish objects that we're attached to to connote deceased relatives. But another deal breaker was the word *cicada*; I just said I stop reading if I come across the word *cicada*. [Laughter] I just think it's usually kind of a shorthand for the melancholy poet. I don't know, it just seems cheaply tugging at some sentimental strings inside me. I don't know. Anyway, it's personal.

Menaker: Well, maybe it's autumnal.

Collins: It's like circadian rhythm? Is there a connection between cicadas and circadian rhythm?

Menaker: No, Sir Cadian.

Collins: Oh, Sir Cadian, yes.

Menaker: Don't you know him?

Collins: Sir Cadian, he's from the Round Table.

Menaker: A medieval knight, yes. [Laughter]

Collins: Oh, here's a question over here.

Audience Member: Hi, I wanted to thank you for coming. I know there's a lot of experience behind it, but I just wanted to know how much time it took you to write the poems, the ones you read.

Collins: How long does it take?

Audience Member: Yes.

Collins: Well, not as long as you'd think. [Laughter] I'm able to spend less time I think with experience. I don't revise as much because I try to make it right as I go along. One analogy might be to the two kinds of kitchen behavior, two kinds of cooks. Either you clean as you go along—you know who you are [Laughter]—or you make a big mess and you clean it later or get someone else to clean it. In the kitchen I make a mess, but when I write I clean as I go along. So I'm trying to write one solid line after another; I'm trying to follow this careful progress of the poem. So that could take a half an hour, it could take four or five hours. But it's almost always done in one sitting, or maybe a little of the next morning. I never stop after a couple stanzas and say, "Well, maybe I'll go to the movies or go out and get an ice cream." It's very much game on with me. I'm trying to figure this poem out, follow some kind of wondering where the poem wants to go, trying to listen to the poem and take impulses from it. So that's done in one sitting.

Then the revisions are not . . . I mean, revision is the wrong word because revision means seeing it again. The conceptual run of the poem is done in one sitting. When I go back to the poem, it's basically refining or with a hope to refine. And my changes are either mostly musical or rhythmic. But the run of the poem from like A to B to C, from "The Suggestion Box" and the guy with the tattoos and the duck looking back at me talking in Irish, that's usually done in one go. And I have a feeling, if I write the thing in one go, that the reader will have a sense that it's happening as they read it.

Audience Member: I first heard you in the Geraldine Poetry Festival in New Jersey. And we really enjoyed that, so I decided to come quite a distance today. But I was born and brought up in a different culture in India. So in our culture, we think that poets, the angels sent by God, they're a chosen one. [Laughter]

Collins: That's what my parents thought. [Laughter] But I don't know about anybody else.

Audience Member: Do you feel you are the chosen one? I don't mean in that egoistic way, but when the words come in your poetry do you think, "Oh, my God, somebody else is writing."

Collins: I mean, we were talking about poems that were a little plainspoken, and we're trying to avoid—that sort of image of the poet is something I'm always trying to dismantle, I guess. That's why I write a lot of poems that are kind of making fun of poetry or making fun of workshops or just kind of gently poking fun at the whole business of it. Whereas, I do take it very seriously, but I think probably one of the reasons I use humor in my poems is so you won't know how seriously I'm really taking it. I'm a little behind this ironic play. But behind that is a serious person who keeps writing poems decade after decade, and I can't think of anything better to do with my life than to do that.

Menaker: Speaking of humor, I've had the misfortune of teaching a workshop next to Collins's workshop, which erupts in laughter every ten seconds regularly, to the point where I became so jealous in Key West that I asked my students to laugh. [Laughter] Because they were having such a good time over there.

Collins: We couldn't hear you; we were laughing so much. [Laughter] Should we close with a poem?

Audience: Yes! [applause]

Collins: May I stand? Thanks, this is a good idea. I'll just read a newer poem. And, again, thank you so much for coming. This has been such a big, full responsive audience. And this library, I can't wait to look around some more. It's just one of the most amazing buildings and amazingly situated buildings I've ever had the pleasure of entering. And it's a poem called "1956" [Reads "1956," later printed in *The Rain in Portugal* under the title "1960"] [applause] Thank you.

When Pastors Learn from Poets: Billy Collins Visits Princeton Theological Seminary

Craig Barnes / 2016

This interview was conducted on November 2, 2016, in the Princeton Theological Seminary Library by seminary president M. Craig Barnes. It is printed with the permission of the Princeton Theological Seminary.

Craig Barnes: I think we'd all rather just hear you read some more rather than have me ask you questions.

Billy Collins: I can *do* that. I have about four hours' worth here. [Laughter]

Barnes: We live in a day that values science and technology and big data. Why do we need poetry?

Collins: Well, because of those things. [Laughter and extended applause]. I guess poetry is little data, or a datum, one datum at a time. That's really my answer. Poetry, if it does nothing, it asks us to tap the brakes, slow down, not only in focusing on something like, as a recent example [alluding to his poem "Digging," which he read earlier], that little car I found digging in the backyard. Just kind of looking at it and stopping, and there it is, and just letting the mind go with unrestrained association about the boy who probably had that toy when it was new. Anybody can do this, really. It's just that some people actually write it down. Also, the form of poetry itself tells you to slow down, in that the lines don't go out to the end of the page. We don't do that because we don't want to write prose, God forbid. [Laughter] So, poets are basically prose-avoidant systems. We turn the line back. Now there used to be a metrical reason for this. Iambic tetrameter, like "Whose woods these are, I think I know," and then you hit the typewriter carriage, and it goes back, and the bell rings. If we don't do that, we still turn back because the turning of the line back into the poem is almost telling the reader's eyes to come back in here. Come back into this thing. Come back into this little soundscape or this little verbal playground where things are going on. Come back in. Come back in. Turn your attention, always back into the dimension of the poem. Prose will ask you to run headlong in a linear way to find out things that lie ahead. And the poem is moving forward, but it's also recirculating your attention that way. So, it's basically just the case for slowing down, and if you slow *completely* down, if you come to a complete stop, then you find yourself in a kind of meditative trance, which is not a bad thing either. So, I think my first answer was better. [Laughs] The short answer. [Laughter]

Barnes: You're not only a poet, but you're a professor of the art. How do you *teach* poetry?

Collins: Oh, I thought you were going to say, "How do you juggle these two things?" I always wanted to be asked that because usually in an interview they say, "How do you manage to be, you know, a film star, and a mother, and a cook, and all that?" With a poet it would be like, "How do you manage to write a poem every three weeks and do nothing at all in between? How do you juggle those things?" [Laughter] You can't *teach* it. You can do matchmaking. You can tell them about poets that they should read. "You're writing this way, have you read Robert Lowell? You haven't? Well, you should." You can set them up with potential influences, but there are a number of things that are completely unteachable. Two of them are a sense of verbal rhythm—you just can't teach that; you can't. It's like being the Arthur Murray Dance Studio: people go there because they can't dance, and I think they leave not being able to dance either, except with each other. You can't teach verbal rhythm; they just don't get it. I have a poem where I talk about being at camp, and I mention going to camp in the Adirondacks. Actually, I went to camp in the Catskills, but *Adirondacks* just sounds better. It's almost like Italian [mimics an Italian accent]: Adiro*nd*acks! And *Catskills* is, like, *Catskills*. So I'm always writing with the ear. But you just can't convey that. And the second thing you can't convey—there could be a longer list here—is a taste for metaphor, a desire, a real thirst and an interest in making unusual connections, connecting dots and making metaphoric comparisons. If you can't do either of those things, you should open up a frame shop in town, take Wednesdays off, but poetry is probably not for you. So that's how you can't teach poetry. [Laughter.]

Barnes: [Deliberately] You have an amazing ability to—

Collins: Slower, please. [Laughter]

Barnes [Slows down dramatically]: *You have . . .*

Collins: Thank you. [Laughter]

Barnes: [Resumes a regular tempo] ability to see something that most of us would pass by—an ordinary object, a dog walking along, a couple of cats, a mailman—but you see something in it, something full of wonder, mysteriousness. Is that a gift, or did you train yourself to do that?

Collins: Well, if you had my teaching schedule, you would see that there's a lot of time left over, [Laughter] but I think you learn that from life. But also, I was an only child. I had a lot of time by myself, which was paradise, really. I never wanted it any different. Being an only child is very good preparation for poetry because poetry doesn't require an interest in other people, for example. [Laughter] Really, I was mentioning earlier that the image I have of the difference between people who write fiction and plays, and on the other hand, poetry, is that the first group,—the novelists, short story writers, and playwrights—are looking into other people's windows. You have to be interested in the domestic lives, and even the erotic and psychological lives, of other people; whereas the poet is inside that house looking *out* the window, and not necessarily at any other people, but at a birdfeeder, or an elm tree, and telling you what he or she is looking at. Flannery O'Connor said, "The writer should never be ashamed of staring." Staring can lead to interesting places. You might not look that smart when you're doing it, especially if your mouth is open. [Laughter] But poets are just looking around for metaphors and different ways to approach these old topics, and you'll settle for anything. If you see a dog or a cat, as you say, or a cloud eating another cloud, or just these little things. We're missing so much. We're missing stuff all the time. Annie Dillard said in her book *Pilgrim at Tinker Creek*, nature is a "now-you-see it, now-you-don't" kind of thing. You don't go out into nature and say, "OK, hit me. Give me the nature stuff." You have to be vigilant. You can sit by a lake for a half an hour and turn around and walk away, and three herons are giving birth or something. [Laughter] You missed it. [Laughs] Probably unlikely, but if you'd stayed longer . . . So it's really a matter of putting time in. A lot of the time you're just staring, and nothing is coming out of it, but at least you're not causing harm to other people.

Barnes: I've heard someone describe you as a poet who puts the *fun* in *profundity*. So as you write, how do you maintain a balance between playfulness and gravitas, between the rapture and the stinky cigar? [Alluding to Collins' celebratory poem "Joy," a rapturous, cosmic reflection that concludes on a playful note, which the poet read earlier.]

Collins: Well, right. [Laughs] I think it's really not balancing it all the time, but it's more of a strategy. It's more of a series of maneuvers and a matter of finding a shift point in a poem where you've been quite serious, as in that poem about the Key West double sunrise and sunset ["Joy"], and then you just want to blow that in a way, or just bring it down to earth with something. Or the other way, where you start with something kind of silly, and it becomes serious. So it's not balancing it all the time. My persona, at least, wants to be a little slippery. I don't think he ever wants to write a poem that's completely grieving or completely silly. He likes to mix the two up in slightly disorienting ways. I think one of the pleasures of literature is disorientation. That is to say, the poem—or the novel, even—takes you to a place that you're not familiar with. I like to say the poem begins in Kansas and goes to Oz. It starts in a familiar place and then lifts you up, and it lands you in some odd or unexpected place that's a little more speculative, or hypothetical, or even surreal. But I think that's the travel of the poem from one place to another. What's wrong with a lot of poems, now that you haven't asked, [Laughter] is that they start in Oz. They start in an already bizarre landscape, and you feel like you have to play catch up, but you don't really want to. I like *being* in Oz. I like being in freaky places, but I like traveling there. Let's start at home and go to some freaky place, but I don't want to just be Medevac'd into this surrealistic landscape of yours. [Laughter] I think a lot of poems are too quick on the reader. I think you've got to be gradual with the reader. Robert Frost is the great prime example. Last week, coincidentally, I was at a place in New Hampshire called Pinkerton Academy, where Robert Frost taught for six years when he was in his twenties. He taught Latin and then English. But Frost is the great master of knowing when to turn cards over and when to leave them face down, when to start simple and end in deeper water. If you've ever studied poetry in textbooks, you've seen that on the side of the page they often have little numbers, like five, ten, fifteen, for the line numbers, to make it easier to discuss the poem. And one of my students, bless her heart, asked me what those numbers were, and I said, "Well, they're like numbers on a swimming pool, the poem gets deeper as it goes along." [Laughter]

Barnes: You opened the door on spirituality, so I want to walk right through it. [Laughter]

Collins: [Laughing] *Pastor!*

Barnes: So much of your poetry, as I mentioned before, takes images from daily life and just finds *wonder* in [them]. To some degree, that's what we're trying to teach our students to do also. Like the poet, we think that's part of the theological task: to look beneath the surface of things and see the miracle and the mystery, or the despair and the heartache, that's at work there. We think that's also where things like spirituality, like the Holy Spirit, are at work. And our job is to attend to that. But we can't do it if we can't see it, and we can't see it if we don't learn how to do it. So this gets back to the question how do you teach people to peer beneath the ordinary?

Collins: Well, I don't know. I don't reject the question; I've never really tried to teach anybody that. For me it's a practice to just look around for things that'll start a poem going. I was reading Juan Jimenez, a poet, and he said, "The worst thing about death must be the first night." [Laughter] I'd heard a lot of images of death, but I never thought it would continue, night and day, but you'd be dead. So it's not so much like boring into the heart of things. So, I have a poem about how he just scared the hell out of me through that image. Is there going to be one long night when you're dead, or a number of nights? And so if there are nights, there must be days, so you just keeping thinking. If there are days, there must be sunsets, and maybe all the dead gather and watch the sun go down. [Laughter] This is the way the poem rolls forward, just in a matter of these speculations.

Barnes: You were made US poet laureate in 2001, which was a very dramatic time for the country. How did 9/11 affect your work that year?

Collins: Well, being poet laureate didn't really affect my work, except that it sort of brought an end to it for a while. [Laughter] You really are dragged out of this little alcove in which you write, and you're given the responsibility of being a public figure. You are not speaking for yourself anymore but speaking on this public platform. And you're almost forced to speak *for* poetry, which I found uncomfortable because most poems I read these days, I don't really finish reading. So it's hard to be a promoter of something you can't finish reading [Laughter] with any enthusiasm. But I was asked by Congress to write a poem on the first anniversary of 9/11, and I did write that poem, and I read it before Congress. So I did respond. I did get off the bench and write a public poem, as public a poem as I've ever written, anyway. And that was a good demonstration of the difference between public and private language. When I got up and read the poem, both houses met in New York City, which was historically very unusual, if not unprecedented. So there they're all gathered, and there were lots of speeches, of course, before there's the Poet Laureate. And I got up and started reading this poem, and the poem begins not with rhetorical talk about heroism or the future of the country. It starts with imagery: it's night, and there's rain against the windows, and there's a mist on the windows, and that kind of thing. So the people in Congress didn't know what to do with that. You could see them looking at me like cocker spaniels who have heard this whistle in the distance. [Laughter] For better or worse, the poem was different language; it was imagery. There was a very clear sense that poetry, as you say, is a matter of observing things and being in touch with the natural world. Certainly, we don't hear that in all the speeches we've been listening to. You never hear anything about a tree or a river or the natural world, and the world of coffee cups and things is obliterated by this rhetoric.

Barnes: I'm turning now to questions from the audience. This one's come up three times, and I've heard it before since you've been on campus: "Did you really make a lanyard?"

Collins: Oh, yeah. Yeah, yeah. You can't lie about that stuff. I went to camp in the Catskills, and lanyard making was and still is going on, I think. Aren't kids still making lanyards? Yes, they even make them in Europe. I have an Italian translator and we've toured around Northern Italy. When he started translating me, I said, "Some of these poems are just too American, they're not going to translate into a European culture, like 'The Lanyard.'" And he said, "Oh no, we make lanyards. We call them Scooby Doo!" In Italy, anyway. I don't know why. So we would give these readings, and I'd read "The Lanyard," and then he'd get up and he'd go, "[Recites mock-Italian phrases] Scooby Doo!" [Laughter] It's not the tone I was looking for. But yeah, I'd make lanyards.

Barnes: Another person asked, "Your poems suggest ambivalent feelings about cats. [Laughter] Can you say something more about your relationship with felines?

Collins: We have two in the house that were rescued, and I've gotten quite fond of them. I'm between dogs. I really am looking around for a dog. It's just a different kind of relationship. I mean they're not glad to see you. [Laughter] Ours aren't. You can be away for two weeks, and then they're not glad to see you, maybe because they've been left alone for two weeks without any food or water. Maybe *that's* the reason. Wait a minute. One of the cats is an indoor-outdoor cat, and the other one—don't tell anybody—but she's not as smart as the first one. So the other one is not allowed to go out, because he did go out once and got the bejeezus kicked out of him in a street fight. He thinks every other cat is like the cat he lives with. So he's gotten out occasionally, but he wears a little collar, and it's got his name and a phone number. Not *his* phone number, but *our* phone number. [Laughter] He also [Laughs] has a little thing on the collar that says, "I'm not supposed to be outside." [Laughter]

Barnes: Bad cat. [Laughter] If you were teaching preachers to preach, what poets would you have them read?

Collins: I guess just John Donne. John Donne's sermons. He's the best. Not only is he the best; he's the only one I know. [Laughter] Because he *is* the best, that's why I know him. John Donne is full of imagery. He's someone who is always supplying titles for poems and novels—*For Whom the Bell Tolls* and all that. It's all lifted from John Donne. And I think even though he's writing in the seventeenth century, his sermons are still forceful today.

Barnes: What habits do you recommend to feed your mind or keep it sharp enough for writing poetry?

Collins: Well, getting up in the morning and not doing anything for a while, like not checking email or reading the newspaper. Just spending a half an hour doing nothing every day. I try to do it. I don't do it every day. It's actually very difficult. It's almost impossible, if you have a life that's . . . even if you *don't* have a life, because you will fill your life with just junk you do. You don't have to have any great set of responsibilities. You don't have to be secretary of agriculture or something. But spend a half an hour doing nothing, absolutely nothing, not writing. Something will happen almost every time; you'll come away a little different. I think Andrew Sullivan—I don't know if you've read him—said, the great enemy of faith today is not hedonism; it's distraction. And someone else said—you mentioned all the big data and stuff—the problem today is not that we're subjected to a flood of information; we're subjected to a flood of insignificance. That really should resonate. So, one way is just to take time out from the flood of insignificance and do nothing for half an hour, and then just read poetry for 10,000 hours, [Laughter] when you're not doing nothing. [Laughs] You just have to read poetry like crazy. People think they can just take a pen and express themselves. It's ridiculous. It's the same thing as picking up a bassoon and saying, "Hey, how do you play this?" You have to take lessons. You wouldn't just buy a big chunk of marble and attack it with a hammer and say, "I'm going to do a bust of my Uncle Charlie, somehow." No! You have to take lessons. But you'll pick up a pen and start telling the world how miserable you are, and the preparation for that is to read for 10,000 hours. Read English poetry, or poetry in any language you understand, for 10,000 hours. Read. Just read, read, read, read, read. It's a huge conversation running back and forth through the centuries. They're all talking kind of about the same thing, you find out. They're talking about grief. They're talking about love. They're talking about not too many things, but in a lot of interesting ways, and with a lot of intensity, as if no one had ever talked about these things before. You have to listen to this huge conversation, and then ask yourself, "Do I have anything to add to this?" Because unless you're just expressing yourself, which is an overrated activity, [Laughing] *vastly* overrated, and it's connected to the self-esteem craze in pernicious ways, I think. But if you want to be *part* of the conversation, you have to listen just out of courtesy, and then find a place where you can insert yourself: "I have something to *add*."

Barnes: Preachers, over time, develop a certain *style* of preaching, maybe even a certain persona, and hopefully it's authentic. It's not put on, but it's not exactly the same persona as the preacher. Is that true for poets?

Collins: Oh, yeah. I have a persona. I pretty much have a sound, in other words. A persona means a verbal personality, and I slip into that. He's almost like another character. If there were Venn diagrams, he and I would overlap heavily, but not completely, because he's an improvement over me. I mean, I wish I were *him*. He doesn't have a job; he doesn't do all the junk I have to do; he doesn't sit in airports, bored. He's this beautiful guy who walks around, falling into speculations. He's got a great life. [Laughter] He has transcended most of the bourgeois concerns that I—and many of you, I think—find ourselves mired in. So, he's a vast improvement. He's like a perch from which things can be seen that I don't have. I need him to get up on that slight elevation in order to gain perspective on things.

Barnes: Did he evolve over time?

Collins: Well, he is based on somebody else. [Laughs] That sounds silly. [Laughter] He's based on a figure in English Romantic poetry, and that's the figure of the dawdler. He's walking through a landscape; he sits on a wayside bench; he falls into a speculation. It's basically the figure of the Romantic lyric, popular in the late eighteenth century and early nineteenth century, in Coleridge and Wordsworth particularly. He's an updated version of that. He's like a rustic *flaneur*, a wanderer through a landscape, who seems to have all the time in the world, a man of reverie and speculation and fairly good natured, I'd say.

Barnes: Another question from the audience: Is there a watershed event in your life that marks some of your work as *before* and your current work as *after*?

Collins: Well, it was when I was in my midthirties. It's not a day, like an epiphanic moment on a Wednesday afternoon. But when I was in my mid-thirties, I figured out how to write. I figured out this persona. Prior to that I didn't know how to do it. Don't ask me what I was doing in those years besides betting on professional football, but I was not developing a persona. I was imitating other poets. I was writing really pathetic beatnik poetry in high school and pathetic beatnik poetry in college. [Laughs] And I was writing really bad Wallace Stevens in graduate school. I was desperate to be a poet. I knew I wanted to be a poet. I didn't think I *would* actually make it, but I kept writing, often covertly. I'd get a poem in some little *Flying Faucet Review* or some little magazine that was about to close. [Laughter] But mostly I was imitating Richard Brautigan. I was imitating all these people, and Gertrude Stein, going through all these periods, right? And then finally many of these influences came together. And then the big permission slip was that I started reading poets who showed me that it was possible to be funny without being silly, to be funny with a point, to be funny and still be serious. I didn't know you *could* be funny. And you *couldn't* because of Wordsworth and Coleridge. Shelley said something like, "I'm sure that the ultimate redemption of mankind is impossible until laughter is banished." So they got rid of humor and sex and substituted landscape. [Laughter] And that's basically where humor went until people like Philip Larkin and the New York School poets like Frank O'Hara and Kenneth Koch and some Los Angeles poets showed that, yeah, you could be funny. You could be not just *serious*; you could be very *dark* like Philip Larkin, who's funny, or Simic. I didn't think Simic was funny until I heard him read, and he started laughing [Laughs] at his own poems. [Laughter] So that was a big permission slip. I'd been repressing my humor because I'd thought you needed to be miserable in poetry, and I found a persona that seems to be less miserable than other peoples' personae. He's actually quite a happy guy, this persona. [Laughter]

Barnes: Can you conclude our evening with one more poem?

Collins: Sure. I'd really like to read a poem that's not mine, if you don't mind. It's a poem by a seventeenth-century English poet, Thomas Traherne, and it's called "The Salutation." It's the only poem I know that's written from the point of view of an infant, a baby who has just, seems to me, come into the world and is looking around with a kind of wonder that we all could try to re-achieve or resurrect. So, "The Salutation," Thomas Traherne. [Reads "The Salutation"] [Applause]

Former Poet Laureate Billy Collins on His New Collection—And How Poetry Is Changing

Diane Rehm / 2016

This conversation was recorded for The Diane Rehm Show, produced by WAMU, which is licensed to American University in Washington, DC, and distributed by National Public Radio (NPR). Broadcast on October 4, 2016, the interview is printed with the permission of WAMU.

Diane Rehm: Billy Collins, it's *always* good to see you.

Billy Collins: Very nice to be here, Diane. Thanks for having me on.

Rehm: Oh, my pleasure. And congratulations on the *birth* of your brand-new book. You've got to talk about this title.

Collins: Today is the birthday of the book. Today is the pub date, and I don't know what sign it is. Maybe it's a Libra? I'm not sure.

Rehm: I think it is, yes.

Collins: I'll have to see if the book and I are compatible according to the stars. [Laughter] I often title a book after a poem in the book, but in this case, it's a line from a poem. I'm not a rhyming poet, at least in the traditional sense of the word. I try to write with my ear, and I try to write poems that sound good. And just to go back—this is a little historical—but when rhyme became an option in American poetry in . . .

Rehm: When was that?

Collins: Well, it starts with Whitman in *Leaves of Grass* [1855]. He was the first one to write a poem without end rhyme or regular meter. Shakespeare, of course, used regular meter without the end rhyme in blank verse, and then it really wasn't picked up until the twentieth century. But what happened was—and this is often a misunderstanding—poets didn't just scissor the rhymes off the right side of the poem and throw them out the window. In the best poetry, the rhymes, you might say, abandoned their

139

little positions at the ends of the lines and invaded the body of the poem. They went inside the poem and became a more organic part of its sound-scape. So I do write with the ear, but I don't have rhymes at the ends of lines, usually. I wrote a poem "On Rhyme." I love formal poetry. I've been teaching English literature for over 30 years, and there's a lot of great formal poetry being written today. But in this poem "On Rhyme," I express my *preference* for unrhymed poetry.

Rehm: *Un*rhymed poetry.

Collins: Yes, so I say, you know, "I like Jack Horner sitting on a sofa," [Laughter] and I've kept subverting some of these rhymes. Instead of "the rain in Spain," I like "the rain in Portugal." Not much rhymes with *Portugal*. So the title of the book, *The Rain in Portugal*, is—I wouldn't call it exactly a trigger warning—[Laughs] but it does imply to the reader that he or she is not in for a traditionally rhymed experience in poetry.

Rehm: I think that that aspect of *un*rhymed poetry leads some people to wonder, "Is a poem without rhyme truly a poem or is it simply a continuing narrative?"

Collins: It is a question for people who haven't been paying attention to poetry [Laughs], quite frankly, because it's become, as I said, an option in poetry. I gave a talk in England many years ago in a rather rural community, and this then-to-me elderly man asked a question. And his question was completely innocent. He said, "Mr. Collins, are all your poems written in prose?" If this was delivered by Oscar Wilde, I would've been devastated, but he missed the little song. He missed the little song that was really synonymous with poetry. Regular rhyme and meter defined poetry until this breakaway from it into what's kind of weakly called *free verse*.

Rehm: And yet, you proclaim that some of the current *modern* poetry is not to your liking, that somehow it strayed too far.

Collins: Well, this is not a recommended aesthetic. It's really just my taste after many decades of reading poetry. The fact is, I don't finish reading a lot of poems, and I think that's the case with a lot of readers. I'll read five or six lines or maybe two lines, in some cases, and I'm out. There are just a lot of deal breakers. And I'll name two of them. Okay? One of them is just the poem is way too obscure to begin with. I don't mind obscurity and difficulty as the poem progresses and finds a way into a rather ambiguous or hazy situation. But if it starts out with something totally mysterious and demanding, I feel the poet and I haven't been introduced yet, and it's a little too much too soon. I like poems that start in simplicity and end in complexity. The way I sometimes put it is that I like poems that start in Kansas and end in Oz. But I don't want to start in Oz. It's too much too soon. And the other poems I don't finish are the type where the poets are presumptuous of my interest in their personal life and usually personal misery. I always start with the indifference of the reader because poets are writing to strangers. We might show our poems to friends and family and colleagues, but basically, we are after what Roger Angel of the *New Yorker* called "the love of strangers." He said writing is really about the love of strangers. In my poetry workshops, I try to introduce this kind of a task. How do you get a stranger to love you or at least be interested, want to date you, maybe, for a minute or two in a poem? And there are techniques and ways of doing that. But one way is not to rush into the poem with a lot of emotional baggage. In fact, when I use the expression "emotional baggage," I say to my students that you are allowed one carryon.

Rehm: [Laughs] And the airlines would totally support you. You talk about formal poetry and the rhyme and the meter of, say, Shakespeare, and yet, you include Shakespeare in one of your poems. And I wonder if you would read that for us on page—*my* page 29.

Collins: Sure.

Rehm: And tell me what inspired this poem.

Collins: This is a little segue from air travel, right?

Rehm: Yes.

Collins: Well, there's a famous line in Shakespeare—it's the fourth line of this poem; I repeat it. I was on an airplane, and often a poem starts where two things that have lane very separate in parts of your mind somehow get synaptically connected. And that's what happened here. It's called "The Bard in Flight." [Reads "The Bard in Flight"]

Rehm: Billy Collins reading a poem titled "The Bard in Flight" from his newest book of poetry titled *The Rain in Portugal*. I *love* the cover. Explain the cover.

Collins: Well, I've been lucky enough to pick all my cover art. I don't know why the art department at Random House lets me do this. I always feel it's a little like going into the kitchen at a restaurant and putting some salt in the soup, and some guy running after you with a cleaver. [Laughter] But I think I'm actually pretty good at it. I just surf the Internet to find images. And in this case, I was hard pressed. I hadn't found an image, and it was time to deliver one. And I found this image. It's a little drawing by an eighteenth-century French artist named Charles-Antoine Coypel. I'd never heard of him. It's a drawing of a woman with a look of I don't know what, anxiety?

Rehm: Quizzicalness?

Collins: Troubled? A quizzicalness.

Rehm: Yes.

Collins: My dear friend Susanna told me that she thought the woman's expression was caused by her trying to figure out what the heck the title means. [Laughter]

Rehm: It works.

Collins: She's actually a figure from the Bible. She's the wife of a fellow named Potiphar. I'd never heard of him either, quite frankly. But she's not a nice lady as it turned out.

Rehm: Oh, really?

Collins: I didn't know the story, so I'm innocent of her doings. But she's famous for trying to seduce a friend of her husband's, and then, having been rejected, accusing him of rape. So I'm sorry if it ruins the cover for you. [Laughs] That's not the kind of subject that usually finds its way into my poems.

Rehm: You have said, elsewhere, that the stuff coming out of a Master of Fine Arts program is not great, that these poems become too cloyingly personal. You've already mentioned that. But what is it about those programs that you think has gotten these students off on the wrong foot?

Collins: Well, I don't think there's anything intrinsically wrong with an MFA course. At the very least, you'll be able to read poetry better. I remember taking oil painting classes a long time ago, not to be a good oil painter—because I don't even do it anymore—but to understand oil painting better. But I do think that the misperception is that you can be taught by a senior poet sitting at the end of a seminar desk, and a series of those poets. I think the real teachers of poetry are on the shelves of the library in the anthologies. I think they are John Donne and Emily Dickinson and Wordsworth and W. H. Auden, X. J. Kennedy, Miller Williams, and Ron Padgett, and I could name 150 other poets. I think that's how you learn, not so much sitting around and comparing each other's work. I'm also just too old for that [Laughs]. When I say that, I mean that when I came out of college, in 1963, it should be said, there were no such thing as MFA programs. I think there were two, actually, one at Stanford and one at Iowa. But it would have been thought of as going into periodontal school, I mean something you'd never consider, [Laughs] or I wouldn't. But the reason I got into poetry as a teenager had a lot to do with being alone. In fact, poetry was something you did with your aloneness, just you and the language. And there was that kind of intimate relationship between *your* expressive desires and the English language. And now it seems to be that it's kind of a quilting bee. People are helping each other, encouraging each other, and giving feedback. And there's probably too much revision going on. Because what can you say about a poem in a class? It's perfect? Put a stamp on it? Send it to the bureau of engraving? I've done that occasionally, but it's rare. No, you say it needs more work. So often, if the revision process becomes too continuous or endless, you lose that initial impulse in the poem. And I don't mean "first thought, best thought," that you should just get high and be spontaneous. You should write with deliberation and care. But you can sap the juice out of the poem by revising.

Rehm: How do you think that differs from the editing process in, say, a novel or a memoir?

Collins: Well, it brings up the whole status of editors these days. I think editors like William Maxwell and Maxwell Perkins, who were almost co-writers, taking sentences and changing them around, would be thought to be kind of intrusive or invasive today. I've never gotten a *line* edit. And I think that's true of other editors. No one's ever come in—except very occasionally and helpfully—and said, "We need to change this stanza all around," or "The fourth stanza should be the first stanza." With my editors, David Ebershoff, Dan Menaker, and Andrea Walker—I've had some really great editors at Random House—I give them 70 poems, say, too many for a book. And I just say, "Find the weak ones. Find six or eight weak ones." And then we pare it down that way.

Rehm: Bob Gottlieb has been my editor since 1998.

Collins: Lucky you.

Rehm: Oh, you bet. And exactly as you say, it's barely touching. It's simply providing the emotional support I've needed to write.

Collins: Yes, that's true of a good editor, I think. You get a sense that they are in your corner, and, if they're not cowriting the book with you, they're co-giving birth to it or something.

Rehm: Absolutely.

Collins: Yes. It is a joint effort, emotionally.

Rehm: Tell me about what you see as the difference between public and private poetry language. Today everybody is talking about politics and how that enters the poetical vision.

Collins: Well, I think of poetry *as* a private language. And I think of it as a very intimate language. I think part of the usefulness of poetry, or one of the pleasures it offers, is that it provides a kind of refuge from the din of public language. With public language, whether it's a political speech or advertising, you get the sense that you're being spoken to as a mass, a part of a crowd. And in some poetry—Whitman is a great example of creating intimacy—you really feel like there's one person speaking to you. Back in the '40s, George Orwell wrote this very important, lasting essay called "Politics and the English Language [1946]." He pointed out even then what rings true today, that the trouble with political language is that it is *hiding* the truth. It uses euphemism, things like *relocation* or *ethnic cleansing*, covering the truth of what's going on. And he says that if you really said the truth, it would be too brutal. So there's this way of being insincere. He then gives guidelines for more direct writing. But he feels that if the language becomes contaminated with euphemism and lying and indirection, it affects our thinking. If that's the language we're exposed to, we begin to think that way.

Rehm: We have a number of calls, but before we open the phones . . . humor really has been your trademark. And you have a very funny poem about dogs on page 27. And it's called "Species." And I happen to have a dog I love deeply. So I'd like you to read that poem.

Collins: Be happy to do that. Well, I'll dedicate it to your dog.

Rehm: Maxie.

Collins: To Maxie. [Reads "Species"]

Rehm: That's just lovely. I really enjoyed that.

Collins: Thanks.

Rehm: I'm going to go to the phones, to Greg here in Washington, DC. You're on the air.

Greg: Thank you, Diane. And thank you, Mr. Collins, for your poetry. I love listening to you. A friend of mine went to one of your workshops and said you discourage your students from using a lot of adjectives. I try to write serious poetry, and I found that very challenging and wondered if you could say more about that?

Collins: Sure. I probably quoted Emerson, who talks about the speaking language of things, that objects and particularly objects in nature are already talking to us. I just find it very refreshing to read Japanese and Chinese poetry, especially earlier works of the seventeenth, eighteenth centuries, where there's just the tree, the bridge, the river, the pot, unadorned. And these objects take on a kind of integrity if you don't cover them in adjectives and other modifiers. So I just try to keep it simple. These objects, if you have any reverence for them, don't really need you to decorate them. They're fine just as they are.

Rehm: I wonder, however, whether you would agree with Greg that perhaps unadorned nouns make it a little more difficult to write poetry?

Collins: Well, it depends on what kind of poetry we're writing. [Laughs] And it should be said, at some point, Diane, that we're using this word *poetry*, which is a very broad word. I like to compare it to the word *sports*. If your program had a sports theme, you wouldn't have a badminton player, someone from the NFL and an Olympic swimmer.

Rehm: Together.

Collins: Together, right?

Rehm: Yeah. Right.

Collins: And have them talk about the future of sports in America. There are so many widely different verbal activities that go on under the umbrella heading of *poetry* that you could get three poets into your studio that would have as little in common with each other [Laughs] as those three athletes. So there is interesting, highly decorative poetry that's lush and full of sound effects. Gerard Manley Hopkins comes to mind.

Rehm: Aha.

Collins: Just amazing.

Rehm: "The Windhover."

Collins: Textural language that you can feel in your mouth and hear in your ear. I'm on a different kind of aesthetic. I love the poet Charles Simic, who writes with the most simple diction. But also, if you have a simple diction and unadorned nouns, once you deploy an interesting adjective, once you throw in a word like *luminescent*, it stands out against the background of that simplicity.

Rehm: You must have encountered a variety of poets and poetry as the poet laureate.

Collins: Well, even before that. But, that's really the beauty of it, the variety of it.

Rehm: Did you enjoy that year?

Collins: Partly. It was good for my self-esteem, for one thing, [Laughs] because you're the lead dog in American poetry for a couple of years. And I was quite honored by it, quite frankly. You'd have to be. But I did feel kind of drawn away from where I write by having a lot of public duties. But that's not to complain.

Rehm: You became involved in this Poetry in Motion project. Tell us about that.

Collins: Well that predated my laureateship, but I continue to be involved in it. I'm on the board of the Poetry Society of America, and we're the ones who came up with the whole idea of Poetry in Motion, putting poems on public transportation—buses and trains and subways. And that continues. Another thing I did was when I was poet laureate was to start a poetry channel on Delta Airlines. I got them to agree to that, somehow. I was really determined to do that, and I found out who does that and talked them into it. We'd pick a theme, like birds or music or love, and I would pick the poems, not my poems, but I'd read them. And then we've had a little jazz in between. So if you were on an airplane, and you didn't want to hear music or watch a movie, you could actually listen to poetry, and that lasted a couple of years.

Rehm: Good.

Collins: I'm all for poetry in public places, getting poetry out of the library, out of the classroom, off the bookshelves, where people tend to sequester it, and into public life.

Rehm: Here's a tweet from Johnny: "I'm curious if your guest has any thoughts about the format of Twitter as an avenue for poetry."

Collins: Well, let me tweet right back to you, Johnny. [Laughs] Interestingly, it's 140 characters, is that right? And there are actually 140 syllables in a sonnet because a sonnet is 14 lines long, and it has 10 syllables per line. I met someone who knew the guy who started it and said there's no connection there whatsoever [Laughs], but there *is* a connection. The postcard, the haiku, the sonnet, and the tweet, all of these give you a limited space in which to work. And that's one of the pressures of poetry, if you're writing formal poetry, a sonnet or a pantoum or a villanelle. And so it *is* a compression. You have to think before you write, or you *should* think before you write. Now there's that famous line of the guy writing his son and saying, "I'm sorry I wrote you such a long letter, I didn't have time to write a short one." You can't just go on and on. So they do have in common, tweeting and poetry, the idea that interesting things happen under compression.

Rehm: Here's a caller in Fort Wayne, Indiana. Billy, you're on the air.

Billy: Hi, Mr. Collins. First, I want to say that I have three books of your poetry. I think your poetry is intelligent, insightful, humorous, and poignant. And I have a question, but I don't think it's really a question. Maybe you've already answered or don't even care to answer. I've found over the years people that seem kind of elitist, who seemed embarrassed to say that they liked a Billy Collins poem. And it dumbfounded me, and I wondered if it was jealousy. I know you talked about how there's all kinds of poetry, and it's a subjective thing what people like. But I was wondering what you think that essence is. You said you like poetry that just speaks, that has very few adjectives. Lots of people whose poetry is wonderful break all the rules, let's say a Bukowski or people that use lots of adjectives, and yet there's something there? What is that essence that makes that poetry so beautiful and good?

Collins: Well that's an interestingly layered question. [Laughter] That last question is interesting. If you get rid of regular rhyme and meter, and you get rid of a sort of lush language, what is there left that is poetry? And the only thing I can say is it's some kind of authenticity of voice. Like Charles Bukowski, you believe in him. Even though the life he's describing is quite extraordinary [Laughs] or unusual, you buy in, and I can't judge that. One of the things we lose when we do lose regular rhyme and meter is a system of trust. A formal poet will never let you down. If Frost starts out, "whose woods these are I think I know," he will continue that beat and those rhymes to the end. So there's a trust system there, and the loss of it means that we have to compensate for that loss through something called "authenticity of voice," and that's very hard to describe, but you know it as soon as you read it.

Rehm: To Jesse in Santa Fe, New Mexico. Hi there.

Jesse: Hello, Diane, thank you so much for having me on. Billy Collins, I hope, will be referred to as "poet laureate emeritus." There's something just unseemly about "the former poet laureate."

Rehm: Okay, I hear you.

Jesse: I don't know if that's really a title he can have, but if I could bestow it upon him and maybe start a trend there. Every time I hear his name, I like to tell a story about the only time I saw him, which was at an event here in Santa Fe almost exactly fifteen years ago, and it was shortly after 9/11, [begins crying] and he spoke to an enormous room, and it was really touch and go. This was just a couple weeks after September 11 in 2001, and you just—you saved it for everybody. You just let everybody exhale, and it was so important.

Rehm: I agree, Jesse, and clearly so important to you. I can hear the emotion in your voice, which clearly you have conveyed to Billy Collins. Do you remember that day?

Collins: No, I don't actually. I'm very moved by his being moved by it, and I thank him for those words. I remember having to travel a lot right after 9/11. I remember being in Santa Fe, but I don't remember the actual experience or the emotional tenor of it.

Rehm: What *was* that like for you, traveling after September 11?

Collins: From September 11 to I think the first week in December, I was on 37 airplanes.

Rehm: Wow.

Collins: I'm fine with flying, but one of them landed in San Diego, and if you've ever landed there, the flight path takes you right through downtown, and the office buildings are higher than you are. You can see people working at their desks. A deep stillness fell over the airplane because here was the confluence of aircraft and skyscraper quite close to each other. Otherwise I was fine, but that was a little scary.

Rehm: Do you remember the emotional reaction of the audiences during that period of time?

Collins: Well, everyone was still very aware of it. My real reaction to 9/11 was caused by being asked by Congress, because I *was* poet laureate, to write a poem on the first anniversary of 9/11, when Congress met jointly in New York City, historically almost unprecedented. And I did write a poem called "The Names," which I recited in front of Congress, which was a good example of public and private language, actually. There had been a lot of speeches before my poem came up. Everyone was quite sincere, and it was sometimes moving, but it was kind of "public" language: heroism and the nation and that kind of thing. And my poem started with an image of rain at night, and the congresspeople looked up like they had heard something strange, like a whistle to a border collie or something. And suddenly they realized it was poetry. But it was a very distinct change of verbal equality and mood that took place there, not to compliment the poem, but to point out the palpable difference between the private language of poetry with imagery and more abstract language of politics.

Rehm: And an email from Margaret, who says, "I've always found the flow of your phrasing to be almost stream of consciousness. Can you tell us about your method of writing, editing and finalizing your poetry?

Collins: Well, it's stream of consciousness with about ten revisions. [Laughs] Yeats said this, too. We labor to sound spontaneous. It takes work to sound convincingly spontaneous. So most of my poems are written in one sitting. That's the run of the poem from beginning, middle, to end. When I do go back, it's not so much *revising* as *refining*, refining the sound and the cadence of it.

Rehm: What about poetry at marriages, poetry at funerals, poetry at staged events?

Collins: Yes, poetry after 9/11. After 9/11 people said we *turn* to poetry at these times, implying that people have had their backs to poetry all the other times. So a poem comes up at a wedding or a funeral or a tragic event as a stabilizing factor, I think. It's something people can even memorize, but because of its form, it tends to stabilize emotion and honor it and also connect you with the past. You can read a poem that was written two centuries ago at a funeral or a wedding and realize that centuries of human beings have felt the same way.

Rehm: To Barry in Ashburn, Virginia, you're on the air.

Barry: Hi, I've got two questions that are unrelated. First is—and I'm kind of an ignoramus when it comes to poetry—I'm trying to understand the difference between blank verse and prose. Is there some sort of dividing line? I think he may have touched upon this a little bit in what you were saying earlier with respect to some poet that's a little more difficult to read. Is it just that you know it when you read it?

Collins: No, well blank verse is a term in English metrics. It means unrhymed iambic pentameter, so ba-dum-ba-dum-ba-dum-ba-dum, five of those, and it's not rhymed at the ends of lines. And prose doesn't have to pay any attention to that.

Barry: My second question, I love the poem "Jabberwocky," and the words in it are completely made up. Why do we like it and kind of understand it even though the words are undefined?

Collins: Well, it's pure language fun: "'twas brillig." It actually sounds like brillig should be a word, so it's not complete nonsense because it's following English syntax. It's sounding like a sentence, but the words don't make any sense. I don't know; it's pure joy. It's like the joy in rock 'n' roll when someone sings "be-bop-a-loo-la" or "koo-koo-ka-joo." There's so much play involved in language. We've defined poetry with phrases like "opening our hearts and memories to encounter the world." I'm quoting from the *New York Times*. But in writing poetry it's pure self-entertainment; it's pure fun, and that's just language. In "Jabberwocky" language is let loose in a dog park to kind of run around and collide into each other.

Rehm: Now here's a tweet from Ronald, who says, "I love listening to poetry, but I have a hard time reading it. What is the secret to reading poetry?"

Collins: Well, when you hear it, you usually are not alone. Maybe the caller is experiencing a difference between being alone and being with other people. You can try reading it out loud, but it takes some gift to read poetry out loud, actually. I would say when you're reading it, just try to hear it in your head. Another poet pointed out that the skull is kind of an auditorium. When we're reading silently, we're actually silently hearing it, if you will. I don't know, I would rather read it alone than hear it, myself.

Rehm: Would you read for us one last poem of your choice as we close?

Collins: Well, let me read this little poem called "December First," and I'll just tell you my mother's maiden name was McIsaak. They were from Scotland or the Hebrides. I mention that. [Reads "December First"]

Rehm: Billy Collins, poet laureate emeritus.

Collins: Thank you, Diane, for having me on your program.

Q and A with Billy Collins

John Cusatis / 2016

This interview appeared in the *Post and Courier* (Charleston, SC) digital edition on October 8, 2016, in a slightly shortened form, as a supplement to John Cusatis's review of Collins's *The Rain in Portugal*. It is reprinted with permission of the *Post and Courier*.

John Cusatis: As US poet laureate you created Poetry 180 to turn readers back to poetry. What do you feel turns people away from poetry, especially since we are so naturally drawn to it as children?

Billy Collins: A critical reason for the absence of poetry in the everyday life of most Americans is that our first exposure to poetry happens in school, in the artificial environment of the classroom. We begin to think of "poetry" as another subject to be learned along with "geometry" and "sociology." So, when we leave school (for many, at the end of college) we leave poetry behind with all the other subjects that seem irrelevant or even useless to our postgraduate pursuits. Poetry 180 was aimed at presenting to high school students clear, hospitable, contemporary poems not to be studied, but to be listened to and enjoyed. It was also meant to balance the classroom emphasis on interpretation by presenting students with poems whose "meaning" was largely apparent and did not require the intervention of teachers.

Cusatis: What kept you from being disenchanted with poetry when you were in high school?

Collins: I was in high school from 1955 to 1959. Interesting times for an adolescent. The birth of rock 'n' roll, the appearance of Elvis, *Rebel without a Cause* (the first movie using a teenage point of view), really good recorded jazz, and the emergence of Beat literature. I'm overlooking the threats of polio and nuclear annihilation, which cast long shadows over those years. I carried around the little City Lights books—Ginsberg's *Howl*, Corso's *Gasoline*, and Ferlinghetti's *Coney Island of the Mind*. They formed a revolutionary disruption of the manners of the traditional poetry we were being taught (by priests and brothers, I might add). The poets in the textbooks were all dead and had three names. I devoted myself to writing dreadfully unconvincing "Beat" poems, decrying the evils of capitalism and called for a radical change in American values. I was sixteen. I didn't even know how to smoke.

Cusatis: You left the East Coast to attend graduate school at UC, Riverside, during the sixties, where you befriended the San Francisco Renaissance poet Jack Spicer. Did you encounter other San Francisco poets?

Collins: I lived in the Haight during the so-called Summer of Love, mostly because I had failed one part of my PhD orals (Colonial American lit). I had to retake that part, but they weren't giving it again until the fall. My girlfriend and I drove north and joined the goings-on. Only—there were no real bars and no bookstores because the movement moved on music and drugs, not alcohol and literature. You had to go to North Beach for that. I hung out in a working-class/literary bar on Green Street. Jack Spicer was a regular and had his own table. Brautigan and others drifted in. Always on the edge of the action, I didn't have any close association with the SF poets. I wasn't really published yet. But we would sit in the park with Spicer some afternoons. You would bring him a couple of quarts of Ranier Ale, and he would talk about poetry.

Cusatis: Speaking of Richard Brautigan, your poems often call his work to mind. I know you've read his legendary novel *Trout Fishing in America*, but did you read his poems as well?

Collins: In 1967–68 I fell under the spell of Brautigan and wrote a lot of little wiggy poems. One magazine editor returned a bunch of these and said they seemed like poor versions of Brautigan, and he was right. I was still learning. A couple of years ago I agreed to write an introduction to a re-issue of *Trout Fishing in America*. I was surprised that the book held up as well as it did.

Cusatis: You studied with the poet Robert Peters, and Miller Williams guided the publication of your first major collection. Were there other mentors along the way?

Collins: Robert Peters was the first teacher I had who taught poetry *as poetry*. His field was Victorian. We might spend an hour on a dozen lines of Tennyson. At first, I found it frustrating. I wanted the big picture, so it took a while before I realized I was learning about sound, rhythm, form, stanzas—the nuts and bolts. And Miller Williams taught me by mail what was good about my poems at the time. He put a paper clip on maybe seventeen of the fifty poems I had sent him. Seventeen good ones. I tossed the rest and began to write poems that lived up to the standard set by the good ones. When I submitted again, almost two years later, he published my first real book, *The Apple That Astonished Paris*. But my best teachers were all waiting for me on the shelves of the library. I never took a workshop; I just read and imitated, sometimes so slavishly the results were travesties of the originals, but I was learning something along the way.

Cusatis: Blues and jazz pervade your work. What about rock 'n' roll? In "Cosmology," from your new book, you imagine the earth balancing on the head of Keith Richards. In a biographical note in *The Ardis Anthology of American Poetry* [1977], you claimed that you were, at the time, "working on a biography of Keith Richards." Were you?

Collins: Saying in a contributor's note that I was "working on a biography of Keith Richards" was a joke. What is there to say? Who would read it? Back then, rock figures did not draw biographical attention. Of course, these days everyone who scores a goal needs a biography, and Keith has told his own story in *Life*. I was fourteen when rock 'n' roll appeared. *Rebel without a Cause*, Elvis, doo-wop all occurred in my teen age years. A contemporary of mine's mother used to call him "the original teenager." So I love rock 'n' roll, as a t-shirt might spell out; trouble is, my persona prefers jazz. We're not the same guy. He drinks tea; I drink coffee. He's more sensitive, probably because he's never had a job.

Cusatis: Like musicians, painters also figure into your new book. When and how did you become interested in the visual arts?

Collins: I have a few abstract expressionist painter friends, but my taste in painting is usually very conservative, favoring still-lifes and nineteenth-century landscape scenes. I think it's possible to love Constable *and* Turner. I took oil painting classes for a while just to be able to better appreciate its difficulties. It's one thing to paint an orange, another to paint a crystal decanter on a glass table-top.

Cusatis: Poems such as "Joy" from *The Rain in Portugal* are reminiscent of the British Romantics, particularly Wordsworth and Coleridge, who called their readers' attention to the extraordinary beauty of ordinary things. You wrote your doctoral dissertation on the Romantics. What was your focus?

Collins: My dissertation was titled "The World's Ear: The Romantic Search for an Audience." I attributed to Wordsworth and Coleridge a problem, that being the lack of an audience for this new kind of poetry. Wordsworth: the poet "must create the taste by which he is enjoyed." They tried to relieve this anxiety by addressing friends, relatives, and especially each other. My dissertation did not have the makings of a book; it was just a dissertation. It's odd to look back on that and realize that I was interested in the question of audience when you consider that my career in poetry could be seen as the gradual acquisition of an audience of readers.

Cusatis: Two writers whom you mentioned when my students at the School of the Arts interviewed you in 2010 are Freud and Sartre. In what ways did these thinkers modify your perception of the world?

Collins: Freud and Sartre: if you hadn't read them when I was growing up, you had to at least pretend you had by conspicuously carrying their books around. The "oceanic feeling" in Freud's *Civilization and its Discontents* gave me a new understanding of religion, and his sense of "civilization" as an inhibiting force only confirmed my worse suspicions. Of course, early on, I equated "civilization" with my parents!

A Conversation with Billy Collins

Anthony Borruso / 2018

This interview was conducted during Collins's visit to Butler University in Indianapolis, Indiana, as part of the Vivian S. Delbrook Visiting Writers Series in the spring of 2018. It appeared in *Booth*, the literary journal of the Butler University MFA Program, on September 21, 2018. It is reprinted with the permission of Anthony Borruso.

Anthony Borruso: During your reading here, you said that as a young man you were under the impression that a poet has to be a miserable and tortured soul. When did you realize that poetry could be funny?

Billy Collins: It wasn't something I realized by myself. Like most information that a poet gets about poetry, I got it from other poets. There were a number of poets I was reading at the time: Philip Larkin, James Wright, James Dickey. And then there was a group of Southern California poets like Ron Koertge.

Borruso: Wright and Dickey are pretty serious.

Collins: Oh, yeah, more serious than not. But there are flashes of humor. Dickey has a poem called "Falling," which is based on the true story of a stewardess being sucked out of an airplane and dying, of course. He imagines her being conscious as she plummets to the ground—her skirt is described as being like a bat wing. He calls her "the greatest thing to ever hit Nebraska." But then we also have the New York School: John Ashbery, Kenneth Koch, and Frank O'Hara. I was reading them a lot in my thirties, and they are all issuing unmistakable permission slips to use humor. Each poet has his own balance of seriousness and levity. Koertge is pretty far out on the levity end of the scale, and Dickey is on the serious end. But they're all closer to humor than poets had been before.

Borruso: I've seen you lumped in with the New York School poets. Is that a style you identify with?

Collins: Well, to some degree. But I don't think anyone wants to be in a school. It's not like they all get together and formulate a group.

Borruso: I guess that could feel reductive.

Collins: Yes, you don't want to be put in a category. David Lehman wrote a book called *The Last Avant-Garde* about the New York poets. He disclaims the school in the beginning, but then he goes on to show a commonality—irony, essentially—that constitutes the general tone of the New York School. With a poet like Ashbery, there is a sense that you are always on the edge of laughter. Nothing is plain and serious unless it arises by mistake, or unexpectedly.

Borruso: When you're reading your work, you have an impeccable sense of timing. You seem to know just how long to linger on a funny line or a poignant image. Is this an innate talent or something you've consciously worked on?

Collins: I think it's God-given. [Laughs]

Borruso: You're the Michael Jordan of poem reading?

Collins: You have to put "laughing" in parentheses; otherwise readers will think I'm crazy. The rhythm that you hear when I'm reading is the rhythm that I have invested in the poem, or placed in the poem as I was writing it. You write with the ear to create sound. Writing with the foot—tapping it, so to speak—is another way of saying that I am always trying to get the cadence right. And it's not just because I might have to read the poem in public. The pauses are there in the poem, like a musical score, telling you when to rest. So it doesn't take any work. When I'm leading a workshop, I deal with the formal parts of a poem much more than the content. I'll point out a line or two that seem a bit flat-footed and say, "If you move the adverb a little closer to the verb, it would have this tripping cadence, and then you could end with an iamb." Some students see that and say, "Wow, that sounds much better," while others don't. It's like telling jokes. It requires timing. People who are bad at telling jokes usually don't have a great sense of rhythm. And it's important to remember that we are practicing an art that began in music. We don't want to completely lose touch with those musical origins.

Borruso: That's true. And music is what makes it memorable, right?

Collins: Sure, and the origins of poetry were probably just having a way to memorize stuff.

Borruso: Do you think this is why so many musicians show up in your poems?

Collins: That's a good question. I think there is some overlap there. I listen to a lot of music.

Borruso: When you write about music, sometimes instruments are transformed into animals: a piano becomes a "curious beast with its enormous moonlit smile," and a saxophone hangs from a musician's neck like "a golden fish." These instruments take on a life of their own, becoming autonomous from the person playing them. Does this connect to the experience of writing poetry?

Collins: It is animating them in a way, but it might have more to do with the metaphor and creating something fresh. When you read the poets of the past, you sometimes find a place for yourself in that work, even if it requires an ironic take. We take the topics of the older poets—love and death—just as seriously. But we cannot use the same language, like a Shakespearean sonnet. One reason to read is to find out what metaphors have been used up and what dots have already been connected. And there are bad metaphors: Some dots were not meant to be connected. If you say you're alone in the woods like Robert Frost and the snow is falling "like confetti," you've yanked us out of the poem totally—now we're at a parade or wedding. It might seem clever to the poet, but we're not in the woods anymore. The theme is ruined.

Borruso: That reminds me of a quote by Reverdy: "The more the relationship between the two juxtaposed realities is distant and true, the stronger the image will be—the greater its emotional power and poetic reality . . ." So the metaphor must be surprising, but also still true or appropriate.

Collins: Yes, that's true. And that might be what's happening with the saxophone and the golden fish.

Borruso: Those are very strange and effective ones. What I was trying to say with my initial question is that the metaphor seems to take control of the writer at a certain point—like the poem is telling you, "I want to be about this!"

Collins: You can employ a single metaphor, and if you get interested in it, it takes over. Then the rest of the poem, or a good part of the poem, engages this metaphor and works out different parts of it. You have what the critics will call an extended metaphor, and you'll find this in Milton and Pope and Wordsworth, just working out a metaphor over many lines. But what you said is very important in poetry—you'll find that a poem can take an interest in itself, or some aspect of itself, and that aspect will take over the poem. It grows out of proportion and escapes the original intention, so that the poem really becomes about the discovery and expansion of one metaphor.

Borruso: You've written a lot of *ars poetica*—poems that take on the idea of poetry as a central subject. Do you think that idea of finding and expanding the correct metaphor is why you write so many of them, so that you can enact that discovery on the page?

Collins: I suppose so, and I think it's also just my personal self-consciousness about being a poet and never wanting to swan into an auditorium with my cape. I'm always a little self-conscious about the serious-sounding high diction that people normally associate with poetry. I'm always trying to undercut that a little bit.

Borruso: That reminds me of your collection *Picnic, Lightning*, which opens with an epigraph by Yeats: "A poet . . . never speaks directly, / as to someone at the breakfast table."

Collins: Yes, I'm undercutting Yeats' seriousness there. I was working on a poem yesterday that had an epigraph from the poet Christopher Morley: "No man is lonely while eating spaghetti." Sometimes you discover a sentence like that and say, "I'm going to put that on the top of a poem and see what happens." Sometimes the epigraph is not just some cute afterthought but the reason why the poem started.

Borruso: There is a lot of absence in your poems. I'm thinking of your imaginary sister in "Only Child" and the dead dog persona in "The Revenant." Why write about what's not there rather than what is?

Collins: I think it's one thing to see what's there. I try to encourage students to write about what's in front of them. But, at the same time, if that's the only place we're able to go, we might as well just take a photograph. The imagination is supposed to, at some point, go to work on what's right there and move to a place where I have an imaginary reaction. I can say, I never wished for a sibling until my parents were ancient, and then I wanted a sister called Mary.

Borruso: Many of your poems take place in the domestic sphere. Why do you think they are such homebodies?

Collins: We're all experts on the familiar, domestic objects that we live with nearly every day. We know the paintings on the wall or whatever kind of decorative evidence of ourselves we put there. For me it's just a good place to start. The conversation poems by Coleridge were very influential for me because they all start at home: he's in his study with the fire going at night, or he's in his backyard under a lime tree, or he's looking at windows that have frosted over, and the poems always move into wide realms of intellectual, even religious speculation. I took those as a model for a lot of my poems. Now it's become kind of reflexive starting a poem. As an only child, I always played games on the floor of my bedroom, which was a very familiar place for me—this place of play. Adorno, or one of those thinkers, talks about defamiliarization, that you should defamiliarize the reader. I usually move the reader from someplace familiar to someplace unfamiliar.

Borruso: Yes, and I guess that's why it makes sense that you usually leave "the trigger" in your poems—that is, whatever object or experience seems to have inspired them.

Collins: That's a great way to get the reader on board, so the reader doesn't think the first line just occurred to you while you were standing on a rooftop yelling at the neighbors. Starting with the composition situation seems to me a good place to start. The thing is, you have to go somewhere; you can't just stay there describing your cabinet or the flowers on your desk.

Borruso: What do you think about poetry's place in considering important historical moments—those that are surprising, or tragic, or extraordinary. Florida poet Peter Meinke has said, "Everyone recognizes that at crucial times prose just doesn't cut it. When we fall in love, when we get married, or have a baby, when somebody dies, prose doesn't do it. We need poetry at these times." Do you agree?

Collins: I agree that poetry picks up where prose leaves off. Apart from highly experimental novels, fiction has certain restrictions that the poet breaks free of, and that's where it seems to take over. Probably we turn to poems in times of crisis, anxiety, and uncertainty because they convey a comforting sense of stability. The poems people traditionally turned to were formal poems stabilized by rhyme and meter. Those two levels of stability made poetry something you could lean on—it was dependable, it was repeatable—whereas prose just goes on and on and on. You have to read maybe forty pages of Emerson before you find a quote that would be helpful at this wedding or this funeral. But the poem is right there, naked on the page, waiting for you.

Borruso: Do you think this current political time is one where poetry seems more important?

Collins: Politically speaking, I think some people in the arts community are starting to feel the effects of these budget cuts, and it might get a lot worse. The NEA and smaller communities that depend on grants might be in trouble. Trump has so much on his plate. I don't even know if he's capable of keeping all those balls in the air at once—certainly not in the situation he's now in, where he wants to break one nuclear deal and make another one. I hope he's so preoccupied with those things he doesn't put the arts in his sights.

Borruso: At your reading you suggested that Trump take up gardening. I was wondering how you thought that would help him.

Collins: Well, it's just funny thinking about him gardening at Mar-a-Lago or the White House. Also, gardening informs you on those most basic things—life and death, the seasons—and it rewards you with blossoms and vegetables. Just getting your hands in the soil is nice. It's one of the things most rich people don't do, like raking leaves or splitting wood. There are so many good physical activities that wealthy people don't do because they have other people do it for them. Shouldn't we see that as a form of impoverishment?

Borruso: That makes me think of the physical and sensual pleasures of cooking that we see in "Osso Buco" and "Clam Ode." Are you big into cooking?

Collins: I don't do most of the cooking at home, but I do like to cook sometimes. I think that's the same pleasure—another thing rich people don't tend to do. William Matthews said, "Happiness begins with an onion." So much of cooking, and particularly Italian cooking, begins with some olive oil in a pan, then you chop up onions and throw them in, and then the whole house smells good . . . like, "Hey, what's for dinner?" That pleasant smell fills you with anticipation. Things like cooking and gardening are good to learn, to some extent.

Borruso: Yeah, it seems to me a gardener would be less likely to hit the nuclear button.

Collins: There should be a rule. Before you hit the button, you have to garden for three hours and think about it, or shoot baskets or something.

Borruso: That's a good idea! To finish up, I was wondering, since you've written so many collections, how do your concerns change from one to the next . . . that is, if they change at all?

Collins: I'm not the best person to ask because I see more similarities than differences. Like most poets, I'm stuck with the same two or three messages, like carpe diem or being a spokesman for being grateful or kind. At the same time, I think of each poem as a new beginning. You know, I write about actual subjects. Once my poems have subjects, they're not just watercolors trying to create some movie. My problem, having written like a dozen collections, is running out of topics, running out of subject matter. Once you write a poem about looking at a match, you have to cross that out like you would cross out a clue in a crossword puzzle. There are very similar veins running through my poems, and the tone of the poems seems to be consistently playful and ironic, shifting into the serious at some points. You have to just be careful not to imitate yourself. You learn a lot about poetry by imitating other poets, but you try not to get to the point where there's no one else to imitate but yourself.

Borruso: Yes, and even in your newest book, *The Rain in Portugal*, I still get the sense that you're surprising yourself. For example, in your poem "Greece," there is a moment when the speaker writes, "Is not poetry a megaphone / held up to the whispering lips of death?" It feels like a moment of true discovery.

Collins: Well, it was such a discovery that I then just threw myself in the ocean with a shout.

Borruso: And that's that carpe diem theme again, but it feels fresh in that moment.

Collins: Thank you. After I wrote that megaphone line, I didn't want to end on this big pronouncement, so I said, "Well, I'd better just go for a swim!"

Poet Billy Collins on Jazz and Poetry

Bob Hecht / 2019

This interview was broadcast on jazz aficionado Bob Hecht's podcast, *The Joys of Jazz*, in August 2019. The two-part show, which included several jazz recordings by musicians who are alluded to in Collins's poetry, can be heard at https://www.thejoysofjazz.com/poet-billy -collins-on-jazz-poetry-part-1/ and https://www.thejoysofjazz.com/poet-billy-collins-on-jazz -poetry-part-2/. Printed with the permission of Bob Hecht.

Bob Hecht: Billy Collins, welcome to *The Joys of Jazz*.

Billy Collins: Well, thank you. Great to be here.

Hecht: As you know, I've been a big fan of your poetry for a long time now, ever since a jazz friend of mine sent me a few of your poems back in the mid-nineties. In a couple of them were references to jazz. Now, for me, jazz poetry can be kind of a self-conscious thing, *quite* self-conscious at times. It doesn't always work for me, but these poems were different. They were simply about everyday life experiences in which jazz sometimes featured a role. And the feeling I got was that here was a guy, the writer, the persona in these poems, who really gets jazz and is writing about it as naturally and unaffectedly as he's writing about everything else. And I've been an avid reader of your work ever since.

Collins: Well, at last someone who understands me. [Laughs] That's pretty much how jazz fits into my poetry, in the same way that any aspect of my life becomes a theme. That includes having a dog or a cat or the clouds passing over the house. And jazz is often playing when I'm at home. If jazz has some metaphoric value or if it is casually mentioned, it becomes the atmosphere of the poem. That's how jazz fits in. There are, in fact, two kinds of jazz poetry, so to speak, that I don't find very interesting. One is when the poem tries to sound like jazz itself, jazzy poetry. The poem is syncopated, or the attempt is there, often ending in a kind of word salad or words spread out across the page in the manner of e. e. cummings. Poetry is poetry, and jazz is jazz. So the attempt to blend one with the other is usually not successful. The other one is kind of a name-dropping jazz poem, where people are mentioned by their nicknames, like "Bird" and "Diz" and "Bud" and "Prez." It's like the poet is saying, "I'm going to shoot pool with "Diz" after I finish writing this poem." [Laughter] The intimacy is pretended. [Laughs] It reminds me of that Terry Southern story called "You're Too Hip, Baby" about a white guy in Paris who is hanging around with all these black musicians at clubs. He's dressing hip, and he's talking hip. He's at the scene every night, and he's being ignored, cold-shouldered. He asks one of the guys, "How come I can't fit in here?" And the guy says, "Well, you're just too hip, baby." [Laughter] In the wrong way. Because of those two errors, I think, I try to let jazz play a more casual role in the poem.

Hecht: There's another difference between jazz and poetry that you've commented on in an earlier conversation with me. That has to do with revision, the fact that when you're playing jazz, you're not revising as you are as a poet.

Collins: Right. I think I might have said that there's no eraser on a saxophone. [Laughter] Improvisation, as we all know, is spontaneous composition. You can't go back and make something better. You can rerecord the tune, but you can't go back and erase notes. And I have heard it said that if you make a mistake in classical music, it's an error. If you make a mistake in jazz, you just repeat the mistake, [Laughs] and it becomes the new theme.

Hecht: Make it part of the creative effort.

Collins: Right. So, another way to deal with the impossibility of on-the-spot revision is just to make the mistake part of the tune.

Hecht: I believe that jazz entered your life fairly early. I wonder if you could tell me how you got onto the music.

Collins: Well, it was, I would say, an epiphanic moment, a big, transitional moment, the first time I heard jazz. I was, I think, fourteen years old. We lived in New York City, but my mother is from what was then rural Canada, in Ontario. Most summers we would go to Canada, which was a great relief from the city for me. I don't have brothers and sisters. If you're an only child, one thing you really enjoy are cousins, and I had tons of cousins in Canada. Cousins are sort of optional, unlike brothers and sisters, [Laughs] but they play the *role* of brothers and sisters. My uncle had a farm there, and he owned a restaurant and inn called the Owaisa Lodge, which was right on Lake Simcoe. One day I was mowing the lawn, and this speedboat pulled up to the dock. Two couples got out. I'd never seen people like them. The guys had goatees, and the girls were wearing Capri pants and ponytails. They were original beatniks, late hipsters, early beatniks. I don't know which. [Laughs] They immediately set up a Victrola record player. You could plug in right there on the dock. They put on a record, and a couple of them were dancing a little bit. The record they put on was the Benny Goodman 1938 concert at Carnegie Hall.

Hecht: Wow.

Collins: Absolutely a desert island recording. This was about 1955, so it wasn't that old. It was, what, seventeen years old, but it wasn't as old as it is now, obviously. In fact, I think the record was not issued until 1950, so it was really just five years out. I just stopped mowing [Laughs] and used the lawnmower to lean on as I listened to "One O'clock Jump" and "Sing, Sing, Sing," "Avalon," all these songs. I had never heard this before. I not only wanted to keep listening to this kind of music for the rest of my life, but I wanted to be one of those guys with a goatee and a girlfriend wearing capris and a ponytail. [Laughter] I bought into the whole thing.

Hecht: An instant conversion.

Collins: That was the magic moment.

Hecht: What was it about the music that really grabbed you, Billy?

Collins: Well, I guess the essence of jazz, the percussion, the steady *driving* percussion on most of these upbeat tunes. And the whole idea of taking a solo. By never hearing jazz, I had never heard the *configuration* of jazz: playing the head, everybody taking a solo, and then going back to the head at the end. It was clear that they were going one at a time, showing off their virtuoso ability to play this instrument, and then the group joined them at the end. That caught my attention right away.

Hecht: There's a famous quotation from Walter Pater about music and art, in which he said, "All art aspires toward the condition of music." Not to belabor this connection between your poetry and music, but I believe you've talked about trying to make your poetry musical, in a sense.

Collins: Well, I don't use metronomic meter. I don't set out to write iambic tetrameter or pentameter, although I've taught English poetry for many decades, and I've spent thousands of hours reading it. And I think I've internalized some of the cadence of English poetry, which is basically an iambic beat. But I'm writing with my ear, and I'm trying to get the rhythm of what Robert Frost called "sentence sounds," that is, not so much tick-tock- tick-tock, iambic, but the rhythms of spoken English.

Hecht: I feel like your poetry is akin to jazz in another way, too. When I read one of your poems, I often feel like you're taking me on a little ride, an unpredictable yet friendly ride, the same way a jazz solo does. It feels spontaneous, like it's being made up on the spot. How do you approach writing? Is it done in one sitting? What's your approach?

Collins: I think what you're getting at is the poem as a kind of reverie, a meditation that starts in one place and, usually by a chain of associations or some other means, leads the poet to another place. In fact, I was just reading this morning on *The Writer's Almanac*, it's the birthday of Alexander Fleming, who discovered Pennsyl . . . [Laughs] Pennsylvania, that's good, *penicillin*. [Laughter] See that's poetry, right there. [Laughs] He discovered penicillin by accident. He left a Petri dish uncovered and came back in the morning and found this thing growing and called it *penicillin*. He said we often discover things when we're not looking for them. I think that's often the way a poem goes, from a known thing to a series of little discoveries. It's always kind of following a thread or following crumbs you find in the woods, but it's a little trip for me. And I do try to write all my poems in one sitting because I want to keep driving through until I get to sniffing out the path of the poem and finally discovering an ending. That's a point of settlement where I'm very confident that I don't want to say anymore, or you don't want to *hear* any more. [Laughter]

Hecht: But you are striving to make it sound natural and of the moment, like a jazz artist does, right?

Collins: Well I have a poem called "Snow," and one of the things it does, at least in the beginning, is that it just focusses on the "o" sound. And I'd be happy to read that.

Hecht: I'd love to hear that.

Collins: Okay, [Laughs] I was hoping you would say that. [Laughter] [Reads "Snow"]

Hecht: So, I think it's safe to say that you admire Thelonious Monk.

Collins: Oh, yes. I think *admiration* is not quite the word. *Revere*, I might throw in there, or some other more intense word. I think everybody does. He's an amazing composer. And no one plays Monk like Monk. Let's just get that out of the way. [Laughs] This sounds a little radicle and dismissive, but I don't see why people cover Monk. Every time I listen to a cover, it just isn't Monk. And it's not an interesting spin, as some covers are; it's just a lesser thing. No one else took advantage of the silences in jazz, and no one else made dissonance an almost constant feature.

Hecht: And, as you mention, his use of silence and space—nobody else plays quite like that.

Collins: Yes. His silences are [Laughs] more silent than other silences. [Laughter] Someone said, and I think this is very true, that you can judge the quality of the poem by the intensity of the silence that exists after you finish reading it.

Hecht: Wow, that's great. So, you play some jazz piano yourself, right?

Collins: Not in front of anybody [Laughs] but, yes, I do. [Laughter] I've had a piano for quite a few years, and I took a couple of years of lessons. I think I took it from the wrong teacher. He was a very good teacher, but I think he was aiming too high. He revered Bud Powell. I was hoping to be maybe a third-rate Horace Silver. I wanted to play bluesy piano. But he taught me the basics. It was certainly worth it, and I began to understand the fundamentals of jazz. I think first hearing jazz as a kid leaning on a lawnmower in Canada, I could tell that there was a sequence of solos, but the rest of it sounded completely wild and crazy, all over the place; just play what you want to, liberated. But when I started to study jazz, I realized it is entirely held together by a sequence of chords, and everybody knows exactly where they are in the song. There is an anecdote about—I'm pretty sure it was Lester Young—who was in a recording studio, and he stopped playing midtune. All the other musicians looked around, and he said that he'd forgotten the words to the song. [Laughter] Not only [Laughs] did he not have a singer, and not only did he know where he was in the chord structure, he knew the *words* to the song. The words were actually guiding his playing, which was an amazing insight.

Hecht: In that poem that you read, "Snow," there is, as there is in so much of your work, an awareness of the present moment. It's kind of like haiku, in a sense, to me. It draws me in and puts me right into the time and the place. And often, I think uniquely, you even include some reference to the moment of composition in the poem.

Collins: Well, that's true. I want to get the reader into the poem in the beginning. The best way to do that, I've found and have learned from others, is to present the compositional moment, the moment of writing. Talk about the weather or what you're listening to or what you're looking at. That's something a reader can't argue with. I want to start with something that the reader has to accept. Stephen Dobyns, a wonderful poet and critic, said that if you get the reader to accept something small in the beginning of the poem, they'll be more susceptible to accepting more demanding, challenging things later in the poem. So it is similar to a haiku moment. I'm sitting here doing this, and then hopefully the poem goes somewhere more interesting than just sitting here doing the same thing. [Laughs]

Hecht: Another poem that, for me, reflects that kind of present moment experience of the world is the wonderful "Man Listening to Disc," which has such a feeling of movement in it, as you're walking in Manhattan, while listening to Monk and Sonny Rollins through earphones. Tell me about that poem.

Collins: This is a really dated poem in a way because I'm listening to a Discman. This was before [Laughs] a lot of innovations in listening technology. It's a poem about how *surrounding* the sound is while walking through a big city, and I start thanking each individual member of the quartet, like Monk and Sonny Rollins and other people for actually accompanying me, literally, down 42nd Street, somehow, with the drums and piano on wheels or some other odd conveyance.

Hecht: Would you read that one for us?

Collins: [Reads "Man Listening to Disc"]

Hecht: The engagement of the reader seems to be very important in your work, and some poets might feel that it would be an insult to label their work "reader friendly," but not in your case. You really care about the reader.

Collins: Well, I don't want to be alone. [Laughs]. Writing, as you know, is a solo activity. It really intensifies your aloneness. I have some company when I'm writing, and that is all the poets I've read, all the poets who are influencing my poem, even though it may be on a subconscious level. But also, in using the speech of English, I'm engaging a listener, so I always feel accompanied by that listener. As I compose a poem, I'm usually flipping back and forth from being the poet to being the reader to see how a reader, a complete stranger, would have read those first five lines that I wrote. I'm writing subjectively, but I try to switch back into a more objective view as I go along. In that way, I'm trying to keep the reader with me.

Hecht: And you often employ humor and conversational language in your poems, which is so refreshing. Is that a purposeful strategy?

Collins: I think a very conversational start is another way to get the reader on board. It's a kind of welcoming voice or an inclusive voice. I'm not making any demands on the reader too early. And that's what's wrong with a lot of poetry, I find, poems that I don't finish reading. It's very easy to stop reading a poem because the investment has been so small. You've invested maybe twenty-five seconds of your life as opposed to reading 150 pages of a novel and quitting. So, one of the reasons that I do quit is that the poem is making unreasonable demands on me right away, in the first few lines, and we haven't really been introduced. In other words, the poet makes her move too soon. I guess by saying that, I'm admitting that I think of the poem as a kind of social engagement. The presence of the reader in the poem is very vital to its continuing.

Hecht: I read an interview in which you talked about your poetic voice, your persona. And you said that your persona is "by nature a daydreamer, whose favorite toys are his thoughts." [See Andy Kuhn, "Interview with Billy Collins"]

Collins: Well, that's a steal from Coleridge, who talked about making "a toy of thought." Being an only child is an excellent preparation for being a poet because you spend a lot of time by yourself, and that leads to the kind of associative daydreaming that poems run by, for the most part. Yes, I think one has to have "downtime," as they call it these days. It was just "time" when I was a child. [Laughs] There was no downtime. It just continued. But I'm more creative when nothing is going on. In a way, I think of boredom as not a blank period to endure. I think of boredom as a prelude to creativity. It's really when I'm flatlining and there is not much to do and nothing on the calendar that poetic possibility opens itself up to me.

Hecht: How often do you write?

Collins: Not as often as you'd think. [Laughs] Not daily, certainly. I don't have a daily habit. Catullus said, "Never a day without a line." But I've let a lot of days go by without writing a single line. I'm getting a book together now to be published late next year, I hope. I get enough good poems every couple of years to make a book. That's really the pace of composition that is, for me, sufficient. It was Max Beerbohm, the humorist, who said that the most difficult thing about being a poet was figuring out what to do with the remaining twenty-three and a half hours of the day. [Laughter] Often the poem comes pretty quickly. I'd love to read this poem, a pretty new poem, about Hank Mobley, who is someone I'm listening to a lot these days. It's got a very long title. It's called "Listening to Hank Mobley around Eleven O'clock after a Long, Fun, Boozy Dinner, the Four of Us at Captain Pig's, Our Favorite Restaurant in Town." [Reads "Listening to Hank Mobley"]

Hecht: That's wonderful.

Collins: The cat comes to the rescue there. I wouldn't know how to end the poem without the cat. [Laughs]

Hecht: There's another poem based on your observations of people listening to music in jazz clubs, the delightful "The Many Faces of Jazz." Would you read that one for us?

Collins: Sure. There is a little play on words in the title, "The Many Faces of Jazz." You would think it's the many *aspects* of jazz, but it's literally the faces. [Reads "The Many Faces of Jazz"]

Hecht: That's great. I love how you poke fun at the ways that people listen to the music, which can be observed regularly in a jazz club. [Laughter]

There is often in your work this mixture of pathos and humor, which of course, that combination of ingredients is also present in the blues and is wonderfully highlighted in another of your poems, titled simply "The Blues." Would you read that one for us?

Collins: Sure. I'd be happy to. [Reads "The Blues"] I wanted to put an epigraph to that poem, but I didn't think about it at the time. The epigraph would be, "Nobody loves me but my mother, and she might be jivin' me, too." [Laughter] I'm not sure who composed that [Laughs] but it's one of my favorite blues lines.

Hecht: The great tenor saxophonist Sonny Rollins makes more than one appearance in your poetry. It's clear you are a fan—do you have a favorite Rollins album?

Collins: *Way Out West* is one of my very favorites, and I even have a poem about desiring to be Sonny Rollins. I think this might be the place for it. I don't know.

Hecht: This would be the perfect place for it.

Collins: I think with most people who listen to jazz, there's a little envy if you're not a player, probably especially if you *are* a player. The poem is called "Being Sonny Rollins." [Reads "Being Sonny Rollins"]

Hecht: [Laughter] That's great.

Collins: Thank you.

Hecht: I read on Marc Myers' JazzWax blog that he actually read that poem *to* Sonny Rollins and got a big guffaw out of him.

Collins: I was aware of that. I know Marc, and I'm a big fan of JazzWax.

Hecht: Well that must have been very gratifying.

Collins: It was the closest I've come to being Sonny Rollins. I'll say that, anyway. [Laughter]

Hecht: Your poetry has reached such an unusually large audience. Did you ever dream that you'd reach so many people through your poems?

Collins: Oh, no. [Laughs] If I had dreamed, I would have picked the wrong genre. I could have dreamed about being a famous movie producer or something. I think what motivates artistic creation is jealousy, basically. Before I was published, I was jealous of just about any poet who was published. And I had publication fantasies, but these fantasies were quite modest in size and scope. I thought if I got published by a university press, which I did, the University of Pittsburgh Press and the University of Arkansas Press, and if my books sold, I don't know, a thousand copies, 1,500 copies? If fifteen hundred people in the world would know who I am, I could die a happy man. [Laughs] So, I had very modest dreams. I'll tell you how it happened, actually, besides just the intrinsic charm of all these poems I'm reading! Basically, it was NPR. Following the publication in 1997 of a book titled *Picnic, Lighting*, I was on Terry Gross's *Fresh Air* and on Garrison Keillor's *Prairie Home Companion*. And there you have a listening audience of, I think, three or four million people. And that actually changed everything. That created a kind of quantum leap in the size of my readership.

Hecht: Well, we're all very grateful for that. And, Billy, I just want to thank you for your time and your willingness to read some of your work. It's been a great pleasure to talk with you. So, thank you.

Collins: Oh, you're very welcome. The pleasure has been completely mutual.

"The Pure Musicality of Language": Billy Collins Speaks with AP Literature Students

Charleston School of the Arts / 2019

This interview was conducted on December 10, 2019, via conference call between John Cusatis's AP English literature class at the School of the Arts (SOA) in Charleston, SC, and Billy Collins, who spoke from his home in Winter Park, Florida. Interviewers were Cusatis and the following students: Hannah Burton, Alex Clifford, Maya Cline, Caroline Conway, Ellen Emge, Hannah Jones, Christina Lewis, Luke Shaw, Layla Wheelon, John White, and Kitty Zheng. It appears in print for the first time in this collection.

School of the Arts: Hello, Professor Collins.
Billy Collins: Hello.
SOA: How are you this morning?
Collins: Doing fine. How's everyone doing?
SOA: Great. We've got eleven students here who are ready to talk to you. Say "hello," students. [Collective "Hi, Professor Collins!"]
Collins: Hello, students!
SOA: We've had a good time discussing your work for the past few weeks. You and I talked about your beginning with an early poem and closing with a new one.
Collins: Right, have you read "Candle Hat"?
SOA: Yes, we have, and we each have a copy in front of us.
Collins: Okay, this is "Candle Hat":

In most self-portraits it is the face that dominates:
Cézanne is a pair of eyes swimming in brushstrokes,
Van Gogh stares out of a halo of swirling darkness,

Rembrandt looks relieved as if he were taking a breather
from painting *The Blinding of Sampson*.

But in this one Goya stands well back from the mirror
and is seen posed in the clutter of his studio
addressing a canvas tilted back on a tall easel.

He appears to be smiling out at us as if he knew
we would be amused by the extraordinary hat on his head
which is fitted around the brim with candle holders,
a device that allowed him to work into the night.

You can only wonder what it would be like
to be wearing such a chandelier on your head
as if you were a walking dining room or concert hall.

But once you see this hat there is no need to read
any biography of Goya or to memorize his dates.

To understand Goya you only have to imagine him
lighting the candles one by one, then placing
the hat on his head, ready for a night of work.

Imagine him surprising his wife with his new invention,
then laughing like a birthday cake when she saw the glow.
Imagine him flickering through the rooms of his house
with all the shadows flying across the walls.

Imagine a lost traveler knocking on his door
one dark night in the hill country of Spain.
"Come in," he would say, "I was just painting myself,"
as he stood in the doorway holding up the wand of a brush,
illuminated in the blaze of his famous candle hat. [Applause]

I just stood up and took a bow. [Laughter] Thank you for your applause.
[Laughs] So, I want to say something about it. The end of the poem goes
back to its very beginning. The last words in the poem are "candle hat,"
which is the title. That's kind of risky, putting the title in the killer line or
the last line, but I did want to say something about the hat, and I did want

to circle back to that to keep the balance. As I'm looking through the poem, I'm noticing a few things that I really wasn't aware of when I wrote it. The state of mind in which a person writes has a great deal to do with the unconscious and training. It has to do with instinctive knowledge about how poems can go.

The first stanza is clearly setting the context. In most self-portraits you just see a big face. Then you have Cézanne, Van Gogh, and Rembrandt, to establish the intelligence of the speaker, maybe. [Laughs] And there are some sound effects there, like "the face dominates," "Van Gogh," "halo," "Rembrandt," "relieve," "breather." I don't put rhymes at the end of lines, usually, but I have rhymes inside the poem. Then in the second stanza, the poem swivels to its real subject: "But in this one Goya stands well back from the mirror." So we see the whole body of Goya. And then in the third stanza something happens: he appears to be smiling out at *us*. Now that's the key word there because now *you're* part of the poem. And "*we* would be amused," right? "By his hat on his head." So "we" and "us" bring the reader further inside the poem, and that is completed in the next stanza, which begins "*You* . . . You can only wonder." So now it's not just the poet who's wondering; it's the reader who's wondering. I'd like *you* to wonder what it would be like to wear this thing on your head "as if *you* were a walking dining room or a concert hall. But once *you* see this hat"—there's another kind of "but" that swivels—"there is no need to read a biography of Goya or to memorize his dates." This is the kind of teacher you want, right? You don't need to read a biography or do anything like that. [Laughs] Just look at this painting and take this hat. That's sort of dismissing the academic approach to learning about a painter, reading his biography and stuff. But in the next stanza, all you have to do "to understand Goya" is use your imagination. Here in this stanza, the imagination is triumphing over a more academic approach to Goya, or art, in the previous stanza. So what you have to do is just imagine him placing the hat on his head and lighting the candles before that. What this does is animate Goya. It really, you might say, "resurrects" him. By lighting and placing, he's doing things, and then he does more things in the next stanza. But, again, the stanza begins with this imperative to you: *imagine* him. Again, the reader is completely included at this point: "Imagine him surprising his wife . . . Imagine him flickering through the rooms of his house." You know how in jokes, things come in threes, right? So many things come in threes, like the three little bears. But in jokes one guy says something, and the next guy says something, and the third is the killer line. So there you have "Imagine him surprising his wife. . . . Imagine him flickering through the rooms of his house," and then finally, "Imagine a lost traveler knocking on his door." I think that becomes interesting right away because [Laughs] you have a sense that Goya is going to answer the door wearing his hat. "'Come in,' he would say, 'I was just painting myself,'" which goes back to the subject of the first line of the poem: self-portraits. And then we just see him there. I use "wand" to describe his brush, as if he can produce artistic magic out of it, and I use "blaze" to describe the hat because I want it to be almost a cartoon at this point, very intense, not just full of candles. And there he stands, "illuminated in the blaze of his famous candle hat." So the reason he did the self-portrait is for us to have a look at him. And the last lines give us a look at him. They resurrect him, as I said, and give you a kind of painterly sense of him standing in this doorway there. [Laughs]

Again, I didn't think of this stuff the way I'm thinking of it now or talking about it, but those are clearly elements of the poem that guide the reader, include the reader, and keep the reader in the poem. So that's very important to me. I feel that the reader is a key element in the poem and that the poem is not completed until it enters the mind of a reader. In this poem you can see now, or *I* can see now, that I'm maneuvering the reader into position so that he or she is completely with me when the lost traveler knocks on Goya's door.

SOA: You've emphasized the importance of the reader to help complete the poem, but do you consider poetry an art form created as much for the poet as for the reader?

Collins: Well, I'd say its 50/50. As I'm writing, I'm always going back to check to make sure that my sense of a reader—just basically a fairly intelligent person that loves poetry, that would be my reader—that that person is still with me. And I try to get the reader early on into, you might say, the sidecar of the poem and make sure that he or she has their safety belt on, [Laughs] and off we go. But I want the *companionship* of a reader. I suppose if you looked at this psychologically, the reader provides company or a companion for the poet, who is never more alone than he or she is when writing a poem. Despite the fact that we have an outbreak of poetry workshops all around the country these days, the actual act of writing a poem is a solo activity. I think when I started writing poems when I was a teenager that was what really appealed to me. I was—well I still am—an only child. I had a lot of time being alone, and I love solitude. Being an only child is a very good preparation for being a poet, by the way. [Laughter] So I think the reader is vital to me. I write in a fairly straightforward, conversational style, and I want you to think I'm talking to you. I've judged a lot of poetry contests. Some offer prizes for a whole book, some for just one poem. I go through stacks of them trying to find the best poem or book, and I move quickly because it will take weeks if I don't. What I look for in the first few lines is whether someone is talking to me or just doing a word painting or throwing out some complicated imagery that I am not willing to stop and examine. So the conversational style is certainly the most basic way to get the reader on board and make the reader feel included.

SOA: If there were no reader, how would your writing differ?

Collins: It would differ because there wouldn't be any. [Laughter] That would be a big difference there. [Laughter] I don't want to make this sound too cozy, that the reader and I are kind of sitting, having a cup of tea together, but the one thing I like to do is play with the reader. I have a poem called "Fishing on the Susquehanna in July," which you might have heard of, and the first lines are "I have never been fishing on the Susquehanna / or any river for that matter." I don't know if I have time to do this, but there is a fairly new poem that is a good example of playing around with the reader. Do I have time to read it?

SOA: Sure, please do.

Collins: Ok, well the title is "Walking My Seventy-Five-Year-Old Dog." So right away the reader should have a problem with that. [Laughter] [Reads "Walking My Seventy-Five-Year-Old Dog"] So there are good memories of walking my dog when she was elderly. I just wanted to play with the reader. No, she's not seventy-five; she is fourteen. No, she is not fourteen. So I'm sort of taking things away. My poems tend to be about things that are missing. Well that's a bigger topic.

SOA: Speaking of missing things, though, the novel *The Catcher in the Rye*, as well as other coming-of-age literary works, treats the idea of growing up as a "fall" rather than an ascent, something is lost in the transition. You treat this theme, though more light-heartedly, in your poem "On Turning Ten." What aspects of childhood do you feel are especially important for the poet or other artists to preserve or revive?

Collins: Well that's a very good question. I really like the way you focus on the word *fall* because he ends up falling and bleeding. It's not a good experience, and I'll say something more about those lines in a minute, but your question expands outward. Don't we think that children love to dance. You put on music, they'll dance. If you give them crayons and something to draw on, they don't need any instructions. They'll just start drawing anything. And they love music; they love dancing; they love rhyming. The trouble is that we all start out that way, but something happens to us, and the name for that is *adolescence*. [Laughter] That's when all of that unself-conscious twirling and singing and dancing comes to an end, and we start wondering about what people think of our noses, or how we look, and how we dress. That often slows people down and stifles their creativity. You are afraid to blow your cool by twirling and dancing and singing. Artists—poets, musicians, dancers, whatever—are people who have not let the child inside wither away. As Wordsworth said, "The child is father of the man." In other words, the child teaches the father how to be a child again. Someone said, "Beware the death called maturity." It's important to keep your child alive inside of you. As for the "fall," "On Turning Ten" is becoming a senti-mental poem towards the end. The kid is alone, and all the steam is drained out of his bicycle. So what I did there was lift a few lines from a famous poem by Shelley called "Ode to the West Wind." In that poem—it's a very romantic poem, full of exclamation points—he says, "I fall upon the thorns of life! I bleed!" So my kid falls upon the sidewalks of life, but if you get that allusion to Shelley you get fifty extra points, right, John? [Laughter]

SOA: In your essay "The Myth of Craft," you describe poetic persona as "the internalization of craft," emphasizing its role as a moving force in the poem, which adheres to your belief that "a poem should not mean but move." How would you characterize the development of your persona, and how did its development influence the movement of your own poetry?

Collins: Well thank you for asking that. It's very important to come up with a persona, and it's a little like inventing a character, the way Shake-speare would invent a character in his plays, or Dickens or Robert Stone, or whoever would invent a character in their fiction. Novelists and playwrights have to invent dozens and dozens of characters, but as a poet, you just have to come up with one character. That character is mainly a voice with a def-inite tone to it. The tone could be jumpy and unpredictable and verbally violent, or the tone could be very dignified and abstract. Or the tone could be witty and conversational, that of a likeable character. I think my persona came from a number of sources, probably my parents to begin with. My first persona was kind of a fatherly voice, maybe not so fatherly. My father was kind of jokey and had a very good sense of humor. He was witty, so my early poems were tricky and jokey. As I developed, I started to allow more feeling into my poems. That's when I was getting my mother's influence. She was a person of more feeling, and he was a person of hiding and being tricky.

The literary influence was probably the Romantic poets, especially Words-worth. If you've read any Wordsworth, you know he's always alone. At least that's the way it starts out. He's in nature. He falls into a kind of speculation about the past or about friendship or whatever. And often he is returned to nature at the end of the poem. I'm just describing what M. H. Abrams called "the greater Romantic lyric." Many of these poems in the Romantic period follow this same pattern. So my persona—like the guy walking his dog—is alone, except for the dog. [Laughs] He's out in nature, and he falls into speculation. So he's kind of a modern or postmodern version of this poetic persona that was very popular at the end of the eighteenth and beginning of the nineteenth centuries in England.

SOA: Our class discussed how your poems tend to end in a surprising, yet tightly fitting, manner. How do you know when you've found the right ending to a poem? Does it arrive organically, and did any of your best-known poems, such as "The Lanyard" or "The History Teacher," lead you toward another possible ending before you considered them complete?

Collins: Okay, well, I have an app, and it tells me when to end the poem. [Laughter] If the typewriter can't type anymore, then that's the ending. No, I don't have that. [Laughs] My poems are always rolling toward an ending. I think that's one of the important characteristics of the poems. They tend to have a beginning, where they are welcoming the reader; they go through a set of maneuvers in the middle; and they're always driving to an end, usually yet to be discovered. When I started the poem about the candle hat, I wasn't thinking about someone showing up at his door in the middle of the night. I arrived at that through the course of the poem, through the process of the poem. One thing I tell students who write poems is that if you're interested in where your poem ends, or should end, your poem ends where the reader stops reading. That's a very blunt way to put it, but it's very easy to stop reading a poem, right? Haven't you not finished poems? Maybe the poems you read for school you *have* to finish, [Laughter] but I'd say maybe seventy-five percent of the contemporary poems that I read, I don't finish for one reason or another. And as far as *my* poems' endings, it's never as if I have multiple possible endings. I never get to that point, I would say, where I think, "Oh, I could end this like three different ways. Which should I pick? What would be the best one?" No, it's always one ending, and it's very clear when I discover the ending that *that's* the ending. It's almost as if the poem has been keeping a secret about itself, and the ending is unlocking the secret of the poem. If you look back from the ending, you see, "Ah, that's what's happening in this poem. It was moving just toward this ending." The poem is the only way to get to the ending, of course, so you can see it as a pathway that it travels through itself and finds a place to stop.

SOA: Our class talked briefly about T.S. Eliot's essay "Tradition and the Individual Talent," in which Eliot argues that poetry should be impersonal, that is, it should not bear the stamp of the poet's personality. Considering the importance of a persona to your writing style and your distaste for poetry that is overly confessional, as you discuss in your introduction to *Best American Poetry*, to what degree do you agree with Eliot's edict?

Collins: Okay, well that's a very smart question. How did you know when to end that question? [Laughter] I've got to ask you the same question. Well, Eliot was one of the champions of impersonality. W. B. Yeats favored "the mask." He took that from Japanese theater, that the poet writes through a mask that both reveals and conceals. For Ezra Pound, I think, translation was his mask. He kind of hid behind his translations. So the result was a lot of poems that didn't give the sense that the poet was talking to a reader. Not only were the poems impersonal, they were, I would say, unconscious of the presence of the reader. In recent years, or at least the last fifty years, we've had a kind of return to personality. You see that in the confessional poets like Robert Lowell, Elizabeth Bishop, Anne Sexton, and others. But then, I think, two roads diverged. One way to have a personality is to be autobiographical about your poems, write about experiences you had in your real life, and reflect on them. The other thing is to be nonautobiographical, and I think of myself. I had a dog, and I took her for walks, but I don't think of myself as an autobiographical poet. If you read all my poems, you wouldn't really know much about me, except that I have a dog, and I have parents, and some pretty basic information like that. The reason I'm not very autobiographical is that I don't think my actual life is interesting enough just to write down and turn into a poem. My persona doesn't seem to be as miserable as most other personas [Laughter] of poets writing today. I've been accused of many things, including a lack of misery. I'm a misery-challenged persona, who seems to be, most of the time, quite delighted with the world around him. I prefer to be what Emerson called a "transparent eyeball." My persona is just present; he's just there. He's not really talking that much about his past. He's talking about where the poem is in the present, and that's a way of keeping the poem alive, keeping the poem animated. I didn't have much family, and I still don't have much family, so I don't write a lot about the family. And I find most poets that write about Mom and Dad and Grandpa and other people that are familiar that way—it just seems very claustrophobic to me, poems that are based completely on memory. I mean when you think of your family, don't you always picture them inside a room? [Laughter] That starts the claustrophobic feeling for me. We're all kind of sitting on the couch together, and I just want to get outdoors. So I think my persona has personality, but it's the personality of a detached viewer, rather than someone who wants to tell you the ups and downs of his past.

SOA: Many artists are known for one piece of work that seems definitive, whether it's Leonardo da Vinci's *Mona Lisa* or the Beatles' "Hey Jude." What would you say is your signature poem according to readers and critics, and what about for you? Do the poems you feel most strongly about get the most enthusiastic response at readings, and have you ever been surprised by a response a certain poem receives?

Collins: Right. That's a good question. I often test new poems out by reading them in public. The one thing I'm pretty sure about them is that they're good. I'm not asking an audience to play the role of a workshop and tell me what's wrong with the poem. But I am surprised by some of the reactions. One of the things is you don't know how an audience is reacting when they're just sitting there because they're not saying anything. It's the same thing with teaching. If you look out at your students, you have no idea what the hell they're thinking about. They might look interested, but it's very easy to pretend to be interested. [Laughter] Everybody has that interested look. The thing about an audience in my readings is that they laugh at some parts of the poem, usually, or giggle or titter or something, and often that's surprising. They find lines funny that I didn't think are funny, and often they don't laugh at lines I think are very funny. That gives me a sense of how foreign I am to these people who come to my readings. [Laughing]

So as far as picking out a signature poem, I only know from reactions that there is a poem called "Forgetfulness" that has become a kind of signature poem. A lot of people who don't know anything about my other work know that poem. It was written some time ago, but it seems to work very well with audiences. So in most readings, I'll read that poem. It's because it takes a fairly humorous look at something that is both funny and *terribly* serious. Alzheimer's, this terribly progressive disease, is a pattern of forgetfulness until you've forgotten who you are. So it's that frightening chasm where memory is basically sanity. But if someone is walking around with their glasses on their forehead looking for their glasses, like Mr. Magoo, that kind of forgetfulness is amusing. And I think, in a broader sense, I'm not often happy with poems of mine that are both funny and serious almost at the same time, and I think that's why that poem works so well.

SOA: You were the national poet laureate at the time of 9/11, and you read your poem "The Names," written in honor of the victims, in front of Congress, a year after the tragedy. How did you manage the pressure of responding to these horrific attacks in such a public arena? And did the form of the poem come to you quickly, or had you considered other approaches?

Collins: Well that's a good question because I know the answer. [Laughter] I had been the poet laureate just a few months, since June or July, and then 9/11 came in September, obviously, and I got a call from Congress. I think it was really a call from the people who were organizing this memorial service in New York. It was the first time both houses of Congress had met outside of Washington, I think, since the British burned down the capital some time ago. They said, "You're the poet laureate; maybe you could write a poem for this occasion." Well, *you* know what I write about—taking my old dog for a walk. They're small poems. They're not about global tensions and uncertainty about the future of the country or our country being threatened. So I actually told them I didn't think I would be able to write anything. There was a great silence on the other end of the line because you don't say "no" to Congress. [Laughter] I told them, if it's okay, I would come and read a poem by somebody else.

Now to get to your question about how I wrote it. I woke up very early one morning, before dawn, and I thought, "I really need to rise to the occasion here. How can I write this poem? It's not a Billy Collins kind of poem but I should write it anyway." And I made two discoveries. One was that I could write an elegy, which is a poem for the dead, right? As an English major, I can name the six great elegies in English literature. I could just make it a poem for the dead; therefore, I could avoid these larger issues, like the fate of our country and political and diplomatic issues. And the other discovery was that if I used the names of the dead, I could go through the alphabet, A to Z, and structure the poem that way. So one name at a time would come up at some point in the poem. They would follow this alphabetical order. It was like having a ladder: every letter of the alphabet was a rung that I could climb as the poem went on. So I had two formal constraints I had to stick to, the alphabet and the elegiac tone. But this is an example of the paradox of writing within a form. Often if you put restraints on yourself—for example, you decide to write a sonnet—it becomes a liberating effect because the energy you put into working within the form, out of that pressure, often, comes nothing, [Laughs] but sometimes creative novelty and inventiveness are the result. So that was the discovery. I couldn't get up and just write it. I had to go in with a plan, and the plan was to write an elegy and follow the alphabet.

SOA: You stated in an interview that early on you were more inspired by those who *discouraged* you rather than those who *encouraged* you. Are

you still motivated by negative criticism even after proving early naysayers wrong? You've been called a "mischievous poet." Does criticism of your
independent, often irreverent, disregard for poetic traditions, as in "Paradelle for Susan" and "Lines Composed Over Three Thousand Miles from
Tintern Abbey," just inspire you to more mischief?

Collins: Well, yeah, that's *me*. I have written a poem called "Taking Off
Emily Dickinson's Clothes." I wrote a poem mocking "The Love Song of
J. Alfred Prufrock." I like turning back on my influences and liberating myself
from them. And, yes, there are plenty of naysayers around these days. I don't
get to *hear* many of them. My books aren't widely reviewed. And I think one
of the problems people have with me is that I sell a lot of books. I give a lot
of readings and I seem to be depriving other poets of their pet grievance,
which is that nobody reads poetry. [Laughter] If you want to make it more
specific, really, nobody reads *their* poetry. [Laughter] It's what they're really
talking about. I was at the University of Houston once, and I was kind of
attacked in class by a little cadre of graduate students, who told me that they
found my work not interesting because it was underconceptualized. I said
to them, "Well why don't you just problematize it. [Laughter] That seems to
be what you people do. So *make* it difficult. Have fun." [Laughter] Early on, I
didn't need encouragement. I needed someone to say I couldn't do it. One of
the inspirations for becoming a poet is not just reading great poetry; that's
one. The other one is reading poetry that's really bad and thinking, "Hell, I
can do better than that." If you feel that you can actually get out in the field
and write better than that, that's a great push towards being a poet. Thank
you for your question.

SOA: Do you think that if you had not been raised Catholic, you would
still have such a passion for both the secular world and the natural world? In
other words, do you think that breaking away from the faith of your upbringing, which you discuss in your introduction to *The Best American Spiritual
Writing*, deepened your appreciation for the physical world? To what degree
do you adhere to Kerouac's idea that there is holiness in everything?

Collins: Right. Well I think there is holiness in a lot of things, not everything. It's hard to answer a question like yours because I don't know what
I would be like if I had not been raised Catholic. I was born and raised in
New York City. I don't know what I would be like if I were raised in a small
town in Nebraska. I imagine I'd be different. I think my Catholicism had a
lot to do with it. I had nuns in grammar school, brothers in high school,
and Jesuits in college, which is the full metal jacket of Catholicism. There is
a great emphasis on language in the Catholic liturgy. Seamus Heaney, also

raised Catholic, talked about the litanies towards the Blessed Virgin. She's called "tower of ivory," "house of gold," images used to describe the mother of Christ. I learned, or memorized, Latin. To be an altar boy you had to pass the Latin examination. I didn't know many words in Latin. I just memorized it syllable by syllable. So it would be like *su-sci-pe a glo-ri-a*, like that. And that's interesting because you don't know what you're saying, but you're saying it. It gives you a sense of the pure musicality of language. It might mean something, but there's a musical and rhythmic package to it that you're receiving before you get the meaning. But that essay in *The Best American Spiritual Writing*, I was shocked that they asked me to introduce that. [Laughing] I don't think of myself as a terribly spiritual person. But that's the simplification of my movement from a church-bound sense of faith to a faith in the natural beauty of the world and in humanity. That's about all I can say about it

SOA: In a past interview you told our graduating class of 2010 that "poetry is a bird and prose is a potato." Are there, however, prose works, particularly fictional works, that you feel reach poetic heights?

Collins: Yeah, good question. I think when poets are asked about their influences, they tend to answer exclusively. But I think influence is much broader and comes in from all sorts of places, including prose: reading John Banville, reading Walter Pater, reading Terry Eagleton. I love to read Nabokov's *Lolita*, or anything by Nabokov. There's the timing of their sentences. There are prose works that are full of metaphoric play. And—I wrote an article for the *Wall Street Journal* about this—one of the influences on me was Looney Tunes cartoons: Bugs Bunny, Daffy Duck, Porky Pig, and those guys. They just gave me, as a kid, a sense that nature was very pliable. You could pull a set of kitchen knives out of your pants, even though you're not wearing pants. [Laughter] Bugs Bunny is not wearing pants most of time. The antigravitational ability of those characters to move around space, I'd name that as an influence. When I said, "prose is a potato," it was just resentful because novels get made into movies, and generally poems don't get made into movies. [Laughter]

SOA: Going back to how being born and raised in New York influenced your writing, the poems in your second book of selected poems, *Aimless Love*, seem to embrace the natural world even more than the poems in *Sailing Alone around the Room*. Did the move to Florida from New York inspire your poetry in new ways?

Collins: Absolutely. I don't know if it's inspired by nature, but it's my surroundings. I often locate my speaker in a place. We're not in outer space somewhere. We're sitting down looking out a window and seeing something, or we're walking and seeing something. So at the house I had in Westchester County, New York, there were woods. There were ash trees and maple and oak trees, and there were stone walls and a river. All that natural environment was not necessarily a big source of inspiration, but a sense of where I was. I am looking out my window in my home in Florida, and I see palm trees and more palm trees. So coming down here, I had to learn a whole new set of flora and fauna, particularly birds. There are very strange birds, as you know, if you've been to Florida or anywhere in the tropics. If you saw birds like these in New York, you would probably call the police [Laughter] because they're so strange looking. I had to learn what an Ibis is and why it's not an egret, and that kind of thing. But poets are expected to know something about botany and the names of plants and animals, and maybe even the names of clouds. Poets are expected to have a vocabulary. Instead of just saying *bird* or *tree*, you know what kind of bird it is or what tree it is. That's also a way of establishing authority in a poem.

SOA: One final question: Many of your poems, such as "Helium," and most recently, "Downpour," address the subject of mortality and the human desire to be remembered. Considering your vast critical and popular success as a poet, does having the assurance of a literary legacy make the thought of mortality any less discomforting, even in light of the unlikely prospect that "Balloon Designs by Pauline" could outlive you?

Collins: [Laughing] Yeah, poor Pauline. I wonder if some of these people will get together and come up to my house one day and announce, "I'm Pauline," and I'm all these other people I'm mentioning that I don't know. [Laughter]

I don't think so. Jacques Lacan, I think, says that there are two deaths. One death in which you die physically, and the next death is when everybody in the world has forgotten about you. So you die twice. Ha! Good! That's so much better than dying once. But if you're a poet, if you're an artist, if you're, say, Shakespeare, that's four hundred years you've got extra on your life because people are not forgetting about you. It's interesting to think of someone reading your book when you're dead. Maybe I'll write about that today. Thanks for mentioning Pauline. She really appreciates it, I'm sure. [Laughter]

SOA: Thank you so much.

Collins: You're very welcome. Thank you everybody for your questions. I think you could tell I had an interesting time responding to them. Shall I read this little poem at the end?

SOA: Yes, that would be great. Thank you for allowing us to spend this time with you.

Collins: You're very welcome. So it's short. It's twelve lines, and it links in with the last question about mortality. It's called "The Garland." [Reads "The Garland"] That was fun. [Laughter]

SOA: Thanks again. This has been a great morning, and we appreciate your taking the time to answer all the questions so thoroughly.

Collins: Great. I'm happy to do it. I'd love for you to take a picture of your class sometime, anytime, and send it to me.

SOA: We took one during the interview, and I'll get it to you for sure. [Applause]

Collins: Okay, good. Bye-bye.

SOA: Take care and enjoy the rest of your day.

Poet Billy Collins on Mortality, Gratitude, and the Importance of Sitting and Doing Nothing

Diane Rehm / 2020

This conversation was recorded for *The Diane Rehm Show*, produced by WAMU, which is licensed to American University in Washington, DC, and distributed by National Public Radio (NPR). Broadcast on November 27, 2020, the interview is printed with the permission of WAMU.

Diane Rehm: Billy Collins, it's great to see you, to have you here for this day after Thanksgiving, and to tell you how much I love your new book of poetry called *Whale Day*. Tell me why you have called this book *Whale Day*?

Billy Collins: [Laughs] You might wonder; it's kind of an odd title. When I title a book, I'm not someone who goes through all the poems and tries to think of the big theme that ties it all together. I don't have titles that are a key to the book. What I do is I look at all the poems I have, and I just pick the one that would seem interesting on a cover of a book. I think of a book as a commodity, among other things. Then I look for cover art to go with it. I've been very lucky with Random House. I've been with them for nineteen years, I think. They've let me choose all my cover art and let me in on the design of the typeface and everything. So it's a real creative process for me to make a book, with their help of course. [Laughs]

Rehm: I wonder if you would begin by reading for us "The Function of Poetry," the poem that begins your new book.

Collins: Well, I'll tell you, it's a very promising title. [Laughs] It's a big title, but you'll see that it's a very small poem. I put it in the book as a kind of prefatory poem. [Reads "The Function of Poetry"]

Rehm: Tell me about that feeling when you had that realization?

Collins: Well, behind the poem, I think, is a comment by Seamus Heaney, who said, I'm not a poet all the time. I'm going to the store or I'm engaged in something else. I'm a poet some of the time. We're really *not* poets more than we *are* poets. We spend more time *not* being poets, that is to say, we're not writing. And then I just thought of my routine. The first stanza is supposed to be very dull. It's just what I do. I go to the post office. Maybe I go to the bank. I have another cup of coffee. [Laughter] It's almost enough to put you to sleep. It does come to this realization as I'm looking out the window that this is the function of poetry: to remind me that there's more to life than what I'm doing when I'm not writing poetry. It's saying that I'm best when I'm reading or writing poetry. That's when I'm connected to life more than when I'm running errands.

Rehm: I had the feeling, reading through many of these poems, that another thing that's on your mind these days is mortality. Your poem "Life Expectancy" made me think of that early on in the book, and there seemed to be several examples like that. "Life Expectancy" is on page 10. Would you read that for us and then let's talk about it?

Collins: Okay, I'd be happy to. [Reads "Life Expectancy"]

Rehm: So, I love the ending with the picture of that cat dressed in black with a touch of red, sitting next to the labradoodle reserved for their kind. I just love that. So, there is humor in this, but there is also that sense of one's own mortality.

Collins: I think in many of these poems I'm trying to blend that. Of course, I'm not the first poet to talk about mortality. I think it's probably the oldest theme in poetry, going back to Roman poetry and the theme of carpe diem, that we must seize the day because we don't have all the diems in the world. An awareness of mortality tends to intensify life rather than a create a morbid fascination with it. But, yes, I think there are only a few themes in poetry, a handful of themes, and certainly the idea of death making more sense of life is one of them. Kafka, I think, was asked, "What is the meaning of life?" And he said, "The meaning of life is that it ends." That's a rather abrupt definition. [Laughs] One of the milestones of becoming aware of death, someone said, is when you notice your dentist is younger than you are. I think we always assume, for example, if we see a squirrel or a robin or an insect, that they have a shorter life than we do. But at a certain point, you can't be that sure. [Laughs] So this is taking a new angle on this ancient theme.

Rehm: And in 2020 the Covid virus—though of course you wrote that poem, I believe, long before we were afflicted with the Covid virus—but, nevertheless, that must be very much on your mind these days.

Collins: I've written a couple of poems in response to the Covid, very short ones. There's also a book edited by Alice Quinn called *Together in a Sudden Strangeness, America's Poets Respond to the Pandemic*. If you'd like to hear those two little poems . . .

Rehm: I'd love to.

Collins: Okay, this is just called "Nurse."

One who spoke by a window in a stairwell,
resting her head on her arm,
said she was so many stumbles beyond tired,
she caught herself envying the dead
for looking like sleepers in their beds.

The other little one is only six lines long, and it takes off from an image in a poem by Shelley called "Ode to the West Wind." The poet notices the wind blowing these leaves on the ground, and they're all different colors. He calls them "pestilence-stricken multitudes," as if they are people fleeing a plague. "Pestilence-stricken multitudes." I'm never going to be able to get that image out of my head. So, here's the little poem called "Comparisons."

In "Ode to the West Wind"
Shelley calls a scattering of blowing leaves
"pestilence stricken multitudes."
and now we are of the stricken,
with no place to scatter
and this year's leaves
have begun to fall.

Rehm: Wow, it's so short but so profound in terms of what we are all feeling these days. I walk my dog through the falling leaves, and I, too, am thinking, "I wonder how many more times I will see those falling leaves."

Collins: I have a poem in which I ask, for example, how many Octobers do I have? A box of Octobers or a suitcase full of Aprils? Once you start thinking about death, there are all sorts of ways of measuring it or looking at it.

Rehm: How many hours each day do you spend writing, or is it that you wait for that poem to come to you?

Collins: Well it's both. As a poet, one develops a habit of paying attention to things with the hope of finding something in an everyday experience that will provoke a poem. The little poem called "Nurse" came from something on television. It was a nurse with her head down in a stairwell in a hospital, saying that she was ashamed of herself that she envied the dead. That's how tired she was. So, in a way, I just organize that in a couple of stanzas. I don't write every day, but I do—I'm confessing this to you—I do often just get up and sit in a chair with a cup of coffee and see what happens. I'll often read somebody else's poems, poems by William Matthews or James Tate or Marie Howe or Charles Simic. I do sit down and open a notebook and see what happens. And if nothing happens, it doesn't. It's kind of a combination of being passively ready to receive an idea for a poem and getting in a kind of irregular habit of sitting down and asking for something to come in.

Rehm: Actually, when the pandemic began, I gather you started streaming a poem a day on Facebook. What did you hope to do by doing that?

Collins: Well it was really my wife's idea, and I think she just wanted to keep me busy [Laughs] so I'd stop bothering her all the time. It was March 23, the day after my birthday, and I had just come back from New York. The virus was just taking hold in America, especially on the East Coast. She's a great follower of Facebook. I have never participated myself, but never say "never." She said, "If you got on Facebook, you could just read a poem or two, and it would be something to do." She said, "Let's decide on a time." I said, "5:30. We'll do it at cocktail time."

Rehm: Good!

Collins: The first one lasted eight minutes. I don't remember what I said, but I read a couple of poems and said "goodbye." Now it's about a half an hour. What happens is I'll play some music, usually some jazz, and I'll put on some cool looking shades and talk about the song I just played. That's my Professor Bebop role. The listeners post comments, hundreds of comments, from thousands of listeners, at this point. I go through the comments and see if there are any interesting ones, and there are lots of interesting ones. So, I have a mail bag, kind of like an old radio show, and I read some comments from the mail bag. Then I read poems, mostly my own in the beginning, but now all sorts of other people's poems. Then I play a little music at the end, and that's it. It does give me something to do. It's every weekday. We just call it *The Poetry Broadcast*, and it's on Billy Collins's Facebook page. Anybody can jump in there. We have people from all over the world listening. I'll give you one little summary of that. There's a woman in Paris who tucks herself in and goes to sleep listening to *The Broadcast*, and another woman in Australia listens with her morning coffee. So, it's in all sorts of time zones.

Rehm: That must really give you a great deal of satisfaction to know that people around the world have come to rely on that half hour, whatever is being read, whether it's your poetry or someone else's.

Collins: Well, I said right in the beginning, on the very first broadcast, "I'm not going to read poems to comfort you or make you feel better about yourself. I'm just going to read good poems." It's not a sentimental comforting of the audience. I say, "I'll never mention the news." There are so many things going on in this country at this time; it's amazing. It's being thought of now as an oasis from the news, something to hear that is not mentioning what is going on. It's mentioning more important things, like life and death, that will always be going on. As Ezra Pound said, "Poetry is the news that stays new."

Rehm: And of course into that mix comes a lot of humor, and, as I mentioned earlier with your reference to the cat draped in black and the labradoodle going to a place for their kind, is there an intention to bring that kind of lightness to that heavy subject of aging?

Collins: Well, yes, it's part of my sensibility. I think if one tries to be funny, it's going to fail. Some people want to write humorous poems, but they're not really humorous people, and you can't really put *on* funny. You can pretend to be serious, right? You and I are sort of pretending to be serious right now. But you can't pretend to be funny. You're either funny or you're not funny. So even though humor is thought of as kind of lower level or unserious poetry, it can be used to access many serious things in life. But it is very authentic, in that you can't fake it.

Rehm: You have a poem in this book about your parents, and I gather in many ways your mother was your first poetry teacher. Can you read us that poem and then tell us about your parents?

Collins: Was this the convergence poem?

Rehm: Yes.

Collins: Yes, of course. [Reads "The Convergence of My Parents"]

My parents didn't marry until they were both in their very late thirties. They met in a hospital in New York, where he was her patient. My father was from Lowell, Massachusetts. My mother was born in a farming town 100 miles north of Toronto. He became an electrician. She became a nurse, which allowed them to go anywhere. For some reason they both had this wanderlust. They traveled around the country mostly by train, my mother going as far as Los Angeles to work in a hospital there. She also worked for a rich woman, who took her up to Banff and Lake Louise [Alberta, Canada]. She was really a proto-feminist, going out on her own, sometimes traveling with a nurse friend. My father was doing the same thing, crisscrossing the country working as an electrician. He worked on the Empire State Building. He worked in the *Daily News* print room, on oil rigs in the Gulf of Mexico. If you think back on it, if your parents had not met, clearly you would not be here, and usually people meet by coincidence. They'll walk into a party or they happen to be at this restaurant. I suppose it would be interesting for *anyone* to think back on how their parents met and give thanks for that moment of serendipity.

Rehm: But your father was actually in a hospital, and your mother was the nurse, and that's how they met?

Collins: That's how they met. They call it the *felix culpa* in Christianity, "the happy fall." If Eve had not eaten the apple, we wouldn't have Christ. So it was a happy accident that this tool hit my father in the forehead, and he had to go to the hospital. [Laughs]

Rehm: And there she was.

Collins: And there she was. It does show you how strangely coincidental life is. People planning on going to college think it is very vital to pick the right college. If you end up at not such a great college, that's where you might meet your wife and have three great children and all that. So no *one* thing gives you control over the rest of your life, I wouldn't think.

Rehm: I want to ask you a little more about your mother. I gather she taught you how to read. She inculcated a love of reading and language in you.

Collins: She did read to me all the time, which I consider one of the great things you can do in life is read to a young person, parent or no parent. She learned a lot of poetry when she was a schoolgirl in Canada, and memorization back then was not only a legitimate way to teach poetry, it was probably the only way to teach poetry. Students were made to memorize it and get into the rhythm of poetry. But she wasn't a literary person. She was smart, and she read a lot of British and Scottish history. But she had a lot of Shakespeare in her head, and she would quote poems on a regular basis. I was hearing poetry before I knew it was poetry. I knew that my mother had two ways of talking: one was the regular way, and the other was the poetry way. And it was like I knew the poetry way was better, or different. Looking back, it was a little like AM and FM radio. The poetry was FM and the regular was AM. [Laughter]

Rehm: I wonder if you'd read another poem for us called "Sleeping on My Side."

Collins: Of course. This is a poem that turned out to be a sonnet. I always try to listen to my poem and not just force upon the poem what I want to say. Sometimes the poem develops its own whimsy. About six lines into this, the poem seemed to be saying it wanted to be a sonnet. So I said to the poem, "Well I'm not going to go back and rewrite the whole thing, but I'll turn you into a sonnet from this point on." [Reads "Sleeping on My Side"]

So that's very much the American East and the American West. It's almost a nineteenth-century poem because the West was full of adventure and the East is sophistication, silverware, theaters, and that kind of thing. Now that's why the poem ends with me with my left ear, always the one that's down, [Laughs] as if listening for hoofbeats in the ground the way the Lone Ranger used to.

Rehm: Would you call that a love poem, Billy?

Collins: Yes, it becomes a love poem, and that's another thing about the poem. It didn't start out as a love poem. I like poems that kind of turn *into* love poems. I'd say love and death—if you can have two magnetic Norths— that's where poems tend to go, toward love or toward death, the two big subjects. It's not until the end, when I say, "yet I hardly care as long as you / are there," that any *you* is mentioned. Then the loved one faces the other way. So we're defended in all degrees, as if we're looking out for danger and listening for hoofbeats. It's from watching too many Westerns, I guess.

Rehm: You were poet laureate during the time of 9/11, and you wrote the poem "The Names." I wonder if you could talk about that experience when you first read it and then read it for us.

Collins: Okay, I'd be happy to. Well, I was named poet laureate, I think, around June of 2001. So it was just a few months before 9/11. There was a memorial one year after the attacks. Both houses of Congress met in New York, which is almost unprecedented to have them meet outside of Washington. I got a call from people in Congress who were arranging this memorial service, asking me, the poet laureate, if I'd write a poem. Well, we now have a sense of what I write about, which is walking the dog and thinking about how that squirrel is going to outlive me, and that kind of thing. And I thought the topic was just way too big for me, like the Covid is way too big for me. I wrote those two little poems, but I can't write a big one about that. So I told them I couldn't do it, but that I'd read something. I'd read Whitman maybe. They were disappointed. So I woke up one morning, and I thought, "My mother would be really disappointed too." I heard her saying, "Get off the bench and get to work." So I thought of two things that made it possible. I could write an elegy, just a poem for the dead, and not worry about geopolitical ramifications, the attack, and all those larger issues. And since I'm mourning people, I could work my way through the poem by using the alphabet, having each letter represented by one of the fallen people. So I wrote it in a couple of hours. The hard part was reading it before Congress. I managed to keep myself together, but the reading did say something interesting about poetry. I had been preceded, of course, by lots of other speakers. When I began to read the poem, which begins by talking about the rain at night, and the breeze, and a glaze on the windows, people looked up like your dog. They're cocking their heads like they had no idea what was being said here, because it wasn't *political* language it was *poetic* language, that used imagery. So it was a good test of the difference between those two languages. Various senators and representatives were attentive in varying degrees. Senator Moynihan was the most attentive of all. He was a poetry lover for sure.

Rehm: It's so interesting how the language of poetry can reach the hearts of people in ways that other writings somehow cannot.

Collins: I like to say that poetry is the history of the human heart. We have lots of histories of warfare and treaties and inventions and exploration, but poetry, going back to Sumerian or Roman times, is really the story of human emotion, and those emotions don't change. What changes are the metaphors and the imagery and the rhythms of the poem, which make the poem unique. But basically, we're wired to the same things that people were wired to thousands of years ago.

Rehm: Billy, now would you read for us "The Names"?

Collins: Sure. [Reads "The Names"]

Rehm: Billy, your mother would have been proud.

Collins: Thank you.

Rehm: Truly, I want to ask you what you are thankful for this year.

Collins: Well, that I'm still alive, not just because I'm older now, but because of the circumstances. I'm still pretty healthy and alive. I'm thankful for everyday experience. I'm thankful for having a loving wife, and also just the experience of walking around. I think we forget so much and we get tied up in our routines. It's really just that cliché of stopping to smell the roses, but there are things everywhere. You don't have to have an actual rose, just the daily experience. Just yesterday, at 7:27 yesterday evening, we were on New Smyrna Beach, and we watched the rocket launch. It lit up the sky with this phosphorescent brightness, and then it settled down and became like an ember at the end of a lit cigarette. Then it disappeared. That's a little too much for me to write about. It's too much in itself. I'd rather pick a small thing and examine it. I think attention is really a form of gratitude, looking at things without any purpose. Also spending a half an hour a day doing nothing. That's something that is very hard to do these days. It sounds easy because you think, "Lots of the time I'm doing nothing." Well, not really, you're doing something almost all the time. If you actually try to do nothing for half an hour, something will happen. You will access something within.

Rehm: Maybe write a poem.

Collins: Maybe even write a poem.

Rehm: Billy, would you finally please read for us "The Garland," which is on the back of your new book.

Collins: I'd be happy to. [Reads "The Garland"]

Rehm: I love it. Billy, what do you consider a good death?

Collins: A good death? I don't think there is . . . well I suppose dying in your sleep, rolling over during a nice dream. One thing about death is that once you're dead, you don't know a lot of things. I'm working on a poem about this. With most religions there is some inclusion of a life after death. If you believe in the afterlife, and if there *isn't* an afterlife, just say hypothetically, you'll never be disappointed, because you'll be dead. You'll never have this realization, "Oh there's no afterlife?" No that doesn't come because you're dead. No believer will be disappointed, and the same goes for the atheists and the skeptics and the agnostics. They'll be dead too, so they won't be able to say, "Well, I told you so."

Rehm: Are you a believer?

Collins: I'm a skeptic, I'd say. I believe in a creator of some kind, something that we can't really conceive of. I could picture the creator saying, "I gave you all *this*, this earth and these planets and this sun and you want *more*? [Laughs] You want to live forever? No, no, no. I'm the one who lives forever. Your life is on Earth." That's why I think that life on earth is so important, because there's no planet B, as they say.

Rehm: Billy Collins, you have tears in your eyes. What brought those?

Collins: [Laughs] It's the Irishness in me. I'm an easy crier.

Rehm: Well, I want to thank you *so much* for being with us today. It was *wonderful* to talk with you.

Collins: Well it's a great pleasure always to be with you, Diane, and I hope we get together again. I think this is the third time we met, and that's not enough for me. So I want to see you again.

Rehm: And I you. And we will.

Collins: Thank you.

Rehm: Thank you.

"One Gift of Sight after Another": Billy Collins on *Whale Day*

John Cusatis / 2021

This interview, conducted in January 2021, focuses on Collins's twelfth full-length collection of poems, *Whale Day*, published by Random House in the fall of 2020. It appears in print for the first time in this collection.

John Cusatis: I'd like to start with the blurb from the poet Alice Fulton on the back of the dust jacket: "Billy Collins puts the 'fun' back in profundity." It's the only blurb on the book, and at eight words, it's both unpretentious and incisive, like the poems it describes. Could you comment on Fulton's observation of your work, which, as *Whale Day* illustrates, can bring together Paul Cézanne and Bugs Bunny in a single poem.

Billy Collins: Some years ago, Alice Fulton introduced me before a reading at Cornell, and when she said that "Billy Collins puts the 'fun' back in profundity," everyone laughed but me. I was too busy writing it down. After the reading, I did something I would strongly advise anyone not to do: ask someone if words not intended as a blurb could be used as one. Lucky for me, she graciously said "okay," and it became my new favorite blurb. As well as being witty, it addressed the heart of the tonal balance of my poems. Ever since I came across poets who had reclaimed humor as a legitimate mode in poetry (Larkin, Koch to name two), I've been trying to even the scales between humor (fun) and seriousness (profundity). I sought to write poems that were "seriously funny." A poem that finds room for both Cézanne and Bugs Bunny is an example of taking advantage of the doors that were thrust open some time ago (see Susan Sontag on "camp" ["Notes on Camp," 1964] between high and low culture, between gravity and play. My preferred order is fun first, then profundity. A poem that follows that order may begin like prose and turn into poetry only later.

Cusatis: The poems in *Whale Day* suggest a fundamental opposition between absence and presence: *absence* meaning not only physical absence, as in the poems concerning the passage of time, but the tendency for things to be *present* in the world, yet *absent* from our daily awareness. The title poem notes, "The earth is busy with whales / even though we can't see any." To some extent is it the poet's task to make the absent present, the invisible visible?

Collins: The tradition of the poet being present to witness a moment in time begins with Wordsworth's innocent little poem about happening upon an array of daffodils on a walk with his sister. From that point on, the poet is typically placed in a setting—be it a pasture or a store window—where the interaction between poet and scene becomes the poem's vital subject. The poet is bilingual. Besides his mother tongue, the poet has as a second language the things of the world. The poet's presence is required in order to bear witness to the scene. The place he finds himself must be clearly described, whereas his reaction to the scene may remain mysterious, invisible. At the end of the poem, the poet disappears, though I sometimes like to erase him a little before that.

Cusatis: In addition to drawing your readers' attention to what they do *not* see, many of these poems direct readers to look more closely at what they *do* see and to pay attention to everything that "is pouring over the mighty floodgates of the senses," as you write in "The Deaths of Friends." "A Sight," for example, pays homage to "a purple flower climbing the fence / one gift of sight after another," and "Arizona" celebrates "the perfect acoustics of birdsong." In the latter poem, the narrator apologizes to the birds for not being "as knowledgeable as the woman / . . . with her binoculars and her bird book," and the former intentionally omits the name of the "purple flower." These poems, as well as "Flashcard" and "Dublin," emphasize the importance and the joy of learning the names for things. How important is naming, an idea you most famously employed in your 9/11 tribute, "The Names," to enhancing one's perception?

Collins: Ever since I read the English Romantic poets, especially Wordsworth and even more especially Coleridge, I've been attracted to the poet as a watcher, a wanderer, a gawker. Staring is his job. How else are clouds supposed to get our attention, though, as Szymborska notes, they are quite happy to sail by without being noticed. It helps if the poet is part botanist, part ornithologist, part arborist. Never "a flower," but "an iris." Never "a bird," but "an oystercatcher." Never "a tree," but "hickory," "a pin oak." Out of this fascination with what's around us comes the fetishistic pleasure of just saying the names of things, listing the many kinds of apples, the types of clouds, the names of horses, as Donald Hall does so well.

Cusatis: "Downpour," which I introduced to my students when it appeared in the *New Yorker*, makes the absence/presence dichotomy, as well as the importance of naming, most vivid in the image of a small piece of paper, one side of which contains a grocery list, the other the names of deceased friends. Can you discuss the genesis of this poem? How did you stumble on this image that so precisely captures the duality of life and death, the mundane and the mysterious? How much of the process was conscious? For example, were you aware, as one student observed, that you were employing a rich instance of the rare rhetorical device known as *zeugma* when the narrator realizes he "had forgotten Terry O'Shea / As well as the bananas and the bread?"

Collins: "Downpour," like a lot of my poems, has an autobiographical beginning. My wife and I were remembering contemporaries that had died. This was before the coronavirus discovered America. Later, I made a list of them on the back of a grocery list. The seriousness of the list on one side against the ordinariness of groceries on the other. The makings were there. All I had to do now was take the list and go shopping. The poem became my trip to the supermarket. The rain was added the way it is in movies. By the way, your student deserves extra credit for recognizing a zeugma. That the phrasing of the ending was very intentional should go without saying, but I was not conscious of "doing a zeugma" any more than I would have to check the owner's manual every time I flicked on my turn signal or flashed my brights.

Cusatis: That the dead were once miraculously alive is a concern of several of these poems, such as "Cremation," "Lakeside Cottage: Ontario," "Wild Barnacle," "Early People," and "April 21st," which imagines John Muir and Charlotte Bronte, both born on that date, alive in their time. Can you comment on your interest in rehumanizing the dead by imagining a day when they were living?

Collins: There's nothing new about exhuming or "rehumanizing" the dead. Historical fiction would not exist without it. Bringing someone back from the dead or even killing off one of the living are well within the scope of poetry's possibilities. I'm now thinking of a poem that would raise an historical figure from the dead then return that person to the dead in the final lines. An abundance of scenarios there.

Cusatis: Yes, but historical fiction does not have the liberty of placing Shakespeare on an airplane next to a contemporary poet, sharing an earbud and listening to Miles Davis, as you do in "The Bard in Flight" from *The Rain in Portugal*. You reimagine deceased figures in ways that make them more real and alive to us. Is this part of what motivates you to resurrect someone like John Muir or the Irish poet Patrick Pearse?

Collins: It might have been Galway Kinnell's poem "Oatmeal," in which he reports having breakfast with John Keats, that made me realize that the partition between the living ("the quick") and the dead (or the predead and the dead) could be penetrated, thus creating a lively transit back and forth between these two realms. Every dead person becomes a Lazarus. The poet can play golf with George Washington or take a walk around a lake with Socrates. In such cases, I have refrained from bluntly asking if there is or is not an afterlife. Their return to life on earth, I suppose, becomes their after-life as far as anyone can tell. Now I feel like making a list of dead people I'd rather play golf with than the father of our country!

Cusatis: You often take the opposite approach as well, speculating on the deaths of the living—a speculation that frequently includes yourself—as in "Vivaci," "My Funeral," "Life Expectancy," "Me First," "The Garland," and others. You've told Diane Rehm that an awareness of death "intensifies life." Some may not see it this way. How have you been able to reconcile living with dying?

Collins: One memorable expression of the way death can intensify or italicize life is Wallace Stevens's "Death is the mother of beauty." We fall in love with other humans, not store window mannikins, except at the cheapest level of fantasy tales. Another comes from Kafka. When asked the meaning of life, he responded that "the meaning of life is that it ends."

Cusatis: You pay homage to William Wordsworth, among several other poets, in *Whale Day*. Another early influence whose work still seems to leave its impression on your poems is Richard Brautigan. Like Wordsworth, Brautigan, too, sought to "bear witness" to ordinary fleeting moments. Unlike Wordsworth, though, Brautigan's work is generally filled with highly liberating humor. Margaret Renkl calls you "the heir of Wordsworth." In what ways might you also be the heir of Brautigan?

Collins: In my introduction to a recent reissue of Brautigan's *Trout Fishing in America*, I tell the fortuitous story of getting my hands on a man-uscript copy some months before the book was published. It really spun me around. I had never read a piece of fiction so odd and playful, and espe-cially so whimsically disrespectful of the conventions of the "novel." When his *Springfield Mine Disaster* book of poems appeared, I got busy trying to write that way. American fiction was Hemingway and Fitzgerald, surrealism was Apollinaire and Breton, separated by an ocean. Brautigan managed to be both at once. I soon gave up writing third-rate Brautigan, but his fanciful take on life left its mark.

Cusatis: While the names and lives of deceased people are invoked in many of these poems, a few poems lament the "rituals and devices" that have also disappeared, devoured by "the gaping maw of obsolescence," as you put it in "My Father's Office." You name such items as "thick tear off calendars," "the black rotary phone," and "the adding machine." What was the inspiration for this poem?

Collins: The poem about my father's office is a study in nostalgia and owes a debt, which I acknowledge with an allusion, to Roethke's "Dolor." All I can do is repeat the fact that the paper clip and the rubber band continue to survive leaps in technology. We should leave one of each on the moon next time.

Cusatis: Yes, the narrator of "My Father's Office" implores paper clips and rubber bands to stay around, calling them, "keepers of order, logic and sense." The idea of order also pervades your work: the office, the library, the museum, and the kitchen appear frequently. Can you comment on this interest in order?

Collins: The role of "order, logic, and sense" in my poems and life were instilled by my mother and the Society of Jesus.

Cusatis: Your poetry has been inspired by so many other artforms. In *Whale Day*, ekphrastic poems abound. "The Floors of Bonnard," "Listening to Hank Mobley," and "A Sight" have their origins in painting, jazz music, and documentary film, respectively. In what ways do works of art invite you to create in ways that the real world may not?

Collins: What is around me gets into my poems, whether it's an osprey flying over the house or some Bonnard paintings I'm paging through, or the eggs in boiling water. I draw on everything around me that seems evocative or even useful.

Cusatis: Many of your poems confront big ontological questions through matter-of-fact, concrete illustrations and language. "The Convergence of My Parents" and "The Yellow Wood" both convey the life-altering, or even life-begetting, effects of choices and chance circumstances, a topic you address memorably in "I Go Back to the House for a Book," from *Picnic, Lightning*. In "Whiskers" the narrator marvels at the growth of "a night's worth of whiskers," which "prove the daily surprise of my being." Can you comment further on this "daily surprise" and how poetry helps to sustain one's capacity to marvel at his or her "being"?

Collins: A favorite poem of mine is "The Salutation" by the seventeenth-century English metaphysical poet Thomas Traherne. It's the only poem I know spoken by a baby, a newborn who is fascinated by his arms and legs, his eyes that see and ears that hear, but mostly by the wonder of his very existence. He was nothing, and now, suddenly, he is here!

> A stranger here
> Strange things doth meet, strange glories see;
> Strange treasures lodged in this fair world appear,
> Strange all and new to me;
> But that they mine should be, who nothing was,
> That strangest is of all, yet brought to pass.

This sense of excited wonder at one's being wears off, as we know. We get used to being alive. And we will continue that way until we sit down in a quiet place and think about it. We might start with the sheer coincidence that our parents met one day. What if she had not gone to that party? What if he had not picked up the umbrella she dropped on a crowded street? These days, poetry is up to all sorts of things, much of it runs according to agendas, but there is still a vital strain of lyric poetry that is largely here to remind us of the amazement of simply being alive. "What will you do with your one wild and precious life?" asks Mary Oliver.

Excellent question, as interviewees like to say.

I'd say not a few of my poems include an awareness of the marvel of being alive, or the poet experiences in the poem a heightening of that awareness in a moment of epiphany. "Joy" contains this exclamation: "What a brazen wonder to be alive on earth / amid the clockwork of all this motion!" For some people, it takes a catastrophe or a brush with death to stimulate a kind of existential awareness. Suddenly, they feel the need to carpe their diems. But poetry by example shows that all it takes is stillness and quiet focus, as in these lines from "The First Night":

> But it is enough to frighten me
> into paying more attention to the world's day-moon,
> to sunlight bright on water
> or fragmented in a grove of trees,
> and to look more closely here at these small leaves,
> these sentinel thorns,
> whose job it is to guard the rose.

Index

About the Editor

Photo credit: Harold Senn

John Cusatis earned a PhD in English from the University of South Carolina in 2003. He is the author of *Understanding Colum McCann*, the first critical study of the Irish-born National Book Award winner, and the editor of *Postwar Literature, 1945 1970*, three volumes of the *Dictionary of Literary Biography*, and, most recently, coeditor of *Conversations with John Banville*. He teaches at the School of the Arts in Charleston, SC.

www.ingramcontent.com/pod-product-compliance
Lightning Source LLC
Chambersburg PA
CBHW020600030726
47497CB00007B/2032